Remnant Missionary Pal

A Reference Guide
for the
Restoration Scriptures

This book can be downloaded for free:
Remnantmissionarypal.com

The Word

In the beginning was the gospel preached
through the Son.
And the gospel was the word,
and the word was with the Son,
and the Son was with God,
and the Son was of God.
The same was in the beginning with God.
All things were made by Him,
and without Him
was not anything made which was made.
In Him was the gospel,
and the gospel was the life,
and the life was the light of men.
And the light shines in the world,
and the world perceives it not.
Testimony of John 1:1

Abbreviations

AoF	=	Articles of Faith
BoA	=	Book of Abraham
BoM	=	Book of Mormon
DS	=	Denver Snuffer
JS	=	Joseph Smith
JSH	=	Joseph Smith History
LDS	=	Latter-day Saint
LoF	=	Lectures on Faith
NC	=	New Covenants
OC	=	Old Covenants
PGP	=	Pearl of Great Price
RS	=	Restoration Scriptures
SP	=	Statement of Principles
SJ	=	Stick of Joseph
T&C	=	Teachings and Commandments
TSJ	=	Testimony of St. John

Blessing upon my people

I bless your ears
that you might hear.

I bless your mind
that you might perceive truth.

I bless your eyes
that you might see…literally.

I bless your throat
that you might absorb and speak truth.

I bless your heart
that you might become one with the Word.

I bless your knees
that you may fall before me.

I bless your feet
that you might walk in my will.

This day, I bless all within the temple,
That we might be
ONE. [1]

Introduction

"The glory of God is intelligence,
or in other words, Light and Truth."
T&C 93:11

In 1959 Keith Marston printed a brilliant little book titled, *"Missionary Pal: Reference guide for missionaries & teachers."*[2] For decades this handy reference guide supported LDS missionaries in their sincere attempt to teach the Gospel of Jesus Christ.

In 2017 the Lord accepted the Restoration Scriptures as His Holy Word and offered a sacred covenant unto His people.[3] At that time the new scriptures became the *"rod of iron"* which all our invited to hold. (1 Nephi 2:8-9).

In 2019 the Lord provided *The Stick of Joseph in the Hand of Ephraim*, thus fulfilling at a deeper level the prophecy recorded in the book of Ezekiel. (RE Ezekiel 19:4)

In response, the *Remnant Missionary Pal* has been compiled to assist those who desire to *transition fully* into the Restoration Scriptures and live the covenant offered by God.

Abide and Receive His Mysteries

"It is not enough to receive my covenant, but you must also abide it. And all who abide it, whether on this land or any other land, will be mine and I will watch over them and protect them in the day of harvest, and gather them in as a hen gathers her chicks under her wings. I will number you among the remnant of Jacob, no longer outcasts, and you will inherit the promises of Israel. You shall be my people and I will be your God and the sword will not devour you. And unto those who will receive will more be given until they know the mysteries of God in full."
Answer and Covenant [4]

Topics summarized begin with foundational truths and expand into principles relevant to offering light and truth to the world. (T&C 166:1).

Restoration references are **bolded** for learning and memorization. Traditional LDS sources are listed in (parenthesis).

When possible, a "<u>notes</u>" section has been added at the end of each topic, that the participant might record personal revelations, references and insights.

When utilizing the *Remnant Missionary Pal* please remember any attempt to summarize God's Holy Word is always subjective and incomplete. With God, "the Truth" is always different, deeper, and more! Thus, any mistakes or mis-application is the error of the authors.

This text is offered in praise and celebration for Almighty God and the gift of His Eternal Word. Let all Glory be given to Father and Mother for the Majesty of their Holy Son!

INVITATION

The *Remnant Missionary Pal* has been compiled for those with a foundation in the Lord Jesus Christ and who seek to support the work of God occurring today.

If the reader is unfamiliar with Joseph Smith, the Restoration Scriptures, and the teachings of Denver Snuffer, they are encouraged first to consider the following:

Learn and live the Holy Word of God.
(Scripture.info) and (StickofJoseph.org)

Repent and accept the Doctrine of Christ.
(Learnofchrist.org) and (Bornofwater.org)

Hear the Teachings and Prophecies of Denver Snuffer.
(Denversnuffer.com) and (Restorationarchives.com)

Join other souls for worship and study
(Fellowshiplocator.info)

Then spoke Jesus, saying, Come unto me, all you that labor and are heavily loaded, and I will give you rest.
Take my yoke upon you and learn of me, for I am meek and lowly in heart. And you shall find rest unto your souls, for my yoke is easy, and my burden is light.
RE Matthew 6:8

TABLE OF CONTENTS

GOSPEL SUBJECTS

11

DOCTRINAL TOPICS

CULTURE SPECIFIC

SCRIPTURE TRANSITIONS

THE MESSIAH

PROPHECIES
In the beginning was the Word. **John 1:1** (John 1:1-3)
Before Abraham was, I AM. **John 6:16** (John 8:58)
Highest council of heaven One who spoke out. **TSJ 1:1**
Prophecy that the Messiah born in Bethlehem. **Matthew 1:6** (Matthew 2:3-6)
Record testifies Jesus is Messiah, Son of God. **TSJ 12:7**
Jesus is following the path of His Father. **TSJ 5:3**
Jesus Christ advanced beyond everyone. **TSJ 1:4**
The worlds and all men made by Him. **TSJ 12:8**
Jesus demonstrates the path of eternal lives. **TSJ 5:4**
We love Him, because He first loved us. **1 John 1:20** (1 John 4:19)
Jesus is born as King of the Jews. **Matthew 1:6** (Matthew 2:2)
Jesus is the Son of the Highest. **Luke 1:5** (Luke 1:32-33)
He is the Way, the Truth, and the Life. **John 9:7** (John 14:6)
None other name under heaven we are saved. **Acts 2:5** (Acts 4:10-12)

MINISTRY
Birth of Jesus Christ. **Luke 2:1** (Luke 2:1-7)
For unto us a child is born. Unto us a Son is given. **Isaiah 4:1** (Isaiah 9:6-7)
He shall be called Jesus, Son of God. **Mosiah 1:14** (Mosiah 3:8)
Family flees to Egypt. **Matthew 1:10-11** (Matthew 2:13-18)
Lord not distracted by the world. **TSJ 10:32**
Returns to Nazareth. **Matthew 1:12** (Matthew 2:19-23)
Jesus waxed strong in spirit. Filled with wisdom. **Luke 2:7** (Luke 2:40)
Jesus about His Fathers business age 12. **Luke 3:2** (Luke 2:49)
Lord's anointed are to preach good tidings. **Mosiah 7:17** (Mosiah 12:21)
Minister to the lost sheep of the House of Israel. **Matt. 8:11** (Matt. 15:24)
Sent to preach the kingdom of God. **Luke 4:7** (Luke 4:43)
Sent to heal the brokenhearted. **Luke 4:2** (Luke 4:18)
Baptized of John. **Matthew 2:4** (Matthew 3:13-17)
Calls His disciples. **Matthew 3:2** (Matthew 4:18-22)
Peter who am I? Thou art the Christ. **Matthew 9:1** (Matthew 16:14-17)
Jesus teaches Sermon on Mount. **Matthew 3:3-49** (Matthew 5,6,7)
Mount of Transfiguration. **Mark 5:5-6** (Mark 9:2-9)
Great Intercessory Prayer. **John 9:20-21** (John 17:19, 21-24)
His works bear witness He is sent of Father. **John 5:6** (John 5:36)
Teaches the doctrine of the Father. **John 6:4** (John 7:16)
Teaches as one who has authority. **Matthew 3:49** (Matthew 7:29)
Jesus Christ fulfilled the law. He is the law. **3 Nephi 7:2** (3 Nephi 15:3-10)
Those blinded by falseness, can see or remain blind. **TSJ 7:8**

Christ's long suffering. **1 Nephi 5:36-37** (1 Nephi 19:9)
Triumphant entry into Jerusalem. **Luke 12:1-4** (Luke 19:29-44)
If disciples held back praise, the rocks would cry out. **Luke 12:3** (Luke 19:40)
Lord's Supper. **Matthew 12:5-6** (Matthew 26:26-29)
Gethsemane sorrow unto death. **Matthew 12:8-9** (Matthew 26:36-45)
Gethsemane agony, great drops of blood. **Luke 13:9** (Luke 22:39-44)
Wounded for our transgressions. **Isaiah 19:2** (Isaiah 53:5)
Brought as a Lamb to the slaughter. **Isaiah 19:2** (Isaiah 53:7)
Lord satisfied demands of justice. **Mosiah 8:7** (Mosiah 15:9)
Trial of Jesus. People say His blood on us. Matt. **12:17-22** (Matt. 27:1-25)
Crucifixion. **Matthew 12:22-25** (Matthew 27:26-37)
Forgive them, for they know not what they do. **Luke 13:21** (Luke 23:34)
Resurrection. **Matthew 13:1-2** (Matthew 28:1-10)
Resurrection of the just. **TSJ 5:5**
Jesus ascends to His Father and our Father. **John 11:2** (John 20:17)
Ministry in Galilee to apostles after resurrection. **TSJ 12:14-21**
Jesus Commands apostles to feed His lambs. **John 11:9** (John 21:15-17)
Commission teach-baptize all nations. **Matthew 13:4** (Matthew 28:19-20)
Jesus visits Nephites and teaches Gospel. **3 Nephi 5:8** (3 Nephi 11:27-30)
Jesus teaches the doctrine of Christ. **3 Nephi 5:8-9** (3 Nephi 11: 22-41)
Teaches Beatitudes to the Nephites. **3 Nephi 5:12-19** (3 Nephi 12:3-12)
Jesus explains gospel to House of Israel. **3 Nephi 7:5** (3 Nephi 16:10-15)
Jesus prays, heals, blesses the little ones. **3 Ne. 8:4-5** (3 Ne. 17:11-23)
Commandments concerning sacrament. **3 Nephi 8:6-7** (3 Nephi 18:1-14)
Lord promises to fulfill covenant, Zion. **3 Nephi 9:8** (3 Nephi 20:22)
Come all ye that labor and rest. **Matthew 6:8** (Matthew 11:28-30)
Receive rest unto your souls. **Matthew 6:8** (Matthew 11:28-30)
Will you not now return unto me? **3 Nephi 4:7** (3 Nephi 9:13-15)
Listen to the voice of your Lord. **T&C 18:1** (D&C 35:1)
We are engraved upon His Hands. **1 Nephi 6:8** (1 Nephi 21:16)
No servant at the gate. **2 Nephi 6:11** (2 Nephi 9:41)
Son of Man comes to save the lost. **Luke 11:4** (Luke 19:10)

PARABLES

Without a parable he did not speak unto them. **Mark 2:19** (Mark 4:34)
Why the Lord speaks in parables. **Matthew 7:2** (Matthew 13:10-15)
Children sitting in the marketplace. **Matthew 6:4** (Matthew 11:16-17)
The sower. **Matthew 7:1** (Matthew 13:3-9)
Wheat and tares. **Matthew 7:5** (Matthew 13:24-30)
Wheat and tares explanation. **Matthew 7:9** (Matthew 13:36-43)
Mustard seed. **Matthew 7:6** (Matthew 13:31-32)
Seed growing secretly. **Mark 2:17** (Mark 4:26-29)
Prodigal son. **Luke 9:13-15** (Luke 15:11-32)
Ten virgins. **Matthew 11:15** (Matthew 25:1-13)
Good Samaritan. **Luke 8:7-8** (Luke 10:29-37)
Kingdom of heaven like leaven. **Matthew 7:7** (Matthew 13:33)
Hidden Treasure. **Matthew 7:10** (Matthew 13:44)
Pearl of great price. **Matthew 7:11** (Matthew 13:45-46)
The draw-net. **Matthew 7:12** (Matthew 13:47-50)
Scribe like a house holder. **Matthew 7:13** (Matthew 13:52)
Lost sheep. **Matthew 9:12** (Matthew 18:12-14)
Unmerciful servant. **Matthew 9:15-17** (Matthew 18:23-35)
Laborers in the vineyard. **Matthew 9:25-26** (Matthew 20: 2-16)
Two sons. **Matthew 10:11** (Matthew 21:28-31)
Evil husbandman of the vineyard. **Matthew 10:12** (Matthew 21:33-41)
Marriage of the king's son. **Matthew 10:17-19** (Matthew 22:1-14)
The talents. **Matthew 11:16-20** (Matthew 25:14-30)
Sheep and goats. **Matthew 11:21-25** (Matthew 25:31-46)
The candlestick. **Mark 2:15** (Mark 4:21-22)
Camel through the eye of a needle. **Mark 5:24** (Mark 10: 23-27)
Fig tree. **Mark 6:9** (Mark 13:28-31)
Two debtors. **Luke 5:20** (Luke 7:41-43)
The importuned friend. **Luke 8:11** (Luke 11:5-8)
Ten pieces of money. **Luke 11:5-6** (Luke 19:11-27)
Parable of the Lost Coin. **Luke 9:12** (Luke 15:8-10)
The rich fool. **Luke 8:22** (Luke 12:16-21)
The barren fig tree. **Luke 8:31-32** (Luke 13:6-10)
King making war. **Luke 9:9** (Luke 14:31-33)
Lost piece of silver. **Luke 9:12** (Luke 15:8-10)
Lazarus and the rich man. **Luke 9:20** (Luke 16:19-31)
The unjust steward. **Luke 9:16-17** (Luke 16:1-12)
The unjust judge. **Luke 10:6** (Luke 18:1-6)
The Pharisee and the Publican. **Luke 10:7** (Luke 18:9-14)
Good shepherd. **John 6:24-26** (John 10:1-16)
Vine and branches. **John 9:10** (John 15:1-7)
Great feast. **Luke 9:7** (Luke 14:16-24)

MIRACLES

He gave sight to the blind. **John 6:17-21** (John 9:1-10)
He calmed the sea and the storm. **Mark 2:20** (Mark 4:36-40)
He cast out devils. **Luke 6:7-9** (Luke 8:27-35)
He healed the deaf. **Mark 4:14** (Mark 7:32-37)
He healed Gentiles. **Matthew 4:2** (Matt 8:5-13)
He healed the lame and palsied. **Luke 4:11** (Luke 5:18-25)
He healed the leper. **Mark 1:9** (Mark 1:40-42)
He healed on the Sabbath. **John 5:2** (John 5:5-9)
He healed when the faithful touched Him. **Matthew 4:11** (Matt 9:20-22)
He healed by His Word. **John 4:12** (John 4:46-54)
He fed the multitudes. **Luke 7:3** (Luke 9:13-17)
He raised the dead. **John 7:1-6** (John 11:1-44)
He walked on water. **Matt 8:6** (Matt 14:25-32)
He knew their thoughts. **Matt 6:12** (Matt 12:24-25)
He healed people among the Nephites. **3 Nephi 8:2-3** (3 Nephi 17:7)

TITLES

I AM THAT I AM. **Exodus 2:5** (Exodus 3:14)
I AM. **John 6:16** (John 8:58)
I AM the Law. **3 Nephi 7:2** (3 Nephi 15:9)
I AM the resurrection and the life. **John 7:3** (John 11:25-26)
I AM the Way, the Truth, the Life. **John 9:7** (John 14:6)
Alpha and Omega. **Revelation 9:3** (Revelation 22:13)
The Word. **John 1:1** (John 1:1)
Wonderful Counselor. **Isaiah 4:1** (Isaiah 9:6)
Mighty God. **Isaiah 4:1** (Isaiah 9:6)
Messiah. **John 1:6** (John 1:41)
Master. **Matthew 4:4** (Matthew 8:19)
The Christ. **John 1:6** (John 1:41)
Immanuel. **Isaiah 3:3** (Isaiah 7:14)
Advocate. **1 John 1:4** (1 John 2:1)
Son of the Most High. **Luke 1:5** (Luke 1:32)
Bishop of your souls. **1 Peter 1:9** (1 Peter 2:25)
Living Water. **John 4:3** (John 4:10)
Spirit of Truth. **TSJ 2:2**
Savior. **1 John 1:20** (1 John 4:14)
Redeemer. **Job 7:9** (Job 19:25)
Beloved. **Ephesians 1:2** (Ephesians 1:6)
Bridegroom. **Matthew 4:9** (Matthew 9:15)
Shepherd **1 Peter 1:9** (1 Peter 2:25)
Good Shepherd. **John 6:26** (John 10:11)

Servant. **Matthew 6:11** (Matthew 12:18)
Mediator. **1Timothy 1:6** (1Timothy 2:5)
Man of sorrows. **Isaiah 19:2** (Isaiah 53:3-7)
Messenger of the Covenant. **Malachi 1:6** (Malachi 3:1)
Light of the World. **John 6:12** (John 8:12)
Rock. **1 Corinthians 1:39** (1 Corinthians 10:4)
He is the Rock. His work perfect. **Deuteronomy 9:14** (Deuteronomy 32:2-4)
He is the Rock. Storm has no power over us. **Helaman 2:17** (Helaman 5:12)
Holy One. **Isaiah 2:1** (Isaiah 6:3)
Lamb of God. **John 1:5** (John 1:29)
Lion of the Tribe of Judah. **Revelation 2:5** (Revelation 5:5)
Lord of lords, King of kings. **Revelation 6:12** (Revelation 17:14)
Names of God. **T&C Glossary: Names of God in Scripture**
Author and Finisher of our faith. **Hebrews 1:51** (Hebrews 12:2)

SECOND COMING
Signs of the Second Coming. **Matthew 11:8-10** (Matt 24:30-36)
Love of men shall wax cold. **T&C 31:6** (D&C 45:27)
False prophets. Wars and rumors of war. **Matthew 11:3,5-7** (Matthew 24:6-11)
Earth is shaken, reels to and fro like drunkard. **Isaiah 7:2** (Isaiah 24:18-20)
Desolating sickness shall cover the land. **T&C 31:7** (D&C 45: 31)
He shall send Elijah before His coming. **3 Nephi 11:4-5** (3 Nephi 25:1-6)
Gospel of Kingdom preached to all the world. **Matthew 11:7** (Matthew 24:14)
All nations gather against Jerusalem to battle. **Zech. 1:38-39** (Zech. 14:1-9)
When Jerusalem compassed armies, desolation nigh. **Luke 12:16** (Luke 21:20)
Destruction of world and great and abominable church. **T&C 9:1** (D&C 29:1)
Remnant gathered. **T&C 31:9** (D&C 45:43)
Vision of Christ's return in glory. **T&C 160**
Prepare ye way of Lord. **Isaiah 14:1** (Isaiah 40:3-5)
Make straight highway for our God. **Isaiah 14:1** (Isaiah 40:3-5)
He shall come in like manner...as you see him go. **Acts 1:2-3** (Acts 1:6-11)
He shall come as a thief in the night. **2 Peter 1:12** (2 Peter 3:10)
Son of man will come in clouds of heaven. **Matthew 12:15** (Matthew 26:64)
When Son of man comes, redemption is nigh. **Luke 12:17** (Luke 21:27-28)
Parable of the ten virgins fulfilled. **T&C 31:12** (D&C 45:56-57)
No man knows day or hour. **Matthew 11:10** (Matthew 24:36)
He comes in hour ye think not. Watch and pray. **T&C 48:9** (D&C 61:36-39)
In mine own due time will I come. **T&C 29:9** (D&C 43:29)
Great day of the Lord will come **T&C 31:9** (D&C 45:39)
Coming of Son comparable days of Noe. **Matthew 11:11** (Matthew 24:37)
Lord returns with thousands of His Saints. **Jude 1:3** (Jude 1:14-15)
Savior shall stand in the midst of His people. **T&C 58:4-8** (D&C 133:41-62)

He comes with clouds, every eye shall see him. **Revelations 1:3** (Rev. 1:7-8)
God shall come and a fire devour before Him. **Psalms 50** (Psalms 50:3-4)
Vengeance as flaming fire those know not God. **2 Thess. 1:2** (2 Thess. 1:7-10)
Who can abide His coming, like a refiner's fire. **Malachi: 1:6** (Malachi 3:2-3)
Who can stand the great day of His wrath? **Revelations 2:12** (Rev. 6:15-17)
Repent and prepare for the great day of the Lord. **T&C 29:7** (D&C 43:17-29)
Howl ye for day of Lord is at hand. **Isaiah 6:2-3** (Isaiah 13:6-14)
Wicked call on rocks to fall and hide them. **Revelations 2:12** (Rev. 6:12-17)
Put on whole armor to withstand evil day. **Ephesians 1:25** (Ephesians 6:11-18)
Righteous caught up to meet him in air. **1 Thess. 1:12** (1 Thess. 4:13-17)
All flesh shall see glory of Lord together. **Isaiah 13:17-14:1-2** (Isaiah 40:1-9)
He will stand at the latter day upon earth. **Job 7:9** (Job 19:25)
Lamb on Mount Zion with 144,000. **T&C 58:3** (D&C 133:18-23)
Lord shall appear in glory and build up Zion. **Psalms 102:2** (Psalms 102:16)
Lord will swallow up death in victory! **Isaiah 7:3** (Isaiah 25:8)
Every knee bow, tongue confess, Jesus is Lord. **Phil. 1:7** (JST Phil. 2:9-11)
Kingdom of God shall stand forever. **Daniel 2:7** (Daniel 2:44-45)
Messiah, King of Zion! **Genesis 4:20** (Moses 7:53)

NOTES:

DOCTRINE OF CHRIST

DOCTRINE OF CHRIST
Must be born of water and of spirit. **John 2:2** (John 3:5)
Doctrine of Christ. **2 Nephi 14:1-3** (2 Nephi 32:1-9)
Doctrine of Christ. **3 Nephi 5:9** (3 Nephi 11:35-41)
Gospel of Christ. **3 Nephi 12:5** (3 Nephi 27:19-21)
Faith, Repentance, Baptism, Holy Ghost. **Moroni 8:5** (Moroni 8:25)
Repent, be baptized and receive Holy Ghost. **Moroni 6:1** (Moroni 6:1-9)
Repent, be baptized and receive Holy Ghost. **Acts 1:12** (Acts 2:37-38)
Result: conversion, consecration, peace, miracles. **4 Ne. 1:1-2** (4 Ne. 1:1-5)
Teach all, baptizing name Father, Son, Holy Ghost. **Matt 13:4** (Matt. 28:19-20)

FAITH
Faith substance of things hoped for. **Hebrews 1:36** (Hebrews 11:1)
the seed of Developing faith. **Alma 16:27-30** (Alma 32:26-43)
All things possible to him that believes. **Mark 5:9** (Mark 9:23)
Faith is not only the principle of action, but of power too. **LoF, First: 13**
Prayer of faith will shall save the sick. **Jacob 1:23** (James 5:14-15)
Faith will move mountains. **Matthew 9:7** (Matthew 17:20)
We walk by faith, not by sight. **2 Corinthians 1:15** (2 Corinthians 5:7)
By grace saved through faith, not yourselves. **Ephesians 1:5** (Ephesians 2:8-9)
Elements required for exercising real faith. **Lecture Third.** (Lecture Third)
Faith is to hope for unseen things that are true. **Alma 16:26** (Alma 32:21)
Greater things for those who exercise faith. **3 Nephi 12:1** (3 Nephi 26:8-10)
Without faith, impossible to please God. **Hebrews 1:38** (Hebrews 11:6)
The just shall live by faith. **Romans 1:3** (Romans 1:17)
Jew and Gentiles must believe or be cut off. **2 Nephi 12:11** (2 Nephi 30:1-2)
If lack wisdom, ask of God and it shall be given you. **Jacob 1:2** (James 1:5-6)
All things denote there is a God. **Alma 16:9** (Alma 30:44)
Receive end of your faith, even salvation of your souls. **1 Peter 1:2** (1 Peter 1:9)
Faith. **T&C Glossary: Faith**

REPENTANCE

Repent, for the kingdom of God is at hand. **Matthew 3:1** (Matthew 4:17)
Parable of the lost sheep. **Luke 9:11** (Luke 15:3-7)
Life is time for men to prepare to meet God. **Alma 16:37** (Alma 34:32-35)
Days of men prolonged that they might repent. **2 Nephi 1:9** (2 Nephi 2:19-21)
Repent and bring forth fruit of repentance **Mathew 2:2** (Mathew 3:8)
Lord desires all to come unto repentance. **2 Peter 1:12** (2 Peter 3:9)
Christ came to call sinners to repentance. **Matthew 4:8** (Matthew 9:10-13)
Repent, be baptized and receive Holy Ghost. **Moroni 6** (Moroni 6:1-9)
Repent, be baptized and receive Holy Ghost. **Acts 1:12** (Acts 2:37-38)
Come unto Christ, broken heart, contrite spirit. **3 Nephi 4:7** (3 Nephi 9:19-22)
Repentance and baptism for those accountable. **Moroni 8:3** (Moroni 8:10-11)
Repentance and baptism as a witness unto God. **3 Nephi 3:12** (3 Nephi 7:24-25)
Repent, come unto Christ and be in His church. **JSH 10:18-19** (D&C 10:62-67)
Godly sorrow worketh repentance. **2 Corinthians 1:24** (2 Corinthians 7:10)
Repent, Lord suffered so others do not. **T&C 17:5** (D&C 19:15-20)
Justice demands suffering if no repentance. **Alma 19:15-16** (Alma 42:22-25)
Christ sacrifice for those broken heart-contrite spirit. **2 Nephi 1:6** (2 Nephi 2:7)
Having these promises, let us cleanse ourselves. **2 Cor. 1:22** (2 Cor. 7:1)
The Lord remembers sins no more. **T&C 45:9** (D&C 58:42)
Parable of the lost coin. Joy over soul that repents. **Luke 9:12** (Luke 15:8-10)
Except ye repent, ye shall all perish. **Luke 8:30** (Luke 13:1-5)
Devils recognize and believe on Christ. Not saved. **Jacob 1:12** (James 2:19)
Devils recognize and believe on Christ. Not saved. **Mark 2:6** (Mark 3:11-12)
Repent, to avoid the fullness of God's wrath. **Ether 1:7** (Ether 2: 11-12)
Repent or receive testimony of destruction. **T&C 29:6-8** (D&C 43:18-25)
Brought to repentance often means driven out land. **Alma 16:44** (Alma 35:14)
This land choice land, serve God or be swept off. **Ether 1:7** (Ether 2:9-12)
Inhabitants of earth repent or be scourged. **JSH 12:4** (D&C 5:19-20)
If Gentiles repent it will be well with them. **1 Nephi 3:26** (1 Nephi 14:5-7)
The goodness of God leads to repentance. **Romans 1:8** (Romans 2:4)
Worth of souls is great. Joy in those who repent. **JSH 15:31** (D&C 18:10-16)
Most worth to teach repentance. **JSH 15:11** (D&C 16:6)
Whatsoever a man soweth, that shall he reap. **Galatians 1:24** (Galatians 6:7-10)
Through Christ all might be saved by obedience. **T&C 146:23** (D&C 138:4).
Lord redeems men from sin, not in their sins. **Helaman 2:17** (Helaman 5:10)
Repent and endure to end. **2 Nephi 13:2-3** (2 Nephi 31:10-16)
Endure to the end to be saved. **Matthew 11:3** (Matthew 24:13)
Repent quickly for the hour is close at hand. **Alma 3:5-6** (Alma 5:27-35)
Hearken unto my voice lest death overtake you. **T&C 31:1-3** (D&C 45: 2-10)
Repentance. **T&C Glossary: Repentance**

BAPTISM AND RE-BAPTISM

Jesus baptized to fulfill all righteousness. **2 Nephi 13:2** (2 Nephi 31:6-12)
Jesus baptized as an example for all. **Matthew 2:4** (Matthew 3:13-17)
He that believeth on me, the works I do he shall do also. **John 9:7** (John 14:12)
Follow me, do the things ye have seen me do. **2 Nephi 13:2** (2 Nephi 31:12)
Gate to enter is repentance-baptism. **2 Nephi 13:3-5** (2 Nephi 31:17-21)
Baptism is the first fruits of repentance. **Moroni 8:5** (Moroni 8:25)
Baptism doth also now save us. **1 Peter 1:14** (1 Peter 3:21)
He that believeth and is baptized shall be saved. **Mark 8:6** (Mark 16:15-16)
Must be born of water and spirit to enter kingdom. **John 2:1-2** (John 3:3-7)
All must be baptized to be saved in kingdom. **2 Nephi 6:7** (2 Nephi 9:23-24)
Must be baptized to ascend into God's presence. **TSJ 2:2**
We have great need of being baptized. **2 Nephi 13:2** (2 Nephi 31:5-7)
Be baptized and forsake sin to ascend into God's presence. **TSJ 2:2**
Baptized in my name, Father gives Holy Ghost. **2 Nephi 13:2 (**2 Nephi 31:12)
Commanded to baptize-lay hands for Holy Ghost. **T&C 18:2** (D&C 35:6)
Baptized unto repentance, cleansed unrighteousness. **Alma 5:4** (Alma 7:14-16)
Garments must be washed white, cleansed all stain. **Alma 3:3-5** (Alma 5:21-27)
Old man of sin crucified, body of sin destroyed. **Romans 1:25** (Romans 6:6)
Buried in baptism-death, raised resurrection life. **Romans 1:25** (Romans 6:4)
Buried in baptism, risen in faith from dead. **Colossians 1:7** (Colossians 2:12)
Walk in newness of life. **Romans 1:25** (Romans 6:4)
Those baptized in Christ, have put on Christ. **Galatians 1:12** (Gal 3:27)
Believe and be baptized. **Mark 8:6** (Mark 16-15-16)
Arise and be baptized, and wash away thy sins. **Acts 12:16** (Acts 22:16)
Adam is baptized. **Genesis 4:7** (Moses 6:51-58)
Adam and Eve baptized and born of Spirit. **Genesis 4:10** (Moses 6:65-66)
John baptizes those confessing sin. **Matthew 2:1** (Matthew 3:1-2)
Jesus baptized of John. **Matthew 2:4** (Matthew 3:13-17)
Peter cries repentance and baptizes thousands. **Acts 1:12-13** (Acts 2:37-41)
Paul is baptized. **Acts 11:5** (Acts 19:17-18)
Cornelius vision, Holy Ghost, Gentile baptism **Acts 6:3-8** (Acts 10:1-48)
King Limhi and his people desire baptism. **Mosiah 9:34** (Mosiah 21:33-35)
Alma re-baptizes those coming out of apostasy. **Mos. 9:7-8** (Mos. 18: 8-17)
Ordained in ministry, baptized unto repentance. **3 Nephi 3:12** (3 Nephi 7:23-26)
Paul re-baptizes disciples. **Acts 11:2 (**Acts 19:1-5)
Philip runs to chariot, baptizes eunuch. **Acts 5:7** (Acts 8:35-39)
Samuel protected. Many believe and baptized. **Hel. 5:18** (Hel. 16:3-5)
Twelve desire Holy Ghost, re-baptized, fire. **3 Nephi 9:2** (3 Nephi 19:9-13)
Sign given, people again baptized unto repentance. **3 Nephi 1:6** (3 Nephi 1:23)
All who repented were baptized. **3 Nephi 3:12** (3 Nephi 7:23-26)
Righteous previously baptized survive. **3 Nephi 4:10** (3 Nephi 10:12)

Lord gives Nephi power to baptize, re-baptize. **3 Nephi 5:8** (3 Nephi 11:18-21)
Nephi is re-baptized. **3 Nephi 9:2** (3 Nephi 19:11-12)
Elders, priests, teachers, repent and are rebaptized. **Moroni 6:1** (Moroni 6:1-4)
Alma invites church members to repent, be baptized. **Alma 3:12** (Alma 5:62)
Priesthood of Aaron restored for baptism. **JSH 14:1** (D&C 13:1)
Apostles commissioned to go and baptize. **T&C 55:2** (D&C 68:8-12)
Blessed are those baptized without being stubborn. **Alma 16:25**. (Alma 32:16)
Come all ye Gentiles, repent and be baptized. **3 Nephi 14** (3 Nephi 30:1-2)

HOLY GHOST

Holy Ghost. **T&C Glossary: Holy Ghost**
Baptizing name of Father, Son, Holy Ghost. **Matthew 13:4** (Matthew 28:19)
Faith, repentance, baptism, and then Holy Ghost. **T&C 35:4** (D&C 49: 11-14)
He shall baptize you with Holy Ghost and fire. **Matthew 2:3** (Matthew 3:11)
Adam baptized with fire and the Holy Ghost. **Genesis 4:10** (Moses 6:66)
Repent, baptized, then remission of sins by fire. **2 Nephi 13:3** (2 Nephi 31:17)
Must be born of water and spirit to enter the kingdom. **John 2:2** (John 3:5)
Christ to go away, that Comforter will come unto us. **John 9:13** (John 16:7)
Another comforter to abide with you forever. **John 9:8** (John 14:16)
When the comforter is come, he will testify of me. **John 9:13** (John 15:26)
I will send Comforter, which promises eternal life. **T&C 86:1** (D&C 88:3-4)
Comforter teaches all things, restores memory of all truth. **TSJ 10:15**
Knowledge by unspeakable gift of Holy Ghost. **T&C 138:21** (D&C 121:26).
Comforter will bring all things to remembrance. **John 9:9** (John 14:26)
Spirit guides you into all truth. **John 9:14** (John 16:13-16)
Truth of all things - by power of Holy Ghost. **Moroni 10:2-4** (Moroni 10:4-19)
Holy Ghost given to those who obey. **Acts 3:7** (Acts 5:32)
Holy Ghost comes upon Gentiles. God no respecter. **Acts 6:6-8** (Acts 10:28-48)
Holy Ghost came, tongues, prophesy. **Acts 11:2** (Acts 19:6)
Meetings are to be led by the Holy Ghost. **Moroni 6:2** (Moroni 6:9)
Fruit of Spirit: love, joy, peace, faith. **Galatians 1:22** (Galatians 5:22-26)
Apostles baptized with Holy Ghost. **Acts 1:7** (Acts 2:1-4)
Paul laid hands-Holy Ghost received. Prophecy. **Acts 11:2** (Acts 19:1-6)
Men ordained by power of Holy Ghost. **Moroni 3** (Moroni 3:4)
Receive the Holy Ghost. **Moroni 2** (Moroni 2:1-3)

SACRAMENT

Lord's Supper. Take, eat, this is my body. **Matthew 12:5-7** (Matthew 26:26-30)
This is my body. Remember me. **Luke 13:3-4** (Luke 22:15-20)
Partake of His flesh and blood to have eternal life. **John 5:17** (John 6:54)
Sacrament a testimony we remember the Son. **3 Nephi 8:6** (3 Nephi 18:7)
Sacrament observed by early Christians. **Acts 1:13** (Acts 2: 46-47)
Disciples break bread on first day of week. **Acts 12:1** (Acts 20:7)
Lord establishes sacrament among Nephites. **3 Nephi 8: 6-7** (3 Nephi 18:1-12)
Jesus breaks bread and blesses it often. **3 Nephi 12:**1 (3 Nephi 26:13)
Partake of sacrament with eye single to glory of God. **T&C 8:1** (D&C 27:2)
Offer up sacraments to stay unspotted from the world. **T&C 46:3** (D&C 59:9)
Offer sacraments in house of prayer on holy day. **T&C 46:3** (D&C 59:9)
Rejoice together-offer sacrament unto Most High. **T&C 49:2** (D&C 62:4)
Does not matter what is used to eat and drink. **TC 8:1** (D&C 27:2)
Wine-strong drink not good except for sacraments. **T&C 89:2** (D&C 89:5)
Wine should be pure wine of grape, of own make. **T&C 89:2** (D&C 89:6)
Be worthy when take sacrament. **1 Corinthians 1:46** (1 Corinthians 11:27-30)
Do not take sacrament of Christ unworthily. **Mormon 4:10** (Mormon 9:29)
Make reconciliation before taking sacrament. **T&C 32:2** (D&C 46:4-5)
Church meets often to fast, pray, take sacrament. **Moroni 6:2** (Moroni 6:5-6)
Prayer for the bread. **Moroni 4** (Moroni 4:3)
Prayer for the wine. **Moroni 5** (Moroni 5:2)

NOTES:

DISCIPLESHIP

KNOW GOD

Seek ye the Lord. **Isaiah 20:2** (Isaiah 55:6)
Eternal life is to know God. **John 9:19** (John 17:3)
Eternal Life. **T&C Glossary: Eternal Life**
Worlds, men, all things made by Him. **T&C 93:2** (D&C 93:10)
Seek me early to find me. **Proverbs 1:36** (Proverbs 8:17)
See my face and know that I am. **T&C 93:1** (D&C 93:1)
Every man shall know the Lord. **Hebrews 1:23** (Hebrews 8:11)
Sheep follow him for they know his voice. **John 6:24** (John 10:4)
Spans the heavens, stand up together! **1 Nephi 6:3** (1 Nephi 20:13)
God can roll earth together as a scroll. **Mormon 2:7** (Mormon 5:23)
His command, the heavens open. **Ether 1:18** (Ether 4:9)
Be still and know that I am God. **Psalms 46:3** (Psalms 46:10)

LOVE GOD

Lord looks upon the heart. **1 Samuel 7:16** (1 Samuel 16:7)
Charity. **T&C Glossary: Charity**
God is love. **1 John 1:19** (1 John 4:8)
First great commandment to love God. **Matt 10:23** (Matt 22:37-39)
Love one another with pure heart. **1 Peter 1:5** (1 Peter 1:22)
Commanded to love one another. **John 9:11** (John 15:12)
If ye love me, keep my commandments. **John 9:8** (John 14:15)
Sign of being my follower, Love each other. **TSJ 10:7**
If ye love one another, you're my disciple. **John 9:5** (John 13:34-35)
Crowns promised to those who love him. **Jacob 1:4** (James 1:12)
We love Him, because he first loved us. **1 John 1:20** (1 John 4:19)
Unto the least of these, done unto God. **Matt. 11:23** (Matt. 25:34-40)
Service of fellow man is service of God. **Mosiah 1:8** (Mosiah 2:17)
Love enemies, bless them that curse you. **Matt 3:26** (Matt 5:44)
Forgive them - know not what they do. **Luke 13:21** (Luke 23:34)
Love neighbor as self. No contention. **Mosiah 11:2** (Mosiah 23:15)
No contention because of love of God. **4 Nephi 1:3** (4 Nephi 1:15)
Sanctified hearts comforted, together in love. **Col. 1:6** (Col. 2:2)
Mercy, peace, and love be multiplied. **Jude 1:1** (Judas 1:2)
Dwell in love, dwell in God. God in us. **1 John 1:20** (1 John 4:16)
Let brotherly love continue. **Hebrews 1:58** (Hebrews 13:1-2)
Without charity we are nothing.**1 Cor. 1:51** (1 Cor. 13:1)

Fear is an opposite of love. **T&C Glossary: Fear**
There is no fear in love. **1 John 1:20** (1 John 4:18)
Perfect love casts out all fear. **Moroni 8:4** (Moroni 8:16)
All things work for good of those love Lord. **Rom 1:35** (Rom 8:28)

JESUS THE CHRIST
Follow me and come to the Father's Throne **TSJ 10:9**
Christ pattern: Here am I send me. **Abraham 6:3** (Abraham 3:27)
Isaiah willing: Here am I. Send me. **Isaiah 2:2** (Isaiah 6:5-8)
Lovest thou me? Feed my lambs. **John 11:9** (John 21:15-17)
Will you not now return unto me? **3 Nephi 4:7** (3 Nephi 9: 13-15)
Must take upon us the name of Christ. **3 Nephi 12:4** (3 Nephi 27:5)
You will accomplish what I have. **TSJ 10:10**
Every upward step I achieve, my loyal followers join me **TSJ 10:9**
If you love each other, it is a sign you as my followers **TSJ 10:7**
Every person loyal to the truth listens to my teachings **TSJ 11:10**
Follow the word, then are ye my disciples. **John 6:14** (John 8:31)
Come unto Christ full purpose of heart.**3 Nephi 4:9** (3 Nephi 10:6)
Follow the Son full purpose of heart. **2 Nephi 13:2** (2 Nephi 31:13)
Turn to the Lord full purpose of heart. **Mosiah 5:10** (Mosiah 7:33)
Lord invites, come follow me. **Luke 10:9** (Luke 18:22)
Treasure my teachings and stand ready **TSJ 10:12**

FAITH DEMONSTRATED
With God all things are possible. **Mark 5:24** (Mark 10:27)
All things can be done in God. **Alma 14:17** (Alma 26:11-12)
Can do all things through Christ. **Philippians 1:16** (Philippians 4:13)
God can do all things even build a ship! **1 Nephi 5:22** (1 Nephi 17:50-51)
Help thou mine unbelief! **Mark 5:9** (Mark 9:24)
Power of Godliness. **T&C Glossary: Power of Godliness**
Obtained mine errand from the Lord. **Jacob 1:4** (Jacob 1:17)
Labor to conquer enemy of all righteousness. **Moroni 9:1** (Moroni 9:6)
Overcame Satan through blood of lamb. **Rev 4:4** (Rev 12:11)
Adam builds an altar and offers sacrifice. **Genesis 3:2** (Moses 5:5)
Able offered a more excellent sacrifice. **Hebrews 1:37** (Hebrews 11:4)
Noah preaches repentance for years. **Gen 5:8-12** (Moses 8:12-30)
Noah builds a great ark. **Gen. 5:12** (Gen. 6:14-15)
Abraham lays Isaac on the altar of sacrifice. **Gen. 8:5-6** (Gen. 22:1-13)
Shadrach, Meshach, Abednego - fiery furnace. **Daniel 3:4** (Daniel 3:21)

Joshua commands the sun to stand still. **Joshua 2:19** (Joshua 10:12-14)
Elijah heavens fire consumes offering. **1 Kings 4:13-19** (1 Kings 18:21-40)
Elisha raises a boy from the dead. **2 Kings 2:8-10** (2 Kings 4:20-36)
Daniel worships God - put into lion's den. **Daniel 6:5-6** (Daniel 6:16-23)
David kills Goliath in Lord's power. **1 Samuel 8:1-18** (1 Samuel 17)
Moses suffers affliction, gives up world. **Hebrews 1:47** (Hebrews 11:25)
Esther risks her life to save her people **Esther 1:20** (Esther 5:1-2)
Jonah obeys and preaches in Nineveh. **Jonah 1:6** (Jonah 3:1-4)
Elijah to come before day of Lord. **Malachi 1:12** (Malachi 3:5-6)
Peter walking on water, sinking save me! **Matt 8:6** (Matt 14:25-31)
Jesus raises the widow's son from the dead. **Luke 5:15** (Luke 7:12-15)
Jesus calms the storm. Peace be still. **Mark 2:20** (Mark 4: 36-41)
Jesus heals blind and lame in the temple. **Matt 10:8** (Matt 21:14-15)
Jesus walks on water. **Mark 4:5-6** (Mark 6:45-51)
Jesus heals many of disease and unclean spirits. **Luke 5:1** (Luke 6:17-18)
Thousands fed with seven loaves - few fish. **Mark 4:15-16** (Mark 8:2-9)
Those that believe will do greater works than Jesus. **John 9:7** (John 14:12)
Paul heals a person crippled. **Acts 9:2** (Acts 14:8-11)
Paul raises a man from the dead. **Acts 12:1** (Acts 20:9-12)
Paul fought good fight. **2 Timothy 1:10** (2 Timothy 4:5-7)
Saints tortured, mocked, imprisoned. **Hebrews 1:49** (Hebrews 11:35-36)
Steven stoned to death. **Acts 4:9-10** (Acts 7:52-60)
Peter to be crucified upside down. **John 11:10** (John 21:18-19)
John banished to isle Patmos. **Revelations 1:4** (Revelations 1:9)
Lehi sees a pillar a fire, overcome with Spirit. **1 Nephi 1:3** (1 Nephi 1:6-7)
Nephi builds a ship for promised land. **1 Nephi 5:15-16** (1 Nephi 17:8-16)
Abinadi calls King Noah-priests to repent. **Mosiah 7:14** (Mosiah 12, 13)
Abinadi: willing to die for the Truth. **Mosiah 9:3** (Mosiah 17:9-10)
Abinadi: scourged, suffers death by fire. **Mosiah 9:5** (Mosiah 17:13-19)
Lehi and Nephi imprisoned. **Helaman 2:20-21** (Helaman 5:20-27)
Ammon protects the Kings flock. **Alma 12:6-10** (Alma 17:26-39)
Moroni waves the title of liberty. **Alma 21:7** (Alma 46:11-13)
Samuel the Lamanite cries unto Nephites. **Hel 5:1-3** (Hel 13: 2-13)
Helaman and the 2,000 stripling warriors. **Alma 24:19-20** (Alma 53:10-17)
Moroni refuses to deny The Christ. **Moroni 1** (Moroni 1:1-3)
Moroni wanders for the safety of his life. **Moroni 1** (Moroni 1:3)
Joseph Smith first vision. **JSH Part 1:4-6** (JSH 1:3-25)
Joseph knew God knew it, not deny. **T&C 1 Part 1:2** (JS. His. 1:25)
Joseph in jail, "Oh God where art thou?" **T&C 138:4-5** (D&C 121:1-6)

No greater love: to lay down life for your friends. **John 9:11** (John 15:13)
Christ has loved us and given Himself for us. **Eph. 1:16** (Eph. 5:2)
Those lay down their lives, partake of glory. **T&C 101:6** (D&C 101:35)
Death is swallowed up in the victory of Christ. **Alma 15:9** (Alma 27:28)
Heirs of God, Joint heirs with Christ. Glorified. **Rom. 1:34** (Rom. 8:15-17)

KNOWLEDGE AND STUDY
Truth Eternal. **T&C Glossary: Truth**
Teachable like a little child. **T&C Glossary: Become as a little child**
Feast upon the word of Christ. **2 Nephi 13:4** (2 Nephi 31:20)
Know the truth, and the truth shall make you free. **John 6:14** (John 8:32)
Intelligence. **T&C Glossary: Intelligence, Light of Christ.**
Currently have less than 1% of records. **Helaman 2:4** (Helaman 3:13-15)
Unbelief. **T&C Glossary: Unbelief,**
Dwindle in Unbelief. **T&C Glossary: Dwindle in Unbelief**
Records kept back because wickedness. **T&C 1 Part 13:13** (D&C 6:26)
Preparatory gospel taught by church **T&C 82:14** (D&C 84:26-27)
Will not endure sound doctrine. **2 Timothy 1:10** (2 Timothy 4:2-4)
A form of Godliness but denying power. **2 Timothy 1:8** (2 Timothy 3:5)
Ever learning, never come knowledge of truth. **2 Tim. 1:8** (2 Tim. 3:7)
Many blinded, know not where to find truth. **T&C 139:15** (D&C 123:12)
If any man lacks wisdom, ask of God. **T&C 1 part 2:3** (JSH 1:11)
Word of God has powerful effect. **Alma 16:16** (Alma 31:5)
Learn the Word of God more perfectly. **Acts 11:1** (Acts 18:26)
Rely Lord's word full purpose of heart. **T&C 1 part 15:14** (D&C 17:1)
Nephi delights in and ponders scriptures! **2 Nephi 3:6** (2 Nephi 4:15)
If you continue in my word, are my disciples. **John 6:14** (John 8:31)
Time devoted to studying scripture. **T&C 6:1** (D&C 26:1)
Spirit prophecy to understand Isaiah. **2 Nephi 12:1** (2 Nephi 25:1-4)
Learn Greater portion of word. **Alma 9:3** (Alma 12: 9-11)
Greater things await the faithful. **3 Nephi 11:1** (3 Nephi 26: 6-11)
The lessor things recorded in the BOM. **3 Nephi 12:1** (3 Nephi 26:8)
Greater views on my gospel. **T&C 1 Part 10:15** (D&C 10:45)
Keep my commandments- taught mysteries. **T&C 50:6** (D&C 63:23)
Mystery hid for ages, now manifest to Saints. **Col 1:5** (Col 1:26)
Why Jesus taught in parables. **Matthew 7:2** (Matthew 13:10-12)
Those who serve God, mysteries revealed. **T&C 69:2** (D&C 76:5-7)
Sanctification leads to unfolding of all revelation. **Ether 1:17** (Ether 4:7)
Strong meat for those who discern good and evil. **Heb. 1:14** (Heb. 5:14)

Only those receive fullness doeth good. **T&C 18:4** (D&C 35:12)
Fullness of the Gospel. **T&C Glossary: Fullness of the Gospel**
Doctrine drops like rain. **Deuteronomy 9:14 (**Deuteronomy 32:2)
If do His will, know doctrine of God. **John 6:4** (John 7:17)
Saints filled knowledge, see eye to eye. **T&C 82:27** (D&C 84:98-99)
Know the truth of all things. **Moroni 10:2** (Moroni 10:3-5)

PRAYER, FASTING, WORSHIP
Thank the Lord Thy God in All Things. **T&C 46:2** (D&C 59:7)
Pray unto the Father with all energy **Moroni 7:9** (Moroni 7:48)
Cry unto the Lord. **T&C Glossary: Cry unto the Lord**
Cry out to God, wax bold mighty prayer. **2 Nephi 3:7** (2 Nephi 4:23-24)
Cry out to God all things. Welfare of others. **Alma 16:35** (Alma 34:17-27)
Call upon God. **T&C Glossary: Call upon God, Prayer.**
Prayer. **T&C Glossary: Prayer, Call upon God.**
Pray unto Father, consecrated performance. **2 Nephi 14:3** (2 Nephi 32:9)
Pray by day, thank His Holy name by night. **2 Nephi 6:13** (2 Nephi 9:52)
Pray vocally, before world and in secret. **T&C 1 Part 18:14** (D&C 23:6)
Sleep in Christ. Lay down unto Lord at night. **Alma 17:14** (Alma 37:37)
Watch and pray always, lest enter temptation. **3 Ne 8: 7-8** (3 Ne 18:15,18)
Pray not to be tempted more than you can bear. **Alma 10:4** (Alma 13:28)
Fervent prayer of righteous avails much. **Jacob 1:24** (James 5:16-18)
Fasted and prayed with exceedingly great joy. **Alma 21:1** (Alma 45:1)
I had fasted many days. **Alma 6:7** (Alma 8:26)
Sacrament and praise, gave Glory to Jesus. **3 Nephi 9:6** (3 Nephi 20:8-9)
Worship! Holiness to the Lord. **Exodus 19:26** (Exodus 39:30)
If disciples praise withheld rocks would cry out. **Luke 12:3** (Luke 19:40)
Gave praise and glory to Jesus. **3 Nephi 9:6** (3 Nephi 20:8-9)
I will boast of my God. In Him all things. **Alma 14:17** (Alma 26:11-12)
I will trust God and His Word! **Psalms 56:1** (Psalms 56:4)
Happy is he whose hope is the Lord. **Psalms 146:1** (Psalms 146:1-5)

NOTES

SACRIFICE
Adam built an altar and offered sacrifice. **Genesis 3:2** (Moses 5:5)
Able offered God more excellent sacrifice. **Hebrews 1:37** (Hebrews 11:4)
Abraham lays Isaac on the altar of sacrifice. **Gen 8:5** (Gen 22:1-13)
Offer whole souls as an offering to Him. **Omni 1:10** (Omni 1:26)
Render unto Him all that you have and are. **Mosiah 1:10** (Mosiah 2:34)
Eye single to glory of God qualify for work. **T&C 1 Part 11:3** (D&C 4:5)
God above family and all things. **Matthew 9:24** (Matthew 19:29)
Forsake houses and family for God. **Matthew 9:24** (Matthew 19:29)
Lose your life for Christ, find your life. **Matthew 9:3** (Matthew 16:25)
Anyone who helps me with harvesting souls will save their own. **TSJ 4:8**
Those willing to sacrifice, = endless lives, worlds without end. **TSJ 9:3**
Minister without purse or script. **Mark 3:7** (Mark 6:7-13)
Give thy cloak also. **Matthew 3:25** (Matthew 5:40)
Strangers and pilgrims upon the earth. **Hebrews 1:42** (Hebrews 11:13-16)
The world will hate you. **JOHN 6:28** (John 10:20)
They will excommunicate you. **John 6:29** (John 10:23)
Prophet not honored in own country and family. **Mark 3:6** (Mark 6:4)
Care for soul, not life of the body. **T&C 101:6** (D&C 101:37)
Death is swallowed up in the victory of Christ. **Alma 15:9** (Alma 27:28)

INTERCESSION
Model of Jesus Christ as great intercessor. **John 9:19-21** (John 17:1-26) -
Model of Joseph Smith first vision. **T&C 1 Part 2:4-7** (JS Hist. 1:15-20)
Workings in the Spirit. **1 Nephi 5:38** (1 Nephi 19:20)
If a man do His will, know doctrine of God. **John 6:4** (John 7:17)
Pour out soul and labor in diligence. **Enos 1:2-3** (Enos 1:9-12)
Thank the Lord Thy God in All Things. **T&C 46:2** (D&C 59:7)
Plead for the Pure Love of Christ. **Moroni 7:9** (Moroni 7:48)
Cry out to God, wax bold in mighty Prayer. **2 Nephi 3:7** (2 Nephi 4:23-24)
Cry out to God over all things, welfare of others. **Alma 16:35** (Alma 34:17-27)
Pray vocally, before world and in secret. **T&C 1 Part 18:14** (D&C 23:6)
Pray He will consecrate performance to the Lord. **2 Nephi 14:3** (2 Nephi 32:9)
Pray continually by day, thank holy name by night. **2 Ne. 6:13** (2 Ne. 9:52)
Nephi waters pillow at night for his people. **2 Nephi 15:1** (2 Nephi 33:3-4)
Faith of Alma Sr. = angel visiting Alma Jr. **Mosiah 11: 26** (Mosiah 27:11-17) -
Prayers consecrated for gain of people. **2 Nephi 15:1** (2 Nephi 33:4)
Labor in Spirit, mighty prayer, pour out Spirit. **Alma 6:4** (Alma 8:10)
Watch and pray always lest enter temptation. **3 Nephi 8:7-8** (3 Nephi 18:15,18)
Call on Holy name, so not tempted more can bear. **Alma 10:4** (Alma 13:28)
Bless the earth for the righteous sake. **Alma 21:3** (Alma 45:15)

Fervent prayer of righteous avails much. **Jacob 1:24** (James 5:16-18)
Fast and pray for the welfare souls know not God. **Alma 4:1** (Alma 6:6)
Fasted and prayed with exceedingly great joy. **Alma 21:1** (Alma 45:1)
I had fasted many days. **Alma 6:7** (Alma 8:26)
This kind goes not out but by prayer and fasting. **Matthew 9:7** (Matthew 17:21)
Blessed are those persecuted for righteousness. **Matt. 3:14** (Matt.5:10-12)
Those willing to sacrifice in this world will obtain endless lives. **TSJ 9:3**
Sacrificial death required for endless glory. **TSJ 12:18**

PURITY AND POWER
Virtue. **T&C Glossary: Virtue**
Righteousness. **T&C Glossary: Righteousness**
Marriage ordained of God. **T&C 35:5** (D&C 49:15-16)
One wife. Procreate that earth answer end of creation. **T&C 35:5** (D&C 49:16)
Broken hearts of wives, sobbing hearts ascend to God. **Jacob 2:9** (Jacob 2:35)
Lord delights chastity of women. **Jacob 2:6-7** (Jacob 2:27-28)
Love thy wife. If lust upon woman-not have Spirit. **T&C 26:6** (D&C 42: 22-25)
Lusting after a woman = adultery in the heart. **Matthew 3:21** (Matthew 5:28)
Warring between law and sinful flesh. **Romans 1:32** (Romans 7:21-25)
Filthy water separates us from tree of life. **1 Nephi 4:5** (1 Nephi 15:27-28)
Let virtue garnish thoughts-confidence strong. **T&C 139:6** (D&C 121:45)
Lord judges the heart. **1 Samuel 7:16** (1 Samuel 16:7)
Lord cannot look sin with least degree of allowance. **T&C 54:5** (D&C 1:31)
Can you look up to God with pure heart and clean hands? **Alma 3:3** (Alma 5:19)
Come with a broken heart and contrite spirit. **3 Nephi 4:7** (3 Nephi 9:20-22)
Those clean hands, pure heart - ascend hill of Lord **Psalms 24:1** (Psalms 24:3-4)
Garments washed white. **T&C Glossary: Garments washed white**
Day soon cometh ye shall see me. Must be pure. **T&C 22:3** (D&C 38:7-8)
Must be pure to abide the day. **T&C 22:3** (D&C 38:8)
Zion is the pure in heart. **T&C 96:7** (D&C 97:21)

HUMILITY AND MEEKNESS
Humility. **T&C Glossary: Humility**
Nothingness of men. Less than dust of earth. **Helaman 4:10** (Helaman 12:7-9)
For this cause I know that man is nothing. **Genesis 1:2** (Moses 1:10)
Many are called but few are chosen. **T&C 139:5** (D&C 121: 34-35)
Whosoever loses his life for my sake, shall find it. **Matt. 9:3** (Matt. 16:25)
Lord shows mercy unto the meek. **T&C 96:1** (D&C 97:1-2)
God gives weakness that we may be humble. **Ether 5:5** (Ether 12:27)
Seek not honor of world, but for glory of God! **Alma 27:11** (Alma 60:36)
With meekness, keep the unity of the Spirit. **Ephesians 1:12** (Ephesians 4:2-3)
People of God smitten, but they do not smite again. **4 Nephi 1:6** (4 Nephi 1:34)
Weak things world called to thrash nations. **T&C 18:4** (D&C 35:13-14)
Weak and simple proclaim fullness. **T&C 54:4** (D&C 1:17-23)

He that is greatest, shall be your servant. **Matthew 10:26** (Matthew 23:11)
He that humbles himself, shall be exalted. **Matthew 10:26**(Matthew 23:12)
Submissive. **T&C Glossary: Submissive, Submission.**
Thank the Lord thy God in all things. **T&C 46:2** (D&C 59:7)
Humble yourselves and call on His holy name. **Alma 10:4** (Alma 13:28)
Become as a little child. **T&C Glossary: Become as a little child**
Call upon God. **T&C Glossary: Call upon God, Cry unto the Lord.**
Cry unto the Lord. **T&C Glossary: Cry unto the Lord, Prayer.**

PEACEMAKER
Peaceable followers of Christ. **Moroni 7:2** (Moroni 7:2-3)
Blessed are peacemakers, called children of God. **Matthew 3:12** (Matthew 5:9)
Let there be no strife between me and thee. **Genesis 7:9** (Genesis 13:8)
The Lord commands men not to contend. **2 Nephi 11:17** (2 Nephi 26:32)
Live peaceably and render every man his due. **Mosiah 2:3** (Mosiah 4:13)
Follow after things that make peace and edify. **Romans 1:72** (Romans 14:19)
Contention. **T&C Glossary: Contention**
Pride causes contention. **Proverbs 2:101** (Proverbs 13:10)
Devil is father of contention. **3 Nephi 5:8** (3 Nephi 11:28-29)
Satan spreads rumors and contention. **Helaman 5:21** (Helaman 16:22)
Children are not to fight with one another. **Mosiah 2:3** (Mosiah 4:14)
Renounce war and proclaim peace. **T&C 98:3** (D&C 98:16)
If war proclaimed, first lift a standard of peace. **T&C 98:6** (D&C 98:32-37)
Do not battle, unless commanded by the Lord. **T&C 98:6** (D&C 98:33)
Righteousness in those that make peace. **Jacob 1:14** (James 3:18)
When come unto a fight, first proclaim peace. **Deut. 6:12** (Deut. 20:10-12)
People of God smitten, but they do not smite again. **4 Nephi 1:6** (4 Nephi 1:34)
Love your enemies. Bless them that curse you. **Matt. 3:26** (Matt. 5:43-44)
Lamanites bury weapons of war, for peace. **Alma 14:9** (Alma 24:19)
Alma bears pure testimony to end contention. **Alma 2:5** (Alma 4:19-20)
People who wrest scriptures contend. **T&C 1 Part 10:18** (D&C 10:63)
Establish my gospel, less contention. **TC 1 Part 10:18** (D&C 10:62–64)
Avoid them that cause contention. **Romans 1:80** (Romans 16:17-18)
Avoid foolish questions and contention. **Titus 1:4** (Titus 3:9)
If you envy or cause strife, not ready for meat. **1 Cor. 1:9** (1 Cor. 3:1-3)
True doctrine, contention decreases. **T&C 1 Part 10:18** (D&C 10:62)
The carnal mind is enmity against God. **Romans 1:33** (Romans 8:7)
Let the mind of Christ be in you. **Philippians 1:7** (Philippians 2:5**)
Until we all come into unity of the faith. **Ephesians 1:13** (Ephesians 4:13)
Conversion to Lord results in no disputation. **4 Nephi 1:1** (4 Nephi 1:2)
If any man quarrel, forgive as Christ forgave. **Colossians 1:13** (Colossians 3:13)
Instead of contention, let there be unity and love. **Mosiah 9:9** (Mosiah 18:21)
Melchizedek establishes peace. Prince of peace. **Alma 10:2** (Alma 13:18)

Peaceable followers of Christ enter rest of Lord. **Moroni 7:2** (Moroni 7:3)
Peace with all men required to see the Lord. **Hebrews 1:54** (Hebrews 12:14)
Let solemnities of eternity rest upon your mind. **T&C 29:10** (D&C 43:34)
Jesus Christ is the Prince of Peace. **Isaiah 4:1** (Isaiah 9:6)

LAW OF GOD
God hath given a law to all things. **T&C 86:6** (D&C 88:42–43)
Light of Christ is the law all things are governed. **T&C 86:1** (D&C 88:7–13)
All laws are spiritual. **T&C 9:9** (D&C 29:34)
Law is schoolmaster to bring us unto Christ. **Gal. 1:10-11** (Gal. 3:19–24)
The law of the Lord is perfect, converting the soul. **Psalms 19:2** (Psalms 19:7)
God gave commandments to Adam. **Genesis 2:9,13**(Genesis 1:28, 2:16–17)
God gave laws to Noah. **Genesis 5:21** (Genesis 9:1)
Mary's purification fulfilled according to law of Moses. **Luke 2:4** (Luke 2:22)
Law of the Lord says every male holy to the Lord. **Luke 2:4** (Luke 2:23)
Where there is no law, there is no punishment. **2 Nephi 6:7** (2 Nephi 9:25)
There is a law given. **Alma 19:15** (Alma 42:17–22)
Men will be judged according to law. **Alma 19:15** (Alma 42:23)
Children of Israel given strict law performances. **Mosiah 8:1** (Mosiah 13:29-30)
Disobedience = law carnal commandments. **T&C 82:14** (D&C 84:23–27)
We keep law of Moses-look forward to Christ. **2 Nephi 11:8-9** (2 Ne. 25:24–30)
Salvation not by law of Moses alone. **Mosiah 7:17-8:2** (Mosiah 12:27–13:32)
In me is the law of Moses fulfilled. **3 Nephi 4:1-2** (3 Ne. 9:17)
Law given unto Moses hath an end in me. **3 Nephi 7:1** (3 Ne. 15:1–10)
The Lord is our lawgiver. **Isaiah 11:5** (Isaiah 33:22)
There is one lawgiver. **Jacob 1:17** (James 4:12)
Jesus Christ is the law. **3 Nephi 7:3** (3 Nephi 15:9)

OBEDIENCE
Choose to obey God over men. **Acts 3:7** (Acts 5:26-29)
To obey is better than sacrifice. **1 Samuel 7:9** (1 Samuel 15:22-23)
Fulfill errand from the Lord. **Jacob 1:4** (Jacob 1:17)
I will go and do the things the Lord commands. **1 Nephi 1:9** (1 Nephi 3:7)
If ye love me, keep my commandments. **John 10:8** (John 14:15)
I the Lord am bound when ye do what I say. **T&C 78:2** (D&C 82:10)
People offended because strictness of the Word. **Alma 16:45** (Alma 35:15)
Confess His hand in all things, obey commandments. **T&C 46:5** (D&C 59:21)
Blessing of keeping commandments, receive good. **T&C 46:1** (D&C 59:4)
Thou shalt not be idle. **T&C 26:12** (D&C 42:42)
You should meet together often. **3 Nephi 8:8** (3 Nephi 18:22)
Stand by my servant Joseph Smith faithfully. **T&C 1 part 13** (D&C 6:18)
Lord invites, come, follow me. **Luke 10:9** (Luke 18:22)

ORDINANCES

Ordinance. **T&C Glossary: Ordinance**

Mankind saved by obedience to laws-ordinances. **T&C 146:23** (AoF 1:3)

Power of Godliness made manifest in ordinances. **T&C 82:12** (D&C 84:20)

Power given disciples to seal on earth and heaven. **T&C 54:2** (D&C 1:8)

First principles and ordinances of Gospel. **T&C 146:24** (AoF 4)

Teach ordinances and laws. **Exodus 11:2** (Exodus 18:20)

Keep my ordinances. **Leviticus 7:4** (Leviticus 18:4)

Keep mine ordinances and ye shall be my people. **Ezekiel** 3:18 (Ezekiel 11:20)

Keep the ordinances as delivered. **1 Corinthians 1:44** (1 Corinthians 11:2)

Keep the performances and ordinances of God. **2 Nephi 11:9** (2 Nephi 25:30)

All things confirmed unto Adam by holy ordinance. **Genesis 3:13** (Moses 5:59)

People keep ordinances, law Moses, feasts, Holy Days. **Alma 16:1** (Alma 30:3)

Passover-feast unleavened bread. Ordinance forever. **Exodus 8:3** (Ex 12:14-17)

Abraham builds altars unto the Lord. **T&C 145 Abraham 4:2** (Abr. 2:17-20)

An altar to minister in the holy place. **Exodus 15:6** (Exodus 28:43)

Lehi makes altar of stones and makes offering. **1 Nephi 1:8** (1 Nephi 2:7)

Isaac builds an altar and makes covenant. **Genesis 9:9** (Genesis 26:24-28)

Thrust hands into side, know God one by one. **3 Ne. 5:5-6** (3 Ne. 11:14-17)

Marriage must be sealed by HSP to endure. **T&C 157:37** (D&C 132:7)

Ordinances of the moon and of the stars. **Jeremiah 12:10** (Jeremiah 31:35)

Ordinances recorded earth and heaven-book life. **TC 151:5**(D&C 128:7-9)

Holy Spirit of Promise. **T&C Glossary: Holy Spirit of Promise**

Repent and be baptized. **2 Nephi 14** (2 Nephi 32:1-9)

He set ordinances to be the same forever **T&C 140:6** (Not in LDS)

Meet often and have the sacrament. **3 Nephi 8:7-8** (3 Nephi 18:15-22)

Blessing of sacrament bread. **Moroni 4** (Moroni 4:1-3)

Blessing of sacrament wine. **Moroni 5** (Moroni 5:1-2)

Need temple to restore fullness of ordinances. **T&C 141:10** (D&C 124:28)

Fullness of the priesthood lost. **T&C 141:10** (D&C 124:28)

Offenders of saints severed from ordinances. **T&C 138:13** (D&C 121:19)

Changed the ordinance, broke everlasting covenant. **Isaiah 7:1** (Isaiah 24:5)

Temple needed for ordinances to be revealed. **T&C 141:13** (D&C 124:40)

Those who strayed from ordinances cut off. **T&C 54:3** (D&C 1:14-16)

Walk blameless in the commandments-ordinances of God. **Luke 1:2** (Lk 1:6)

CALLED AND ORDAINED OF GOD

Whom shall I send? Who will go for us? **Isaiah 2:2** (Isaiah 6:8)
Son of Man: Here am I, send me. **Abraham 6:3** (Abraham 3:27)
If desire to serve God, ye are called to the work. **T&C 1 part 11:2** (D&C 4:3)
Be anxiously engaged in a good cause. **T&C 45:6.** (D&C 58:27)
Jesus calls His disciples. **Matthew 3:2** (Matthew 4:18-22)
Apostle. **T&C Glossary: Apostle**
Apostles sent out to teach and baptize all world. **Matt 13:4** (Matthew 28:19)
Paul not ashamed. Power in his holy calling. **2 Tim. 1:2-3** (2 Tim. 1:6-12)
Paul is a prisoner of Jesus Christ. **Ephesians 1:8** (Ephesians 3:1)
Several called to preach and testify of Christ. **3 Nephi 3:4** (3 Nephi 6:20)
How shall they preach except they be sent? **Rom. 1:48-50** (Rom. 10:13-17)
Called to the ministry of a holy work. **Moroni 8:1** (Moroni 8:1-2)
Calling to be apostles and cry repentance. **T&C 1 part 15:30** (D&C 18:9-14)
I have commanded my sanctified ones. **Isaiah 6:1** (Isaiah 13:3)
I have called my mighty ones. **Isaiah 6:1** (Isaiah 13:3)
I have chosen you and ordained you. **John 9:11** (John 15:16)
If you continue in my word you are my disciples. **John 6:14** (John 8:31)
Temple instruction for those called unto ministry. **T&C 96:4** (D&C 97:13-14)
A teacher of truth teaches only what God tells him. **John 6:5** (John 17:19-24)
Anyone who helps me harvest souls, saves their own **John 4:8** (John 9:27-30)
Lord looks upon the heart. **1 Samuel 7:16** (1 Samuel 16:7)
Only a few who are not prideful. **Mormon 4:5** (Mormon 8:35-36)
Few humble followers of Christ. **2 Nephi 12:2** (2 Nephi 28:14)
I am not ashamed of Gospel of Christ. **Romans 1:3** (Romans 1:16)
I will boast of my God. In Him I can do all things. **Alma 14:17** (Alma 26:12)
Weak things of the world called to thrash nations. **T&C 18:4** (D&C 35:13)
Sent to teach the gospel. Confound enemies in Lord. **T&C 62:1** (D&C 71:3-7)
Servants labored with might. Lord labored with them. **Jacob 3:27** (Jacob 5:72)
Reap while day last, treasure up salvation. **T&C 1 part 15:4** (D&C 14:3)
Thrust in sickle and reap, same is called of God. **T&C 1 part 15:4** (D&C 14:4)
Anyone awaiting direction shall not be overtaken by death **TSJ 6:20**
Open your mouth and it shall be filled. **T&C 16:2** (D&C 33:8)
Bear record of the land of Zion. **T&C 45:2** (D&C 58:7)
Preached with power, thousands converted. **Helaman 2:19** (Helaman 5:18)
I am disciple of Christ called to declare His word. **3 Nephi 2:17** (3 Nephi 5:13)
Mormon repents of refusing to help Nephites. **Mormon 2:4** (Mormon 5:1)
I Moroni will not deny the Christ. **Moroni 1:1** (Moroni 1:3)
Many called. Few are chosen. **T&C 139:5** (D&C 121:34-35)
Children of God become joint heirs with Christ. **Romans 1:34** (Romans 8:17)

TRIALS AND TRIBULATIONS

Lord chastens whom He loves. **T&C 94:1** (D&C 95:1)

Lose your life for Christ, find your life. **Matthew 9:3** (Matthew 16:25)

Paul glories in tribulation. Loves God **Romans 1:22** (Romans 5:3-5)

Joseph Smith glories in tribulation like Paul. **T&C 150:3** (D&C 127:2)

Rejoice in persecution. **Matthew 3:14** (Matthew 5: 11-12)

Praised God while perishing under sword. **Alma 14:10** (Alma 24:23)

Expect to be rejected and smitten. **4 Nephi 1:6** (4 Nephi 1:31)

Prophet not honored in own country. **Mark 3:6** (Mark 6:1-4)

The world will hate you. **TSJ 10:20**

They will excommunicate you. **TSJ 10:23**

After Apostles fall asleep, tares choke the wheat. **T&C 84:1** (D&C 86:2-3)

Blessed when men revile and persecute you. **Matt 3:14 (**Matt 5:11-12)

We are refined in the furnace of affliction. **1 Nephi 6:2** (1 Nephi 20:10)

Lord eases burdens-visit us in afflictions. **Mosiah 11:9** (Mosiah 24:14-15)

Those converted are firm and steadfast. **3 Nephi 3:2** (3 Nephi 6:14)

Father forgive them, know not what they do. **Luke 13:21** (Luke 23:34)

Overcame Satan through blood of the lamb. **Rev 4:4** (Rev 12:11)

We shall look at Lucifer narrowly. **2 Nephi 10:6** (2 Nephi 24: 12-16)

Offer your whole souls, endure to the end. **Omni 1:10** (Omni 1:26)

He that endures to the end shall be saved. **2 Nephi 13:3** (2 Nephi 31:15)

HARVEST AND FRUIT

Men are that they might have joy. **2 Nephi 1:10** (2 Nephi 2:25)

In this world joy not full, but in me joy is full. **T&C 101:6** (D&C 101:36)

In this life I shall have joy. **Genesis 3:4** (Moses 5:10-11)

Worth of souls great in the sight of God. **T&C 1 part 15:31** (D&C 18:10)

Joy to be instrument in hands of God. **Alma 15:13** (Alma 29:9)

Bringing souls to Christ is of most worth. **T&C 1 part 15:11** (D&C 15:6)

Bring souls unto me, rest in the kingdom. **T&C part 15:11** (D&C 15:6)

Bringing souls to Christ results great joy. **T&C 1 part 15:31** (D&C 18:16)

Great shall be your joy - kingdom Father. **T&C 1 part 15:34** (D&C 18:15)

What joy, and what marvelous light I beheld. **Alma 17:4** (Alma 36:20)

My Spirit shall fill your soul with joy. **T&C part 1 14:12** (D&C 11:13)

The fruit filled my soul with great joy. **1 Nephi 2:8** (1 Nephi 8:12)

The fruit of the Spirit is love, joy, peace. **Galatians 1:22** (Galatians 5:22)

Your joy no man taketh away from you. **John 9:16** (John 16:22)

The joy of the righteous shall be full forever. **2 Nephi 6:7** (2 Nephi 9:18)

Jesus prays for people unto the Father. Joy! **3 Nephi 8:4** (3 Nephi 17:17)

Multitude overcome with prayer of Jesus. **3 Nephi 8:5** (3 Nephi 17:18)
Because of faith, joy within Jesus is full. **3 Nephi 8:5** (3 Nephi 17: 20)
Behold your little ones! Joy of Jesus full. **3 Nephi 8:5** (3 Nephi 17:21-23)
Give up all that I possess to receive great joy. **Alma 13:9** (Alma 22:15)
Dwell with God, snever-ending happiness. **Mosiah 1:12** (Mosiah 2:41)
Spiritual Fruit. **T&C Glossary: Fruit**

NOTES:

BORN OF GOD

BORN OF GOD

Natural man is an enemy to God. **Mosiah 1:16** (Mosiah 3:19)

Mankind carnal, sensual, devilish. **Mosiah 8:13** (Mosiah 16:3)

Men in carnal state, gall of bitterness. **Alma 19:10** (Alma 41:11)

Warring between law and sinful flesh. **Romans 1:32** (Romans 7:21-25)

Nothingness of men. Less than dust of earth. **Hel. 4:10** (Hel. 12:7-9)

Children of men unsteady and false. **Helaman 4:9** (Helaman 12:1)

Natural man receives not the spirit. **1 Cor. 1:8** (1 Cor. 2:14)

They who are sick need the Physician. **Luke 4:12** (Luke 5:31)

This life time to prepare to meet God. **Alma 16:37** (Alma 34:31-32)

Believe I am sent by Most High, or die burdened with sins. **TSJ 6:15**

Whoever born of God, does not continue in sin. **John 1:14** (1 John 3:8-11)

Garments washed white. **T&C Glossary**: Garments washed white

Must be born of God- receive title son/daughter. **Mos. 11:28** (Mos. 27:25)

Receive Christ to become son of God. **Mosiah 4:7** (3 Nephi 9:17)

Children of God. **T&C Glossary**: Children of God

BORN OF SPIRIT

Adam born of spirit, quickened in inner man. **Genesis 4:10** (Moses 6:65)

All must be born of water and of spirit. **John 2:2** (John 3:5)

Must have a broken heart and contrite spirit. **3 Nephi 4:7** (3 Nephi 9:20)

Broken heart, contrite spirit required. **2 Nephi 1:6** (2 Nephi 2:7)

His Gospel is Holy Ghost, sanctifies. **3 Nephi 12:5** (3 Nephi 27:13-21)

Sanctification. **T&C Glossary: Sanctification**

Doctrine of Christ = purity. 2 Nephi 14:1 (2 Nephi 32:1-6)

Lord looks on the heart. **1 Samuel 7:16** (1 Samuel 16:7)

All must become new creature. **Mosiah 11:28** (Mosiah 27:25-27)

Become a new creature in Christ. **2 Cor. 1:118** (2 Cor. 5:17)

Lord visits Nephi and softens his heart. **1 Nephi 1:9** (1 Nephi 2:16)

Mighty change, no evil, desire good continually. **Mosiah 3:1** (Mosiah 5:2)

No more desire to do evil. **Alma 12:26** (Alma 19:33)

New heart and new spirit. **Ezekiel 3:18, 18:9** (Ezekiel 18:31)

New heart. Be His people. **Ezekiel 3:18; 18:9** (Ezekiel 11:19-21; 36:24-28)

BORN AGAIN

All invited to believe and enter heaven. **Helaman 2:7** (Helaman 3:27-30)
Lord cannot look sin-least degree of allowance. **T&C 54:5** (D&C 1:31)
Must be born again for title son - daughter. **Mosiah 11:28** (Mosiah 27:25)
Have you been born again? **Alma 3:3** (Alma 5:14)
What must I do to be born again? **Alma 13:9** (Alma 22:15)
Garments white and cleansed from all stain. **Alma 3:3-5** (Alma 5:21-27)
Must be cleansed by blood of Lamb. **Mormon 4:6** (Mormon 9:3-6)
Clean, but not all, with none else is He pleased. **T&C 22:4** (D&C 38:10)
Those who believe and follow His Son escape limitations of sin. **TSJ 2:4**
Have you felt to sing the song of redeeming love? **Alma 3:5** (Alma 5:26)
Come with a broken heart - contrite spirit. **3 Nephi 4:7** (3 Nephi 9:20-22)
Hearts changed-no more desire to do evil. **Alma 12:26** (Alma 19:33)
Mighty change, desire to do good continually! **Mosiah 3:1** (Mosiah 5:2)
Spirit, water, and blood all bear witness. **1 John 1:22** (1 John 5:6-8)
Altar of Sanctification. **Isaiah 2:1-2** (Isaiah 6:1-13)
Sanctification results in more revelation. **Ether 1:17** (Ether 4:7)
Sanctification is plan of salvation. **Genesis 4:9** (Moses 6:58-63)
Sanctification. **T&C Glossary: Sanctification**
Righteousness. **T&C Glossary: Righteousness**
Purity and Virtue. **T&C Glossary: Virtue**
God cleanses inner and outer vessel. **Alma 27:8-9** (Alma 60:23).
Sanctified by yielding their hearts to God. **Helaman 2:8** (Helaman 3:35)
Sanctified by the blood. **Genesis 4:9** (Moses 6:57-63)
Jesus sheds purification/oneness. **3 Nephi 9:4** (3 Nephi 19:25-29)
Alma the younger born again. **Mosiah 11:28** (Mosiah 27: 23-26)
Garments washed White. **T&C Glossary: Garments washed white**
When born again, get the new name of Christ. **Mosiah 3:2** (Mosiah 5:9)
Receive Christ to become son of God. **3 Nephi 4:7** (3 Nephi 9:17)
Joy of being born again. **Alma 17:4-6** (Alma 36:17-26)

BAPTISM OF FIRE

O wretched man that I am. **2 Nephi 3:7** (2 Nephi 4:17-8)

Trust in the Lord, not the arm of flesh. **2 Nephi 3:7-8** (2 Nephi 4:19-35)

Heal me and Save me! **Jeremiah 7:1**(Jeremiah 17:14)

Children of God, we cry Abba, Father **Romans 1:34** (Romans 8:15-16)

Cry out to God. **Alma 16:35** (Alma 34:17-27)

Transcend temptation, no filthiness. **1 Nephi 4:5** (1 Nephi 15:27)

Adam baptized fire and the Holy Ghost. **Genesis 4:10** (Moses 6:64-66)

Repent, baptized, remission of sins by fire. **2 Nephi 13:3** (2 Nephi 31:17)

Jesus shall baptize with Holy Ghost and fire. **Matt. 2:3** (Matt. 3:11)

After baptism, cleansed power Holy Ghost. **Moroni 6:1** (Moroni 6:4)

Partakers of the Divine nature. **2 Peter 1:1** (2 Peter 1:4)

Who can abide His coming, like refiner's fire. **Malachi 1:6** (Malachi 3:2-3)

Garments washed White. **T&C Glossary: Garments washed white**

Must be pure to abide the day. **T&C 22:3** (D&C 38:8)

Zion is pure in heart. **T&C 96:7** (D&C 97:21)

Pure in heart shall see God. **Matthew 3:11** (Matthew 5:8)

NOTES:

THE FAMILY OF GOD

<u>KNOW GOD</u>
Eternal life is to know God. **John 9:19** (John 17:3)
How does a man know the Master without serving? **Mosiah 3:3** (Mosiah 5:13)
Able to bear his presence in the flesh. **T&C 69:29** (D&C 76:116-118)
Requirements to see God. **T&C 93:1** (D&C 93:1)
Requirements to ascend to God's presence in this life. **TSJ 2:2**
Pure in heart shall see God. **Matthew 3:11** (Matthew 5:8)
He which is of God hath seen the Father. **John 5:16** (John 6:46)
Will find God if seek with all heart. **Jeremiah 11:1** (Jeremiah 29:13)
Christ is the Spirit of Truth. **TSJ 10:24**
All who are born anew...receive the Spirit of Truth. **TSJ 2:2**
Lord's friends receive Second Comforter. **T&C 86:1** (D&C 88:3)
Peace with all men required to see the Lord. **Hebrews 1:54** (Hebrews 12:14)
I will come to you and manifest myself. **John 9:7-8** (John 14:14-21)
I will personally minister to them. **TSJ 10:12**
I will be by your side to guide you by my voice. **TSJ 10:25**
When I arise, I will prepare places for you and be your companion. **TSJ 10:9**
I will visit each of you, so that where I travel you may journey also. **TSJ 10:9**
Open the door, Jesus will come and sup. **Revelations 1:20** (Revelations 3:20)
Will ye not now return unto me? **3 Nephi 4:7** (3 Nephi 9:13)
Sanctified to receive Lord. **T&C 82:16-17** (D&C 84:32-39)
He shall appear second time to those who look. **Hebrews 1:28** (Hebrews 9:28)
When Jesus comes in flesh-observe His word. **2 Nephi 14:1** (2 Nephi 32:6)
Fullness requires receiving Second Comforter. **T&C 69:23** (D&C 76:74-77)
He comes in His own time, own way. **T&C 86:12** (D&C 88:68)
Moses sees the Lord face to face. **Genesis 1:1** (Moses 1:1-4)
Enoch sees the Lord face to face. **Genesis 4:12** (Moses 7:2-4)
Abraham sees the Lord face to face. **Abraham 5:3** (Abraham 3:11)
Jacob sees God face to face. **Genesis 9:44** (Genesis 32:30)
Isaiah sees Lord sitting on a throne. **Isaiah 2:1** (Isaiah 6:1-5)
Stephen sees Son of Man on right hand of God. **Acts 4:10** (Acts 7:54-56)
Isaiah, Nephi, and Jacob all saw the Lord. **2 Nephi 8:2** (2 Nephi 11:2-3)
Brother of Jared sees Lord-redeemed fall. **Ether 1:13** (Ether 3:13)
Emer saw Son of Righteousness and rejoiced. **Ether 4:5** (Ether 9:21-22)
Mormon visited of the Lord. **Mormon 1:4** (Mormon 1:15)
Moroni sees Jesus face to face. **Ether 5:8** (Ether 12:38-39)
Joseph sees God and Jesus face to face. **JSH 2:9** (J.S. History 1:25)
Look for the appearing of the great God and Christ. **Titus 1:3** (Titus 2:13)
Sacred Embrace. **T&C Glossary: Sacred Embrace**

COME UNTO FATHER

One God and Father of all, who is above all. **Ephesians 1:12** (Ephesians 4:6)
Glorify your Father which is in heaven. **Matthew 3:16** (Matthew 5:16)
Christ was in the beginning with the Father. **T&C 93:8** (D&C 93:21)
Men were in the beginning with Father. **T&C 93:8** (D&C 93:23)
No man cometh unto the Father, but by me. **John 9:7** (John 14:6)
Lord gives sayings to know how and what to worship. **T&C 93:7** (D&C 93:19)
Do will of the Father to enter kingdom of heaven. **3 Nephi 6:5** (3 Nephi 14:21)
Will of the Father. **T&C Glossary: Will of the Father, Meekness.**
Pray in your families unto the Father. **3 Nephi 8:8** (3 Nephi 18:21)
Pray to thy Father which is in secret. **Matthew 3:28** (Matthew 6:6)
Father-Son will come and take up their abode. **John 9:8** (John 14:23)
Father-Son personal appearance. **T&C Glossary: 2nd Comforter** (D&C 130:3)
We will come and visit him and continually abide by his side **TSJ 10:13**
If a man stands ready, we will come and visit him. **TSJ 10:13**
When He manifests himself unto you in the flesh. **2 Nephi 14:1** (2 Nephi 32:6)
No man has seen the Father without hearing Him testify of Christ. **TSJ 1:4**
Voice of God in Father Whitmer's chamber. **T&C 151:15-16** (D&C 128:21)
I and my Father are one. **John 6:29** (John 10:30)
Jesus is both Father and Son. **Mosiah 8:5** (Mosiah 15:2-3)
Christ is in the Father, and the Father in Christ. **3 Nephi 4:7** (3 Nephi 9:15)
Christ is Father because conceived by power of God. **Mosiah 8:5** (Mosiah 15:3)
Intercessory prayer,.One as Jesus is with Father. **John 9:20-21** (John 17:11, 22)
Receive the Lord to receive the Father. **T&C 82:17** (D&C 84:37, 40)
My Father is greater than I. **John 9:9** (John 14:28)
Worship the Father in spirit and in truth. **John 4:6** (John 4:23)
Prophets worship Father in the name of Christ. **Jacob 3:2** (Jacob 4:5)
Spirit of adoption, whereby we cry, Abba, Father. **Romans 1:34** (Romans 8:15)
If we confess Jesus, He will confess us before Father. **Matt. 5:6** (Matt. 10:32)
Lord confesses to the Father those that overcome. **Revelation 1:16** (Rev. 3:5)
Come unto Father in my name and receive fullness. **T&C 93:7** (D&C 93:19)
Receive fullness = received of Christ and Father. **T&C 82:17** (D&C 84:35-37)
Continue to end to have eternal life with the Father. **T&C 52:3** (D&C 66:12)

NOTES

DIVINE MOTHER

The Gods formed the heavens and the earth. **Abraham 7:1** (Abraham 4:1)
Divine Wisdom with Father before the creation. **Prov. 1:37** (Prov. 8:22)
She was present during the creation. **Jeremiah 4:16** (Jeremiah 10:12)
We are created in the image of male and female. **Genesis 2:8** (Genesis 1:27)
Man and woman uniting is eternity. **Proverbs of Denver Snuffer 159:21**
Adam left Father and Mother, to cleave to his wife. **Gen.2:14** (Gen. 2:21-24.)
Eve is named the mother of all living. **Genesis 2:18** (Genesis 3:13-20)
Mother wove the Messiah. **Psalm 2:2** (Psalm 2:6) (Hebrew "nacak" weave)
Mary. **T&C Glossary Mary, The Mother of Christ.**
Nephi witnessed the Mother come down as Mary. **1 Ne. 3:7-8** (1 Ne. 11:8-18)
Mary will be the mother of the Son of God. **Mosiah 1:14** (Mosiah 3:8)
Mary is the servant of God. **Luke 1:6** (Luke 1:38)
Blessed art thou among women. **Luke 1:5** (Luke 1:28)
Woman anoints Jesus' head. **Matthew 12:1** (Matthew 26:6-13)
Wisdom. **T&C Glossary: Wisdom**
Wisdom to know we are saved through Christ. **Alma 18:3-4** (Alma 38:9,11)
Wisdom to serve Christ and our fellow beings. **Mosiah 1:8** (Mosiah 2:17)
If we lack wisdom, ask God. **Jacob 1:2** (James 1:5)
To learn Wisdom we must be humble. **Alma 16:24** (Alma 32:12)
Wisdom cries out to her children. **Proverbs 1:2** (Proverbs 1:20-21)
Wisdom is more precious than rubies. **Proverbs 1:11** (Proverbs 3:15.)
Her ways are pleasant and full of peace. **Proverbs 1:11** (Proverbs 3:17.)
She is a tree of life to them that lay hold upon her. **Prov. 1:11** (Prov. 3:18)
Don't forsake Wisdom and she will preserve you. **Proverbs 1:16** (Proverbs 4:6)
Mankind is slow to walk in Wisdom's paths. **Helaman 4:9** (Helaman 12:5)
Mankind does not seek Wisdom and allow her to rule. **Mos. 5:14** (Mos. 8:20)
Words of Wisdom, given to the saints, concerning health. **T&C 89** (D&C 89)
Lord desires we seek not for riches but for wisdom. **JSH 13:5** (D&C 6:7)
Wisdom counsels mankind to align their words with their hearts. **T&C 157:4**
Follow Spirit into Wisdom's paths, be blessed. **Mosiah 1:11** (Mosiah 2:36)
We should seek words of Wisdom **T&C 86:29** (D&C 88:118)
The Mother will give a crown to the faithful. **Proverbs 1:16** (Proverbs 4:9)
By Wisdom, kings reign. **Proverbs 1:36** (Proverbs 8:15)
Wisdom has sent prophets and apostles. **Luke 8:17** (Luke 11:46-49)
Wisdom is justified by her children. **Matthew 6:4** (Matthew 11:16-19)
Wisdom from above is pure, peaceable, gentle. **Jacob 1:14** (James 3:17)
Gift of the spirit is to teach the word of Wisdom. **Moroni 10:3** (Moroni 10:9)
New moons, set feasts, holy things, offerings. **Neh. 2:40** (Neh. 10:33)
Forsake not the law of thy mother. **Proverbs 1:1** (Proverbs 1:8)
Those who find the Mother find life. **Proverbs 1:38** (Proverbs 8:35)
Divine Wisdom rejoices over earth and Her children. **Prov. 1:37** (Prov. 8:31)

Our Father counsels in Wisdom over his works. **Alma 17:8** (Alma 37:12)
Wisdom in Father, Gentiles came promised land. **Alma 32:6-13** (Alma 16:24)
Lamanite remnant will be gathered in the day of wisdom. **Hel. 5:16** (Hel. 15:16)
Wisdom has built her Household. **Prov. 1:39** (Prov. 9:1)
A woman in heaven clothed with sun. **Revelation 4:1-5** (Revelation 12:1-17)
Testimony of stars, thundering and earthquakes. **T&C 86:18** (D&C 88: 89-91)
Hills and mountains quake. **Helaman 4:10** (Helaman 12:9)
Moon shall turn to blood. Weeping-wailing. **T&C 9:5** (D&C 29:14-15)
Sun darkened and moon not causing her light to shine. **Isaiah 6:2** (Isaiah 13:10)
Moon shall withhold its light. Blown out. **T&C 58:6** (D&C 133:49)
Gaze upon Eternal Wisdom. **T&C 83:7**

NOTES

ENTER HIS REST (Second Comforter)

Seek ye the Lord. **Isaiah 20:2** (Isaiah 55:6)
Make your calling and election sure. **2 Peter 1:3** (2 Peter 1:10)
Calling and Election. **T&C Glossary: Calling and Election**
Receive more sure word of prophecy. **2 Peter 1:5** (2 Peter 1:19)
More sure word of prophecy. **T&C Glossary: More sure word of prophecy**
That ye may know the hope of his calling. **Ephesians 1:3** (Ephesians 1:18)
Come unto Christ that you might enter into His rest. **Jacob 1:1** (Jacob 1:7)
His Rest is to enter the fullness of His glory. **T&C 82:13** (D&C 84:24)
Remission of sins proceeds entering rest of the Lord. **Alma 10:1** (Alma 13:16)
Repent and harden not your heart to enter my rest. **Alma 9:8** (Alma 12:34)
Washed from all sin to enter into His rest. **3 Nephi 12:5** (3 Nephi 27:19)
Need sufficient hope to enter rest of the Lord. **Moroni 7:2** (Moroni 7:3)
Have love of God *always* in heart to enter His rest. **Alma 10:4** (Alma 13:29)
Seek Him early, to find rest to the soul. **T&C 41:2** (D&C 54:10)
I will not leave you comfortless: I will come unto you. **John 9:8** (John 14:18)
Soul forsakes sin - comes unto me, shall see my face. **T&C 93:1** (D&C 93:1)
Those ordained higher priesthood enter his rest. **Alma 9:10** (Alma 13:6)
Lord speaks to those chosen to enter into His rest. **T&C 4:2** (D&C 19:9)
Power rest upon thee. Lord go before thy face. **T&C 23:3-4** (D&C 39:11-13)
Father and Son will come and take up their abode. **John 9:8** (John 14:23)
If a man stands ready, we will come and visit him. **TSJ 10:13**
Fullness priesthood with Christ and Father. **T&C 82:17** (D&C 84:35-37)
No man has seen the Father without hearing Him testify of Christ. **TSJ 1:4**
We will come and visit him and continually abide by his side. **TSJ 10:13**
Labor to enter into His rest. **Hebrews 1:9-10** (Hebrews 4:1, 3, 11)
Enter into rest of the Lord. **T&C Glossary: Rest of the Lord**
Sacred Embrace. **T&C Glossary: Sacred Embrace**

Notes

FURTHER LIGHT AND KNOWLEDGE

<u>LESSER PORTION</u>

If any man lacks wisdom, ask of God. **JSH 2:3** (JSH 1:11)

Joseph Smith first vision. **JSH 1:2-2:9** (JSH 1:3-25)

Religious creeds are an abomination. **JSH 2:5** (JS History 1:18-19)

Fullness of Gospel will go to the Gentiles. **3 Nephi 7:4** (3 Nephi 16:7)

Fullness sent through my servant Joseph Smith. **T&C 18:5** (D&C 35:17)

Fullness = Principles in Bible and Book of Mormon **T&C 26:5** (D&C 42:12)

Fullness = Sanctification. **T&C 23:6** (D&C 39:18)

Gentiles offered fullness of the Gospel. **1 Nephi 3:4** (1 Nephi 10:14)

Gentiles reject fullness of Gospel. **T&C 31:6-7** (D&C 45:26-30)

Church condemnation for vanity and unbelief. **T&C 82:20** (D&C 84:54-55)

Angels cease to teach because of unbelief. **Moroni 7:6-7** (Moroni 7:29-31, 37)

Fullness of the Priesthood lost. **T&C 141:10** (D&C 124:28)

Preparatory gospel taught by LDS church. **T&C 82:14** (D&C 84: 26-27)

Currently have less than 1% of records. **Helaman 2:4** (Helaman 3:13-15)

Dwindle in Unbelief. **T&C Glossary: Dwindle in Unbelief. Unbelief.**

Records kept back because of wickedness. **JSH 13:12** (D&C 6:26)

Many will not endure sound doctrine. **2 Timothy 1:10** (2 Timothy 4:3-4)

Last days will be perilous times. **2 Timothy 1:8** (2 Timothy 3:1-7)

Believe all is well in Zion, we have enough. **2 Nephi 12:4-7** (2 Nephi 28:24-27)

If carnal in strife-division, not ready for meat. **1 Cor. 1:9** (1 Cor. 3:1-3)

Sanctification leads to unfolding of all revelation. **Ether 1:17** (Ether 4:7)

Keep my commandments and be taught Mysteries. **T&C 50:6** (D&C 63:23)

Have much of my Gospel. There are other books. **1 Ne. 3:23** (1 Ne. 13:34)

Part of my gospel. **JSH 10:17** (D&C 10:52)

Greater and lesser portion of word. **Alma 9:3** (Alma 12: 9-11)

Only those receive fullness doeth good. **T&C 18:4** (D&C 35:12)

Fullness required: parts of gospel denied. **4 Nephi 1:6** (4 Nephi 1:27)

Need fullness to please god. **T&C 18:4** (D&C 35:12-13)

Learn the Word of God more perfectly. **Acts 11:1** (Acts 18:26)

Zion only built on laws of Celestial Kingdom. **T&C 107:1** (D&C 105:5)

Fullness from Gentiles to House of Israel. **3 Nephi 7:5** (3 Nephi 16:10-11)

No more children, tossed to-fro every wind doctrine. **Eph. 1:13** (Eph. 4:14)

Saints filled knowledge of Lord, see eye - eye. **T&C 82:27-28** (D&C 84:98-99)

GREATER THINGS

Come unto Christ and receive greater things. **Ether 1:18-19** (Ether 4:12-15)
Lord has reserved sacred things for future generation. **JSH 12:3** (D&C 5:9)
Greater things available. LDS test. **3 Nephi 12:1** (3 Nephi 26:6-13)
Greater views on my gospel. **JSH 10:15** (D&C 10:45)
Know the truth of all things. **Moroni 10:2** (Moroni 10:3-5)
Great Knowledge and Greater Knowledge. **T&C Glossary: Great Knowledge**
  Fullness. **T&C Glossary: Fullness, Fullness of Priesthood.**
Fullness of the Gospel. **T&C Glossary: Fullness of Gospel**
Requirements for celestial glory. **T&C 69:10-22** (D&C 76:52-70)
Babes utter marvelous things forbidden to write. **3 Nephi 12:2** (3 Nephi 26:16)
Fullness required: parts of gospel denied. **4 Nephi 1:6** (4 Nephi 1:27)
Greater/lesser portion of word. **Alma 9:3** (Alma 12: 9-11)
Greater things await the faithful. **3 Nephi 12:1** (3 Nephi 26: 6-11)
Keep commandments-given mysteries of kingdom. **T&C 50:6** (D&C 63:23)
Mysteries and why Jesus taught in parables. **Matthew 7:2** (Matthew 13:10-15)
Those who serve God, have mysteries revealed. **T&C 69:2** (D&C 76:5-7)
Find mysteries-bring many to knowledge of the truth. **JSH 13:7** (D&C 6:11)
Find mysteries-convince many of error of their ways. **JSH 13:7** (D&C 6:11)
Judging good from evil. **Moroni 7:3** (Moroni 7:15-16)
We are to make righteous judgments. **John 6:5** (John 7:24)
Strong meat. **Hebrews 1:14** (Hebrews 5:14)
Doctrine drops like rain. **Deuteronomy 9:14** (Deuteronomy 32:2)
True doctrine decreases contention. **JSH 10:18** (D&C 10:62-63)
Contending against word of God = accursed. **Ether 1:18** (Ether 4:8)
Intelligence attained rises with us. **Glossary Intelligence** (D&C 130:18-19)
Many blinded-know not where to find the truth. **T&C 139:15** (D&C 123:12)
Help thou my unbelief. (real definition) **Mark 5:9** (Mark 9:23-24)
If do His will, know doctrine of God. **John 6:4** (John 7:17)
Scriptures given for the salvation of elect. **T&C 18:6** (D&C 35:20–21)
Weak and simple proclaim fullness. **T&C 54:4** (D&C 1:17-23)
Disciples continue in Lord's word. **John 6:14** (John 8:31)
Nephi delights in and ponders scriptures! **2 Nephi 3:6** (2 Nephi 4:15)
Word of God more powerful effect. **Alma 16:16** (Alma 31:5)
THE WORD made flesh. **John 1:2** (John 1:1-3, 14)
Rely upon the word **T&C 15:28** (D&C 18:2-3)
Know the Truth, and the truth shall make you free. **John 6:14** (John 8:32)
Jesus Christ is the law. **3 Nephi 7:2** (3 Nephi 15:9)
Jesus Christ received Fullness of All Truth. **T&C 93:9** (D&C 93:26)

LATTER DAY APOSTASY

God and His Word confirm that The Church of Jesus Christ of Latter Day Saints is currently in a state of apostasy. Observing how the LDS institution is violating scripture, while simultaneously fulfilling prophecy, is useful only if it results in personal repentance. The following summary is provided to encourage all who trust in the Lord Jesus Christ to choose truth over tradition.

RESTORATION and BOOK OF MORMON
1805: Joseph Smith is born. **JSH 1:2** (JS History 1:3)
1820: First vision with Father and Son. **JSH 2:4** (JS History 1:16-17)
1820: Joseph told religious creeds abomination. **JSH 2:5** (JSH 1:18-19)
1823: Joseph visited by angel and instructed. **JSH 3:1-12** (JSH 1:29-47)
1827: Joseph obtains the plates. **JSH 6:1** (JS History 1:59)
1828: Book of Lehi and 116 pages are lost. **JSH 9, 10** (D&C 3:5-15)
1829: Aaronic priesthood given to Joseph+-Oliver. **JSH 14:1** (D&C 13:1)
1829: 3 and 8 Witnesses shown gold plates. **JSH 15:16-22** (D&C Intro)
1829: Oliver Cowdery scribe for Joseph. **JSH 13:24-25** (D&C 9:1, 4)
1830: Book of Mormon printed. **BOM Intro** (BOM Intro)
1830: Church of Christ is established. **T&C 54:5** (D&C 1:30)
1831: Joseph to translate New Testament. **T&C 31:13** (D&C 45:60-61)
1831: Book of Commandments coming. **T&C 54:1-2** (D&C 1, Preface)
1833: Commanded build house for translation. **T&C 97:3** (D&C 94:10)
1834: Print the fullness of scriptures. **T&C 105:13** (D&C 104:58)
1835: Translation of Book of Abraham. **T&C 145** (Book of Abraham)
1835: Lecture first of Lectures on Faith. **T&C 110** (Lecture First)
1835: Doctrine and Covenants published. **T&C 54** (D&C 1, Preface)
1842: Facsimiles Book of Abraham published. **T&C 145:1-7** (Abr. 1-5)
1842: Wentworth letter, articles of faith. **T&C 146:21-33** (AoF: 1-13)
1844: Joseph and Hyrum martyred for Christ. **Heb. 1:42** (Heb. 11:13)

RELIGIOUS LEADERS
Jesus Christ is the only keeper of the gate. **2 Nephi 6:11** (2 Nephi 9:41)
Trust in Jesus Christ, not the arm of flesh. **2 Nephi 3:8** (2 Nephi 4:34)
Trust in Lord; cursed is he that trusts in man. **Jer. 6:12** (Jer. 17:5-7)
Looking past the mark of Christ. **Jacob 3:5** (Jacob 4:14)
Know a true or false prophet by his fruits. **Matt. 3:46** (Matt. 7:15-16)
Fruit of Spirit: love, joy, peace, faith. **Galatians 1:22** (Galatians 5:22-26)
Samuel Lamanite warns of popular prophets. **Hel. 5:7** (Hel. 13:26-27)
Prophets can lie. **Ezekiel 5:3-4** (Ezekiel 13:7-8)
Do not trust a prophet more than God. **1 Kings 3:11-20** (1 Kings 13:1-32)
A Prophet can be deceived. **Ezekiel 5:9** (Ezekiel 14:9)

Shepherds feed themselves-not the flock. **Ezekiel 17:5** (Ezekiel 34:2-3)
Lost shepherds and wandering sheep. **Ezekiel 17:5-7** (Ezekiel 34:6-13)
Do not feed flock for filthy lucre. **1 Peter 1:19** (1 Peter 5:2)
Priestcraft: get gain and praise of world. **3 Nephi 11:17** (2 Nephi 26:29)
Priestcraft led to the crucifixion of Jesus. **2 Nephi 7:1** (2 Nephi 10:5)
The true shepherd does not profit from sheep. **TSJ 7:11**
Enforced priestcraft leads to destruction. **Alma 1:2** (Alma 1:12)
Spiritual wickedness high places. **Ephesians 1:25** (Ephesians 6:12)
Prophets prophecy falsely and people love it. **Jer. 3:7** (Jer. 5:30-31)
Cursed for hearkening to precepts of men. **2 Nephi 12:6** (2 Nephi 28:31
Traditions of fathers limit light-truth received. **T&C 93:11** (D&C 93:39)
Why have ye transfigured the holy word of God? **Mor. 4:5** (Mor. 8:33)
False prophets deceive many. **Matt. 11:3,6** (Matt. 24:11-12, 23-24)
Beware of false prophets in sheep's clothing. **Matt. 3:46** (Matt. 7:15)
Apostles fall asleep, tares choke the wheat. **T&C 84:1** (D&C 86:2-3)
Satan sows tares, drive church into wilderness. **T&C 84:1** (D&C 86:3)
Leaders cause people to err and be destroyed. **Isaiah 4:3** (Isaiah 9:16)
Because you claim, "We see", therefore your sins remain. **TSJ 7:8**
False prophets do not profit people. **Jeremiah 8:19** (Jeremiah 23:32)
Lord against them that prophecy false dreams. **Jer. 8:19** (Jer. 23:32)
False prophets follow own spirit. **Ezekiel 5:3** (Ezekiel 13:1-3)
Those preach from own understanding, gratify their pride. **TSJ 6:5**
If message unpopular, say false prophet. **Hel. 5:7** (Hel. 13:26-27)
If message popular, say a prophet. **Hel. 5:7** (Hel. 13:26-27)
Rebellious desire smooth language-deceit. **Isa. 9:7, 9** (Isa. 30:1, 8-11)
Famine in the land of hearing word of Lord. **Amos 1:27** (Amos 8:11)
False prophecy and the people love it. **Jeremiah 3:7** (Jeremiah 5:30-31)
Prophets have erred. **Isaiah 8:2** (Isaiah 28:7-8)
Teachings are tables full of vomit. **Isaiah 8:2-3** (Isaiah 28:8-9)
Unrighteous dominion of leaders. **T&C 139:5-7** (D&C 121: 34-44)
Priests cast poor out of synagogue. **Alma 16:23** (Alma 32:5)
Lord cannot look upon sin with any allowance. **T&C 54:5** (D&C 1:31)
Those who labor for money shall perish. **2 Nephi 11:17** (2 Nephi 26:31)
Gentiles who worship men destroyed. **Matt. 10:15-16** (JST Matt. 21:56)
Idolizing deceived prophets = destroyed. **Ezek. 5:9** (Ezek. 14:9-10)
Grievous wolves come in among the flock. **Acts 12:4** (Acts 20:29-31)

RELIGIOUS CULTURE

Two Churches Only. Church Lamb, Church devil. **1 Ne. 3:27** (1 Ne. 14:10)
Traditions of Fathers limit receiving light and truth. **T&C 93:11** (D&C 93:39)
Pattern of idolatry and apostasy. **Judges 1:6** (Judges 2:17-23)
Idols in the heart. Separated from Lord. **Ezekiel 5:8** (Ezekiel 14:2-7)
Cursed for hearkening to precepts of men. **2 Nephi 12:6** (2 Nephi 28:31)
Samuel Principle. People rejecting God. **1 Samuel 4:2** (1 Samuel 8:7-9)
All must follow God over a prophet. **1 Kings 3:11-20** (1 Kings 13:1-34)
Laman incorrectly believes Jerusalem righteous. **1 Ne. 5:17** (1 Ne. 17:21-22)
All is well in Zion. **2 Nephi 12:4** (2 Nephi 28:21)
Signs of religious apostasy. **1 Nephi 7:4** (1 Nephi 22:23)
People wrest scriptures and do not understand them. **JSH 10:18** (D&C 10:63)
Moroni sees our doing and mourns. **Mormon 4:5** (Mormon 8:35-41)
BOM to come forth in due time by way of the Gentile. **BOM Title Page**
LDS identified with the Gentiles. **T&C 123:18** (D&C 109:60)
Warning to Church. **T&C 50:14-15** (D&C 63:60-64)
Church pride. Grind on poor. **2 Nephi 11:15** (2 Nephi 26:20)
Repent or condemned church will be cut off. **T&C 50:14** (D&C 63:61-64)
Proud and drunkards of Ephraim. **Isaiah 8:1-4** (Isaiah 28:1-18)
Church can be overthrown if people transgress. **Mosiah 11:20** (Mosiah 27:13)
Temple defiled, ordinances changed. **Isaiah 7:1** (Isaiah 24:5)
Losing fullness of priesthood, temple needed. **T&C 141:10** (D&C 124:28)
Glory of God is intelligence. **T&C 93:11**(D&C 93:36)
Grow line upon line. **2 Nephi 12:6** (2 Nephi 28:30)
To know not mysteries, is to be in chains of hell. **Alma 9:3** (Alma 12:11)
Find mysteries-bring many to knowledge of truth. **JSH 13:8** (D&C 6:11)
Find out mysteries-to convince many of error. **JSH 13:8** (D&C 6:11)
Wo unto him that sayeth he has enough. **2 Nephi 12:6** (2 Nephi 28:27-29)
Receive the light or lose it. **T&C 29:3** (D&C 43:9-10)
The lesser and greater portion of the word. **Alma 9:3** (Alma 12:10)
Some have wrested scriptures-gone far astray. **Alma 19:9** (Alma 41:1)
Church teaching the preparatory gospel. **T&C 82:14** (D&C 84: 26-27)
Gentiles rejecting the fullness. **T&C 31:6-7** (D&C 45:26-29)
Contention, jarrings, envy, strife, pollute inheritance. **T&C 101:2** (D&C 101:6)
Church Pride, Grind on Poor. **2 Nephi 11:15** (2 Nephi 26:20)
Tithing is for the Poor. **Genesis 7:21** (JST Genesis 14:39)
All is well in Zion, need no more. **2 Nephi 12:5** (2 Nephi 28:24)
False prophets cause people to err. **Jeremiah 8:19** (Jeremiah 23:15-32)
Rebellious desire smooth language and deceits. **Isaiah 9:7, 9** (Isaiah 30:1, 8-11)
Unbelief. **T&C Glossary: Unbelief**
Dwindle in Unbelief. **T&C Glossary: Dwindle in Unbelief.**
Tares persecute wheat-drive church into wilderness. **T&C 84:1** (D&C 86:1-7)

The real Church of Christ **JSH 10:19** (D&C 10:67)
Those who follow the Lord know how to worship. **TSJ 4:5 (John 4:22-24)**
Fullness of the Priesthood Lost. **T&C 141:10** (D&C 124:28)
Need Nauvoo temple done to restore lost fullness. **T&C 141:10** (D&C 124:28)
Church Breaking Up because of pride. **3 Nephi 3:2** (3 Nephi 6:7-14)
Gentiles shall be destroyed. **Matthew 10:16** (JST Matthew 21:56)

PROPHETIC WARNINGS TO LATTER DAY SAINTS
Moroni sees our day and mourns. **Mormon 4:5** (Mormon 8:35-41)
God cannot look upon sin any degree of allowance. **T&C 54:5** (D&C 1:31)
Church comes under condemnation. **T&C 82:20** (D&C 84:54-56)
Condemnation is to receive not the light. **T&C 93:10** (D&C 93:32)
LDS identified with the Gentiles. **T&C 123:18** (D&C 109:60)
Gentiles rejecting the fullness. **T&C 31:6-7** (D&C 45:26-29)
Two Churches Only. Church Lamb, Church devil. **1 Ne. 3:27** (1 Ne. 14:10)
Priestcraft. **T&C Glossary: Priestcraft**
Unbelief. **T&C Glossary: Unbelief, Dwindle in Unbelief**
Fullness of the Priesthood lost. **T&C 141:10** (D&C 124:28)
Warning to church. **T&C 50:14-15** (D&C 63:60-64)
Repent or be condemned - church cut off. **T&C 50:14-15** (D&C 63:61-64)
Church can be overthrown by transgression. **Mosiah 11:26** (Mosiah 27:13)
Last days will be perilous times. **2 Timothy 1:8** (2 Timothy 3:1-7)
Many will not endure sound doctrine. **2 Timothy 1:10** (2 Timothy 4:3-4)
Having a form of Godliness but denying power. **2 Timothy 1:8** (2 Timothy 3:5)
Ever learning, never come knowledge of truth. **2 Timothy 1:8** (2 Timothy 3:7)
Many blinded, know not where to find the truth. **T&C 139:15** (D&C 123:12)
Satan lulls church away into carnal security. **2 Nephi 12:4** (2 Nephi 28:21)
Masses erroneously say "All is well in Zion." **2 Nephi 12:4** (2 Nephi 28:21)
Why have ye transfigured Word of God? **Mormon 4:5** (Mormon 8:33)
Fullness of the Priesthood lost. **T&C 141:10** (D&C 124:28)
Temple defiled by changing ordinances. **Isaiah 7:1** (Isaiah 24:5)
Unrighteous dominion = Amen to priesthood. **T&C 139:5** (D&C 121:36-37)
Priesthood keys and authority. **T&C Glossary Keys**
Tares persecute wheat-drive church into wilderness. **T&C 84:1-2** (D&C 86:1-7)
Lord's church overthrown by transgression. **Mosiah 11:20** (Mosiah 27:13)
Church of God polluted. **Mormon 4:5** (Mormon 8:38)
Proud and drunkards of Ephraim. **Isaiah 8:1-4** (Isaiah 28:1-18)
Church breaking up because of pride. **3 Nephi 3:2** (3 Nephi 6:10-14)
Churches built for gain/popularity, consumed. **1 Nephi 7:5** (1 Nephi 22:23)
Members chose money over Zion. **T&C 107:2** (D&C 105:8)
Famine in the land of hearing word of Lord. **Amos 1:27** (Amos 8:11)
Satan soweth tares, church driven into wilderness. **T&C 84:1** (D&C 86:3)

Falling away before the coming of the Lord. **2 Thess. 1:4** (2 Thess. 2:1-3)
An End of Authority through Denver Snuffer. **T&C 166**
Upon my house it shall begin. **T&C 124:6** (D&C 112:25-26)
Gentiles shall be destroyed. **Matthew 10:15** (JST Mathew 21:56)
Zion can only be built on laws Celestial Kingdom. **T&C 107:1** (D&C 105:6)
Few only that do not lift themselves in pride. **Mormon 4:5** (Mormon 8:36)
Humble overcome false precepts of men. **2 Nephi 12:2** (2 Nephi 28:14)
Few humble followers of Christ in latter-days. **2 Nephi 12:2** (2 Nephi 28:14)

APOSTASY AFTER JOSEPH SMITH

God cannot look upon sin any degree of allowance. **T&C 54:5** (D&C 1:31)
Joseph Smith identifies LDS as Gentile Church. **T&C 123:18** (D&C 109:60)
Christ prophesies Gentiles will lose fullness. **3 Nephi 7:5** (3 Nephi 16:10-11)
Christ confirms church lost fullness of priesthood. **T&C 141:10** (D&C 124:28)
Gentiles perceive not the light, reject it. **T&C 31:6-7** (D&C 45:28-30)
Wo unto the Gentiles…they will deny me **2 Nephi 12:7** (2 Nephi 28:32)
Why have ye transfigured Word of God? **Mormon 4:5** (Mormon 8:33)
Church comes under condemnation. **T&C 82:20** (D&C 84:54-56)
Condemnation is to receive not the light. **T&C 93:10** (D&C 93: 32)
Gentiles rejecting the fullness as remnant gathered **T&C 31:6** (D&C 45:26-29)
Moroni sees our day and mourns. **Mormon 4:5** (Mormon 8:35-41)
Temple defiled by changing ordinances. **Isaiah 7:1** (Isaiah 24:5)
Unrighteous dominion = Amen to priesthood. **T&C 139:5** (D&C 121:36-37)
Priesthood keys and authority. **T&C Glossary Keys**
Tares persecute wheat-drive church into wilderness. **T&C 84:1-2** (D&C 86:1-7)
Lord's church overthrown by transgression. **Mosiah 11:20** (Mosiah 27:13)
Church of God polluted. **Mormon 4:5** (Mormon 8:38)
Tares persecute wheat-drive church into wilderness. **T&C 84:1-2** (D&C 86:1-7)
House of God still needs to be set in order. **T&C 83:4** (D&C 85:7)
Upon Lord's house shall troubles begin. **D&C 124:6** (D&C 112:25)
Gentile stewards of Gospel to be destroyed. **Matt. 10:16** (JST Matt. 21:56)
Destroyed unknowingly. **T&C Glossary: Destroy**

NOTES

TIMES OF THE GENTILES

Times of the Gentiles. **T&C Glossary**: Times of the Gentiles
Fullness of the Gospel will go to the Gentiles. **3 Nephi 7:4** (3 Nephi 16:7)
Book of Mormon to come forth by way of Gentile. **BOM Title Page**
LDS are identified with Gentiles. **T&C 123:18** (D&C 109:60)
Gentiles invited into House of Israel. **3 Nephi 14:1** (3 Nephi 30:1-2)
Much of my Gospel brought to Gentiles. **1 Nephi 3:23** (1 Nephi 13:34)
Gentiles reject fullness, precepts of men. **T&C 31:6-7** (D&C 45: 26-31)
Lord will set his hand second time. **Jacob 4:1** (Jacob 6:2)
Several called to preach and testify of Christ. 3 **Nephi 3:4** (3 Nephi 6:20)
John sees angel preaching gospel in last days. **Rev. 5:2** (Rev. 14:6)
If Gentiles repent-enter covenant, part of Jacob. **3 Ne. 10:1** (3 Ne. 21:22)
Bible-other books convince Gentiles of truth. **1 Ne. 3:24** (1 Ne. 13:38-39)
Repentant Gentiles assist New Jerusalem. **3 Ne. 9:12-10:1** (3 Ne. 21:11-29)
Gentiles are to restore Jews/Lamanites. Mormon 2:6-7 (Mormon 5:13-24)
Repentant Gentiles numbered House of Israel. **3 Ne. 7:5** (3 Ne. 16:13)
A few humble followers of Christ. **2 Nephi 12:2** (2 Nephi 28:14)
Come unto Christ, receive greater things. **Ether 1:18-19** (Ether 4:12-13-15)
New Heaven/New Earth. New Jerusalem. **Ether 6:1-3** (Ether 13:1-12)
Remnant scattered until times Gentiles fulfilled. **T&C 31:5-6** (D&C 45:22-25)
Gentiles reject fullness. Gospel to House Israel. **3 Nephi 7:5** (3 Nephi 16:10-12)
Gospel given to remnant of Lehi's seed. **1 Nephi 4:3** (1 Nephi 15:13-14)
House of Israel. T&C Glossary: House of Israel
Remnant. T&C Glossary: Remnant

PRESERVING THE RESTORATION

Christ is only keeper of the gate. **2 Nephi 6:11** (2 Nephi 9:41)
The course of the Lord is one eternal round. **1 Nephi 3:5** (1 Nephi 10:19)
The Lord gives pattern in all things. **T&C 39:4** (D&C 52:14)
Truth is things as they really are, really will be. **Jacob 3:4** (Jacob 4:13)
Truth: things as they are, were, and are to come. **T&C 93:8** (D&C 93:24)
Men are free to choose. **2 Nephi 1:10** (2 Nephi 2:27)
Lords church can be overthrown by transgression. **Mos. 11:26** (Mos. 27:13)
Satan lulls church away into carnal security, **2 Nephi 12:4** (2 Nephi 28:21)
Masses say "All is well in Zion" **2 Nephi 12:4** (2 Nephi 28:21)
Joseph identifies church as a Gentile Church. **T&C 123:18** (D&C 109:60)
Christ prophesies Gentile church loses fulness. **3 Nephi 7:5** (3 Nephi 16:10-11)
Gentiles receive not the fulness, but reject it. **T&C 31:7** (D&C 45:28-30)
Wo unto the Gentiles...they will deny me **2 Nephi 12:7** (2 Nephi 28:32)
House of God needs set in order. **T&C 83:4** (D&C 85:7)
Lord sets hand second time to restore people. **2 Nephi 11:6** (2 Nephi 25:17)
Lord offers hand second time to nourish and prune. **Jacob 4:1** (Jacob 6:2)

Joseph's marvelous work has yet to occur. **JS History 11:2** (D&C 4:1)
The Lord brings forth His strange act. **T&C 101:20** (D&C 101:95)
Strange act to prune vineyard last time. **T&C 94:1** (D&C 95:4)
Dispensation. **T&C Glossary**
Dispensation of the Fullness of Times. **T&C Glossary**
Fullness of the Gospel. **T&C Glossary**
Entering Lord's real church through repentance. **JS History 10:19** (D&C 10:67)
Few only that do not lift themselves in pride. **Mormon 4:5** (Mormon 8:36)
Few humble followers Christ. **2 Nephi 12:2** (2 Nephi 28:14)
Humble overcome false precepts of men. **2 Nephi 12:2** (2 Nephi 28:14)
Scriptures wrested to their own destruction. **2 Peter 1:14** (2 Peter 3:16)
Scriptures given for salvation of elect. **T&C 18:6** (D&C 35:20–21)
Remnant of Israel receives revelation. **T&C 129:5** (D&C 113:9-10)
Lord sends his angels then and now. **Alma 19:3** (Alma 39:19)
Everlasting Gospel comes with the angels. **T&C 86:24** (D&C 88:103)
Several called to preach and testify of Christ. **3 Nephi 3:4** (3 Nephi 6:20)
Blessings or cursing Israel? Repent-obey covenant. **Lev. 13:8-16** (Lev. 26:1-46)
Righteous Gentiles offered covenant in last days **3 Nephi 10:1** (3 Nephi 21:22)
Gentiles offered covenant, Christ in midst. **3 Nephi 10:1** (3 Nephi 21:22-25)
Incline ear to everlasting covenant, mercies David. **Isaiah 20:1** (Isaiah 55:3)
New name of David given unto Denver Snuffer. **T&C 162:1**
God has given David for a witness unto the people. **Isaiah 20:1** (Isaiah 55:3-4)
Covenant of Peace through servant David. **Eze. 17:10-11** (Eze. 34:22-27)
The Pass through Denver Snuffer. **T&C 163:1-4**
Gethsemane through Denver Snuffer. **T&C 161:1-31**
A Sign through Denver Snuffer. **T&C 160:1-5**
An End of Authority through Denver Snuffer. **T&C 166:1-4**
Seven Women through Denver Snuffer. **T&C 167:1**
The Resurrection through Denver Snuffer. **T&C 169:1-4**
His Return through Denver Snuffer. **T&C 164:1**
The Train through Denver Snuffer. **T&C 172:1-5**
Prayer for Covenant through Denver Snuffer. **T&C 156:1-8**
Answer and Covenant through Denver Snuffer **T&C 157:1-66**
Servant marred-but spared in God's hand. **3 Nephi 9:12** (3 Nephi 21:9-10)
Need plates to preserve language of fathers. **1 Nephi 1:12** (1 Nephi 3:19)
Watchmen see eye to eye when Lord brings Zion. **3 Nephi 7:6** (Isaiah 52:8)
Old things are done away, all things new. **3 Nephi 5:31** (3 Nephi 12: 47)
All invited heaven, to sit down Holy Fathers. **Helaman 2:7** (Helaman 3:27-30)
Seeking for the blessings of the Fathers. **Abraham 1:1** (Abraham 1:2-3)
Elijah keys to seal hearts of fathers to children. **TC Ref.** (D&C 27:9-12)
Elijah hearts of fathers to children, children to fathers. **Mal. 1:12** (Mal. 4:4-6)
Fathers and children must be welded together. **T&C 151:14** (D&C 128:18)
Promises made to fathers, in the hearts of children. **JS History 3:4** (D&C 2:1-3)

Dispensation fullness. Glory-keys since Adam. **T&C 151:14** (D&C 128:18)
Priesthood from the Fathers. **Abraham 1:1** (Abraham 1:4)
Those called to bring Zion with priesthood. **T&C 129:4** (D&C 113:7-8)
God will gather in one all things. Fullness of times. **TC Ref.** (D&C 27:13)
Fullness of the Gospel. **T&C Glossary**
Brought to repentance often = driven out of the land. **Alma 16:44** (Alma 35:14)
Upon my house it shall begin. **T&C 124:6** (D&C 112:25)
Gentiles. **T&C Glossary**
Parable that Gentiles would be destroyed. **Matt 10:16** (JST Matt 21:56)
Do not gather in haste, brings confusion - pestilence. **T&C 50:6** (D&C 63:24)
God's message to those who seek for Zion at last day **Isaiah 18:7** (Isaiah 52)
Lord takes one of a city and two of a family to Zion. **Jeremiah 2:3** (Jer. 3:14)
Believing Gentiles numbered among Lamanites. **3 Nephi 10:1** (3 Nephi 21: 22)
The first shall be last and the last first **Jacob 3:25** (Jacob 5:63)
Restitution of all things. **Acts 2:3** (Acts 3:21)
New Heaven. **T&C Glossary**
New Earth. **T&C Glossary**
New Heaven/New Earth. New Jerusalem. **Ether 6:3** (Ether 13:1-12)

NOTES:

PRESERVING THE RESTORATION

ETERNAL PATTERN
Course of the Lord is one eternal round. **1 Nephi 3:5** (1 Nephi 10:19)
Lord gives pattern in all things. **T&C 39:4** (D&C 52:14)
God does not change. **Lectures on Faith, Lecture Third**
Truth is things as they really are and will be. **Jacob 3:4** (Jacob 4:13)
Truth is things as they are, were, and are to come. **T&C 93:8** (D&C 93:24)
Men are free to choose. **2 Nephi 1:10** (2 Nephi 2:27)
Jesus Christ is the only keeper of the gate. **2 Nephi 6:11** (2 Nephi 9:41)
Entering Lord's real church requires repentance. **JSH 10:19** (D&C 10:67)
Scriptures wrested to destruction. **2 Peter 1:14** (2 Peter 3:16)
Scriptures given for salvation of elect. **T&C 18:6** (D&C 35:20-21)
Need plates to preserve language of fathers. **1 Nephi 1:12** (1 Nephi 3:19)
Lord sends his angels then and now. **Alma 19:3** (Alma 39:19)
Everlasting Gospel comes with the angels. **T&C 86:24** (D&C 88:103)
Several called to preach and testify of Christ. **3 Nephi 3:4** (3 Nephi 6:20)
Blessing or cursing? Repent-obey covenant. **Lev. 13:8-16** (Lev. 26:1-46)
Repentant are driven out of the land. **Alma 16:44** (Alma 35:14)

JOSEPH SMITH AND THE BOOK OF MORMON
God is unchanging. **Hebrews 1:59-63** (Hebrews. 13:8-20)
Lord will do nothing save reveals His secret to prophets. **Amos 1:9** (Amos 3:7)
Can know a true or false prophet by fruits. **Matthew 3:46** (Matthew 7:15-16)
Fruit of Spirit: love, joy, peace, faith. **Galatians 1:22** (Galatians 5:22-26)
Spirit guides you into all truth. **John 9:14** (John 16:13-16)
Gain knowledge by the gift of Holy Ghost. **T&C 138:21** (D&C 121:26).
Words spoken by the Holy Spirit are scripture. **D&C 55:1** (D&C 68:3-4)
Man not live bread alone, but every word of God. **Matthew 2:5** (Matthew 4:4)
Only part of what Jesus said and did recorded in Bible. **John 11:3** (John 21:25)
Jesus teaches there are other sheep not of this fold. **John 6:26** (John 10:16)
Gospel will be given to another nation. **Matthew 10:13** (Matthew 21 :43)
Know ye not there are more nations then one? **2 Ne. 12:9-10** (2 Ne. 29: 7-12)
Stick of Judah, Stick of Joseph. Together. **Ezekiel 19:4** (Ezekiel 37:15-19)
Book of Mormon contains the fullness of the gospel. **JSH 16:3** (D&C 20:9)
Everlasting gospel comes with the angels **D&C 86:24** (D&C 88:103)
John sees angel preaching gospel in last days. **Revelation 5:2** (Revelation 14:6)
Several called to preach and testify of Christ. **3 Nephi 3:4** (3 Nephi 6:20)
Prophecy occurring after the death of Jesus. **Acts 11:2** (Acts 19:6)
Gentiles say, have a Bible-need no other Bible. **2 Ne. 12:8-9** (2 Ne. 29: 3-5)
Other scriptures wrested to their own destruction. **2 Peter 1:14** (2 Peter 3:16)

Choose things true, pure, of good report. **Philippians1:15** (Philippians 4:8)
Ask God, He will manifest the truth to you. **Moroni 10:2** (Moroni 10:4)

MARVELOUS WORK AND WONDER

Marvelous work and wonder to occur in latter days. **JSH 11:2** (D&C 4:1)
A mighty servant to restore much. **2 Nephi 2:7** (2 Nephi 3:24)
Marvelous work after restoration of gospel. **1 Ne. 3:25-26** (1 Ne. 14:1-7)
Marvelous work causes division. **1 Nephi 2:25-26** (1 Nephi 14:1-7)
Marvelous work occurs after Lehi's seed scattered. **1 Ne. 7:3** (1 Ne. 22:8)
Marvelous work after Lord reveals arm. **1 Nephi 7:3** (1 Nephi 22:8-11) *
Marvelous work gathers lost tribes. **1 Nephi 7:3** (1 Nephi 22:12)
Marvelous work comes through covenant servant. **1 Ne. 6:7** (1 Ne. 21:8)
Marvelous work gathers righteous to lands. **1 Ne. 7:3** (1 Ne. 22:8-12)
Greater work to reveal hidden mysteries. **Ether 1:19** (Ether 4:13-14)
Greater work to "recover my people." **T&C 23:3** (D&C 39:11)
Great revelatory work to reveal folly of Gentiles. **T&C 18:3** (D&C 35:7)
Fullness of gospel includes restoring Israel. **T&C 23:3** (D&C 39:11)
Fullness of gospel is the everlasting covenant. **T&C 58:7** (D&C 133:57)
Marvelous work to restore covenant people. **1 Ne. 6:6-7** (1 Ne. 21:4-6)
Lord set himself again to recover covenant people. **2 Ne. 5:5** (2 Ne. 6:14)
Lord sets His hand second time. **2 Nephi 11:6** (2 Nephi 25:17-18)
Lord offers hand second time to nourish and prune. **Jacob 4:1** (Jacob 6:2)
Lord sets his hand again to recover remnant. **2 Ne. 9:22** (2 Ne. 21:11)
Second time is when gentiles repent. **2 Nephi 12:7-8** (2 Nephi 28:32; 29:1)
Purpose of marvelous work is restoration. **2 Nephi 11:6** (2 Nephi 25:17)
Restoration of all things. **T&C 74:14** (D&C 77:14)
Lehi's seed restored to knowledge of Christ. **2 Nephi 7:1** (2 Nephi 10:2)
Restoration to lands of inheritance. **2 Nephi 11:4** (2 Nephi 25:11)
Elias has calling to restore all things. **T&C 74:9, 14** (D&C 77:9, 14)
Latter-Day Elias must restore all things. **Matt. 9:5** (JST Matt. 17:9-14)
Christ was "Moses" to hear or be cut off. **1 Nephi 7:5** (1 Nephi 22:20-21)
Joseph Smith was the "Moses" in his day. **T&C 104:4** (D&C 103:15-17)
Strange act completes division. **T&C 101:20** (D&C 101:93-95)
Strange act is to prune vineyard for the last time. **T&C 94:1** (D&C 95:4)

NOTES

LAST DAYS SERVANTS
Incline your ear to covenant, sure mercies David. **Isaiah 20:1** (Isaiah 55:3)
Servant comes as messenger before Jesus. **T&C 31:3** (D&C 45:9)
Root servant to do latter-day work. **T&C 129:3** (D&C 113:5)
Branch servant to do latter-day work. **Isaiah 5:4** (Isaiah 11:10)
Servant comes from the East. **T&C 74:9** (D&C 77:9)
Servant comes from East far country. **Isaiah 15:21** (Isaiah 46:11)
Servant will have the correct lineage. **T&C 129:3** (D&C 113:5)
Restorative prophet becomes marred Servant. **3 Ne. 9:12** (3 Ne 21:9-11)
Hear Christ's words through servant or be cut off. **1 Ne. 7:5** (1 Ne. 22:20)
Servant unites Israel and Gentiles. **3 Nephi 10:1** (3 Ne 21:22)
Servant will rule over nations and kings. **Isaiah 15:1** (Isaiah 41:2)
David servant shall be a prince. **Ezekiel 17:10** (Ezekiel 34:23-25)
David servant shall be a king. **Ezekiel 19:6** (Ezekiel 37:24-25)
Servant's name is David. **Isaiah 13:12** (Isaiah 37:35)
Lord will raise up the tabernacle of David. **Amos 1:31** (Amos 9:11)
Servant/Messenger to bring knowledge. **Isaiah 15:10** (Isa 42:18-20)
Servant embodies covenant from Lord to people. **1 Nephi 6:7** (1 Ne 21:8)
Root servant is set up as an ensign. **Isaiah 5:4** (Isaiah 11:10-12)
Servant/messenger is a rallying point to the gentiles. **T&C 31:3** (DC 45:9)
Servant is a witness/leader/commander. **Isaiah 20:1** (Isaiah 55:3-4)
Servant coordinates building New Jerusalem. **Isaiah 15:18** (Isa 45:12-13)
Servant is like unto Moses. **JSH 3:4** (JS-H 1:40)

DENVER SNUFFER AND CONTINUING REVELATION
New name of David unto Denver Snuffer. **T&C 162**
God has given David for a witness unto the people. **Isa. 20:1** (Isa. 55:3-4)
Covenant of peace through servant David. **Ezek. 17:9-11** (Ezek. 34:22-27)
The Pass through Denver Snuffer. **T&C 163**
Gethsemane through Denver Snuffer. **T&C 161**
A Sign, prophecy given by Denver Snuffer. **T&C 164**
An End of Authority through Denver Snuffer. **T&C 166**
Seven Women through Denver Snuffer. **T&C 167**
His Return through Denver Snuffer. **T&C 160**
The Train through Denver Snuffer. **T&C 172**
Prayer for Covenant through Denver Snuffer. **T&C 156**
Answer and Covenant through Denver Snuffer **T&C 157**

Repentant Gentiles numbered with Remnant of Israel

Gathering in haste brings confusion and pestilence. **T&C 50:6** (D&C 63:24)
Remnant of Israel receives revelation. **T&C 129:7** (D&C 113:9-10)
Righteous Gentiles offered covenant in last days **3 Nephi 10:1** (3 Nephi 21:23)
Gentiles offered covenant, Christ in midst. **3 Nephi 10:1-2** (3 Nephi 21:22-25)
Lord takes one of a city and two of a family to Zion. **Jeremiah 2:3** (Jer. 3:14)
Believing Gentiles numbered among Lamanites. **3 Nephi 10:1** (3 Nephi 21: 22)
God's message to those who seek Zion at the last day. **Isaiah 18-19** (Isaiah 52)

SEALED TO THE FATHERS

Sealing Power. **T&C Glossary: Sealing Power**
Priesthood. **T&C Glossary: Priesthood, Priesthood Power.**
Fullness of the Priesthood. **T&C Glossary: Fullness of the Priesthood**
The Fathers. **T&C Glossary: Fathers, The; Powers of Heaven.**
Hearts turned to the Fathers. **T&C Glossary: Hearts turned to the Fathers**
Rights belonging to the Fathers. **T&C Glossary: Rights belonging to Fathers**
Blessings of the Fathers. **T&C Glossary: Blessings of the Fathers.**
Powers of Heaven. **T&C Glossary: Powers of Heaven, Priesthood.**
All invited heaven, to sit down Holy Fathers. **Helaman 2:69** (Helaman 3:27-30)
Seeking for the blessings of the Fathers. **Abraham 1:1** (Abraham 1:2-3)
Adam given dominion over every living thing. **Gen. 2:8-9** (Gen. 1:26-28)
God covenants with Adam and Eve. **Genesis 4:10** (Moses 6:64-66)
Adam first father given priesthood. **Abraham1:1** (Abraham 1:3)
Adam and Eve are after the order of God. **Gen. 4:10** (Moses 6:67)
All things confirmed unto Adam by holy ordinance. **Genesis 3:13** (Moses 5:59)
Abraham promised his posterity to be numerous. **Genesis 7:29** (Genesis 17:2-6)
Seed of Abraham blessed with Gospel, salvation. **Abr. 3:1** (Abr.2:11)
Blessings of Abraham passed Isaac to Jacob. **Genesis 9:20** (Genesis 28:10-16)
God covenants Jacob/Israel. Given land-seed. **Gen. 9:55-56** (Gen. 35:10-15)
Covenant: Abram given land for seed forever. **Genesis 7:11** (Genesis 13:14-16)
Covenant: Abraham's posterity as sands of sea. **Genesis 8:7** (Genesis 22:17-18)
Elijah keys seal hearts fathers to children. **JS History 3:4** (JS History 1:38-39)
Hearts fathers to children, children to fathers. **Malachi 1:11-12** (Malachi 4:4-6)
Fathers and children must be welded together. **T&C 151:14** (D&C 128:18)
Promises made to the fathers-in hearts of children. **JS History 3:4** (D&C 2:1-3)
Becoming heirs to Christ. (Abrahamic covenant) **Galatians 1:12** (Gal. 3:26-29)
Israel invited keep covenant-kingdom of priests. **Exodus 12:1** (Exodus 19:1-6)
Receive priesthood-become seed of Abraham. **T&C 82:16** (D&C 84:34)
Receive priesthood, receive Christ and Father. **T&C 82:17** (D&C 84:35-37)
Promises made to fathers, in the hearts of children. **JSH 3:4** (D&C 2:1-3)
Hearts of fathers to children, children to fathers. **Mal. 1:11-12** (Mal. 4:4-6)

67

Fathers and children must be welded together. **T&C 151:14** (D&C 128:18)
Men are free to choose. **2 Nephi 1:10** (2 Nephi 2:27)
Cry out, Abba Father! Receive adoption. **Romans 1:34** (Romans 8:15-17)

STRANGE ACT
God is unchanging. **Hebrews 1:59-63** (Hebrews. 13:8-20)
Course of the Lord is one eternal round. **1 Nephi 3:5** (1 Nephi 10:19)
Lord gives pattern in all things. **T&C 39:4** (D&C 52:14)
Truth is things as they really are and will be. **Jacob 3:4** (Jacob 4:13)
Truth is things as they are, were, and are to come. **T&C 93:8** (D&C 93:24)
Great and marvelous work begins words Christ. **3 Nephi 9:12** (3 Nephi 21:9-10)
Men are free to choose. **2 Nephi 1:10** (2 Nephi 2:27)
LDS Church under condemnation, vanity-unbelief.**T&C 82:20** (D&C 84:54-55)
Satan lulls church away into carnal security, **2 Nephi 12:4** (2 Nephi 28:21)
Masses say "All is well in Zion" **2 Nephi 12:4** (2 Nephi 28:21)
Joseph identifies church as a Gentile Church. **T&C 123:18** (D&C 109:60)
Christ prophesies Gentile church loses fulness. **3 Nephi 7:5** (3 Nephi 16:10-11)
Gentiles receive not the fulness but reject it. **T&C 31:6**-7 (D&C 45:28-30)
Few only that do not lift themselves in pride. **Mormon 4:5** (Mormon 8:36)
Few humble followers of Christ. **2 Nephi 12:2** (2 Nephi 28:14)
Humble overcome false precepts of men. **2 Nephi 12:2** (2 Nephi 28:14)
Scriptures wrested to their own destruction. **2 Peter 1:14** (2 Peter 3:16)
Wo unto the Gentiles…they will deny me **2 Nephi 12:7** (2 Nephi 28:32)
Ordinances changed, broken everlasting covenant. **Isaiah 7:1** (Isaiah 24:5-6)
House of God needs to be set in order. **T&C 83:4** (D&C 85:7)
Lord will set hand second time to restore people. **2 Nephi 11:6** (2 Nephi 25:17)
Lord will offer hand second time to nourish and prune. **Jacob 4:1** (Jacob 6:2)
Lord set himself again to recover covenant people. **2 Ne. 5:5** (2 Ne. 6:14)
Lord sets his hand again to recover remnant. **2 Ne. 9:22** (2 Ne. 21:11)
Second time is when gentiles repent. **2 Nephi 12:7-8** (2 Nephi 28:32; 29:1)
Lord brings forth His strange act. **T&C 101:20** (D&C 101:95)
Strange act to prune vineyard last time. **T&C 94:1** (D&C 95:4)
A mighty servant to restore much. **2 Nephi 2:7** (2 Nephi 3:24)
Marvelous work has yet to occur. **JS History 11:2** (D&C 4:1)
Marvelous work and wonder to occur in latter days. **JSH 11:2** (D&C 4:1)
Marvelous work after restoration of gospel. **1 Ne. 3:25-26** (1 Ne. 14:1-7)
Marvelous work causes division. **1 Nephi 2:25-26** (1 Nephi 14:1-7)
Marvelous work occurs after Lehi's seed scattered. **1 Ne. 7:3** (1 Ne. 22:8)
Marvelous work after Lord reveals arm. **1 Nephi 7:3** (1 Nephi 22:8-11) *
Marvelous work gathers lost tribes. **1 Nephi 7:3** (1 Nephi 22:12)
Marvelous work comes through covenant servant. **1 Ne. 6:7** (1 Ne. 21:8)
Greater work to reveal hidden mysteries. **Ether 1:19** (Ether 4:13-14)

68

Greater work to "recover my people." **T&C 23:3** (D&C 39:11)
Great revelatory work to reveal folly of Gentiles. **T&C 18:3** (D&C 35:7)
Fullness of gospel includes restoring Israel. **T&C 23:3** (D&C 39:11)
Fullness of gospel is the everlasting covenant. **T&C 58:7** (D&C 133:57)
Marvelous work to restore covenant people. **1 Ne. 6:6-7** (1 Ne. 21:4-6)
Gentiles offered covenant in last days **3 Nephi 10:1** (3 Nephi 21:23)
When men covenant they are salt of the earth. **T&C 101:7** (D&C 101:39-40)
Covenant with His laws in their heart-mind. **Hebrews 1:31** (Hebrews 10:16)
Gentiles who repent are covenant people. **2 Nephi 12:11** (2 Nephi 30:1-2)
Whosoever repents, comes unto me, my church. **JS History 10:19** (D&C 10:67)
Willing to enter covenant, be called name of Christ. **Mosiah 3:1** (Mosiah 5:5)
Baptism and re-baptism covenant. **Mosiah 9:7-8** (Mosiah 18:8-13)
If Gentiles repent, covenant established. **3 Nephi 10:1** (3 Nephi 21:22)
Because of covenant made, become children of Christ. **Mos. 3:2** (Mos. 5:7)
Gentiles experience Christ in midst. **3 Nephi 10:1-2** (3 Nephi 21:22-25)
All invited heaven, to sit down Holy Fathers. **Helaman 2:69** (Helaman 3:27-30)
Seeking for the blessings of the Fathers. **Abraham 1:1** (Abraham 1:2-3)
Hearts of fathers to children, children to fathers. **Mal. 1:11-12** (Mal. 4:4-6)
Elijah keys seal hearts fathers to children. **JS History 3:4** (JS History 1:38-39)
Fathers and children must be welded together. **T&C 151:14** (D&C 128:18)
Promises made to fathers, in the hearts of children. **JSH 3:4** (D&C 2:1-3)
Dispensation fullness of times, keys since Adam. **T&C 151:14** (D&C 128:18)
I will make an everlasting covenant with you. **Isaiah 20:1** (Isaiah 55:3-5)
I will make an everlasting covenant in the last days. **Isaiah 23** (Isaiah 61:8)
Lord will do nothing save reveals His secret to prophets. **Amos 1:9** (Amos 3:7)
Can know a true or false prophet by fruits. **Matthew 3:46** (Matthew 7:15-16)
Fruit of Spirit: love, joy, peace, faith. **Galatians 1:22** (Galatians 5:22-26)
Spirit guides you into all truth. **John 9:14** (John 16:13-16)
Gain knowledge by the gift of Holy Ghost. **T&C 138:21** (D&C 121:26).
Words spoken by the Holy Spirit are scripture. **D&C 55:1** (D&C 68:3-4)
Man not live bread alone, but every word of God. **Matthew 2:5** (Matthew 4:4)
Only part of what Jesus said and did recorded in Bible. **John 11:3** (John 21:25)
God's message to those who seek Zion at the last day. **Isaiah 18-19** (Isaiah 52)
Several called to preach and testify of Christ. **3 Nephi 3:4** (3 Nephi 6:20)
Remnant of Israel receives revelation. **T&C 129:7** (D&C 113:9-10)
Incline your ear to covenant, sure mercies David. **Isaiah 20:1** (Isaiah 55:3)
Servant comes as messenger before Jesus. **T&C 31:3** (D&C 45:9)
Root servant to do latter-day work. **T&C 129:3** (D&C 113:5)
Branch servant to do latter-day work. **Isaiah 5:4** (Isaiah 11:10)
Servant comes from the East. **T&C 74:9** (D&C 77:9)
Servant comes from East far country. **Isaiah 15:21** (Isaiah 46:11)
Servant will have the correct lineage. **T&C 129:3** (D&C 113:5)
Restorative prophet becomes marred Servant. **3 Ne. 9:12** (3 Ne 21:9-11)

Hear Christ's words through servant or be cut off. **1 Ne. 7:5** (1 Ne. 22:20)

Servant unites Israel and Gentiles. **3 Nephi 10:1** (3 Ne 21:22)

Servant will rule over nations and kings. **Isaiah 15:1** (Isaiah 41:2)

David servant shall be a prince. **Ezekiel 17:10** (Ezekiel 34:23-25)

David servant shall be a king. **Ezekiel 19:6** (Ezekiel 37:24-25)

Servant's name is David. **Isaiah 13:12** (Isaiah 37:35)

Lord will raise up the tabernacle of David. **Amos 1:31** (Amos 9:11)

Servant/Messenger to bring knowledge. **Isaiah 15:10** (Isa 42:18-20)

Servant embodies covenant from Lord to people. **1 Nephi 6:7** (1 Ne 21:8)

Root servant is set up as an ensign. **Isaiah 5:4** (Isaiah 11:10-12)

Servant/messenger is a rallying point to the gentiles. **T&C 31:3** (DC 45:9)

Servant is a witness/leader/commander. **Isaiah 20:1** (Isaiah 55:3-4)

Servant coordinates building New Jerusalem. **Isaiah 15:18** (Isa 45:12-13)

Servant is like unto Moses. **JSH 3:4** (JS-H 1:40)

Denver Snuffer is given the *new name of David.* **T&C 162**

God has given David for a witness unto the people. **Isa. 20:1** (Isa. 55:3-4)

Covenant of peace through servant David. **Ezek. 17:9-11** (Ezek. 34:22-27)

The Pass through Denver Snuffer. **T&C 163**

Gethsemane through Denver Snuffer. **T&C 161**

A Sign, prophecy given by Denver Snuffer. **T&C 164**

An End of Authority through Denver Snuffer. **T&C 166**

Seven Women through Denver Snuffer. **T&C 167**

His Return through Denver Snuffer. **T&C 160**

The Train through Denver Snuffer. **T&C 172**

Prayer for Covenant through Denver Snuffer. **T&C 156**

Answer and Covenant through Denver Snuffer **T&C 157**

God has given David for a witness unto the people. **Isaiah 20:1** (Isaiah 55:3)

One mighty and strong to set the House of God in order. **T&C 83:4** (D&C 85:7)

Those who will not believe what man declares. **3 Nephi 9:12** (3 Nephi 21:9)

Don't condemn things God, because of man. **Mor. 8:3-4** (Mor. 8:12-17)

Servant marred, but life of servant in God's hand. **3 Nephi 9:12** (3 Nephi 21:10)

Come-hear everlasting covenant, sure mercies David. **Isaiah 20:1** (Isaiah 55:3)

Blessings or cursing Israel? Repent-obey covenant. **Lev. 13:8-16** (Lev. 26:1-46)

Strange act completes division. **T&C 101:20** (D&C 101:93-95)

Strange act is to prune vineyard for the last time. **T&C 94:1** (D&C 95:4)

Those willing to observe covenants are accepted. **T&C 96:3** (D&C 97:8)

Disbelieving cut off from covenant people. **3 Nephi 9:12** (3 Nephi 21:11)

Lord takes one of a city and two of a family to Zion. **Jeremiah 2:3** (Jer. 3:14)

Covenant people blessed-safe in wilderness. **Ezekiel 17:9-11** (Ezekiel 34:22-31)

Marvelous work gathers righteous upon the land. **1 Ne. 7:3** (1 Ne. 22:8-12)

Lord will reestablish Ephraim in last days. **Jeremiah 12:5-10** (Jeremiah 31)

Lord create new covenant with Judah. **Jeremiah 5-10** (Jeremiah 31)

Everlasting gospel preached unto those on earth. **Revelation 5:2** (Rev. 14:6-7)

Dispensation of the fullness of times. **T&C 151:14** (D&C 128:18)
Dispensation fullness. Glory and keys since Adam. **T&C 151:14** (D&C 128:18)
Purpose of marvelous work is restoration. **2 Nephi 11:6** (2 Nephi 25:17)
Restoration of all things. **T&C 74:14** (D&C 77:14)
Restitution of all things. **Acts 2:3** (Acts 3:21)
Old things are done away, all things new. **3 Nephi 5:31** (3 Nephi 12: 47)
New Heaven/New Earth established for the pure. **Ether 6:1-3** (Ether 13:1-12)
Redeemer will keep His word and come to Zion. **Isaiah 21:2** (Isaiah 59:20-21)
Shall we not go on in so great cause! **T&C 151:15, 18-20** (D&C 128: 19, 22-23)

NOTES:

SATAN AND SECRET COMBINATIONS

SATAN
Satan. **T&C Glossary: Satan**
Lucifer. **T&C Glossary: Lucifer**
Satan rebellious from beginning, fought against truth, prefers lies. **TSJ 6:19**
Devil desired honor of God. Hell prepared. **T&C 9:11** (D&C 29:36-38)
War in heaven, dragon cast out. **Revelations 4:3** (Revelations 12:7-9)
Angel before God thrust down in preexistence **TC 69:6** (D&C 76:25-28)
Angel fallen from heaven. **2 Nephi 1:9** (2 Nephi 2:17-18)
Lucifer, son of morning, fallen from heaven. **Is. 6:6** (Isaiah 14:12-15)
Many spirits followed after Lucifer. **Abraham 6:3** (Abraham 3:27-28)
Third part turn away because of agency. **TC 9:11** (D&C 29: 36-38)
Satan deceives the whole world. **Revelations 4:3** (Revelations 12:9)
God of this world blinds minds. **2 Corinthians 1:12-13** (2 Corinthians 4:3-6)
Powers of darkness prevail upon earth. **T&C 22:4** (D&C 38:11)
Satan deceives, seeking to destroy souls of men. **JSH 10:11** (D&C 10:22-25)
Satan can overcome those confused and fearful. **TSJ 10:16**
He is the source of deceit in this fallen world. **TSJ 6:19**
Satan attempts to destroy freedom of all lands. **Ether 3:17-19** (Ether 8:15-25)
Satan overcome by blood of lamb, testimony. **Revelations 4:4** (Rev. 12:11)
Satan shall be bound. **T&C 29:9** (D&C 43:31)
Satan is bound. **1 Nephi 7:5** (1 Nephi 22:26)
Satan will be bound. **Revelation 8:4** (Revelation 20:1–3).
Satan has no power to tempt. **T&C 101:4-5** (D&C 101:22–31)
Satan has no place in the hearts of children of men. **T&C 31:12** (D&C 45:55)
Satan loosed for little season. **T&C 29:9** (D&C 43:31)
Satan loosed little season end of Millennium. **T&C 86:28** (D&C 88:111-115)
Satan loosed, gathers to battle. **Revelation 8:6** (Revelations 20:7–10)
Armies of devil fight against hosts of heaven. **T&C 86:28** (D&C 88:111–115).
Satan and his followers defeated and cast out. **T&C 86:28** (D&C 88: 111-115)
Battle of Great God. Devil-his angels cast out. **T&C 86:28** (D&C 88:111-115)
Michael shall overcome him who seeks the throne. **T&C 86:28** (D&C 88:115)
Lucifer looked upon narrowly. **2 Nephi 10:6** (2 Nephi 24:12-17)
Kingdom delivered unto the Father. **1 Cor. 1:63** (1 Cor. 15:23-28)

KINGDOMS OF THIS WORLD
Satan rebellious from beginning, fought against truth, prefers lies. **TSJ 6:19**
Devil desired honor of God. Hell prepared. **T&C 9:11** (D&C 29:36-38)
War in heaven, dragon cast out. **Revelations 4:3** (Revelations 12:7-9)
Satan deceives the whole world. **Revelations 4:3** (Revelations 12:9)
Powers of darkness prevail upon earth. **T&C 22:4** (D&C 38:11)

Satan deceives, seeking to destroy souls of men. **JSH 10:11** (D&C 10:22-25)
Satan can overcome those confused and fearful. **TSJ 10:16**
He is the source of deceit in this fallen world. **TSJ 6:19**
God of this world blinds minds. **2 Corinthians 1:12-13** (2 Corinthians 4:3-6)
Satan attempts to destroy freedom of all lands. **Ether 3:17-19** (Ether 8:15-25)
Behold, the enemy is combined. **T&C 22:4** (D&C 38:12)
Spiritual wickedness in high places. **Ephesians 1:25** (Ephesians 6:12)
Political oppression we live under. **T&C 139:14-15** (D&C 123:7-11)
Defend country and your little ones. **Alma 27:10** (Alma 60:29)
Secret murders, oaths and covenants. **Helaman 1:1-3** (Helaman 1:3-12)
Secret band objective to murder and get gain. **Helaman 1:10** (Helaman 2:8)
Secret combinations to get gain. **Alma 8:6-7** (Alma 10:27-32)
Kingmen seeking for power and authority. **Alma 27:7** (Alma 60: 17)
Factions/divisions in government. **Alma 26:33** (Alma 58:36)
America land of liberty-no king. **2 Nephi 7:2** (2 Nephi 10:11)
Government indifferent to freedom. **Alma 27:4** (Alma 59:13)
Laws corrupted, judgments of God coming. **Helaman 2:14** (Helaman 4:22)
High judges let wicked go. Satan's covenant. **3 Nephi 3:5** (3 Nephi 6:27-30)
Judges let guilty go. Head government corrupt. **Helaman 3:1** (Helaman 7:4-5)
People could not be governed by the rule of law. **Helaman 2:15** (Helaman 5:3)
More part Nephites join Gaddiantons. **Helaman 2:31, 35** (Helaman 6:21, 38)
Gaddianton's sole management of government. **Helaman 2:35** (Helaman 6:39)
Robbers administering oaths to destroy the kingdom. **Ether 4:16** (Ether 10:33)
Words of prophets rejected because of secret society. **Ether 4:21** (Ether 11:22)
Powers of darkness on earth. Eternity is pained. **T&C 22:4** (D&C 38: 11)
Enemy is Combined. Angels ready to burn. **T&C 22:4** (D&C 38:12)
More choose evil than good = Destruction. **Helaman 2:15** (Helaman 5:2)
False security that country can't fall. **Helaman 3:6** (Helaman 8:6)
America greatest nation on the earth. **Ether 1:4** (Ether 1:43)
Nation must serve God or be swept off. **Ether 1:6-7** (Ether 2:8-12)
Nation upholds secret combinations destroyed. **Ether 3:17-18** (Ether 8:15-25)
Awake awful situation. **Ether 3:17-19** (Ether 8:15-25)
Bad government, thrones, prisons, taxes, death. **Ether 4:10** (Ether 10:6)
Rule of law gone. Robbers and gangs unrestrained. **Ether 6:6** (Ether 13:31)
Destruction in last days. **T&C 31:7-8** (D&C 45:32-35)
More settled parts land destroyed firsts. **Helaman 2:6** (Helaman 3:23)
Wicked slay the wicked. Consumed with fire. **T&C 50:8** (D&C 63:33-34)
Judging between good and evil. **Moroni 8:3** (Moroni 7:15-16)
Mother of abominations fights the Lamb. **1 Nephi 3:25** (1 Nephi 14:13)
Abominations shall not reign. **T&C 9:6** (D&C 29:21)
Great abominable church cast down by fire. **T&C 9:6** (D&C 29:21)
Wicked consumed with fire. **T&C 50:8** (D&C 63:34)
Spirit of Moroni and covenant of freedom. **Alma 21:13** (Alma 46:34-36)

Spirit of Moroni and the Cause of Christ. **Alma 21:32-33** (Alma 48:10-12)
Patriots preserve rights for God and family. **Alma 20:3** (Alma 43:9)
Remember them that be with us are more. **2 Kings 2:20-22** (2 Kings 6:8-17)
Hope in a better world is anchor to our soul. **Ether 5:1** (Ether 12:4)
If all men were like Moroni. Powers of hell shaken. **Alma 21:34** (Alma 48:17)
Kingdoms of world, become Kingdoms of our Lord! **Rev. 3:15** (Rev. 11:5)

CLEANSING THE EARTH
Destruction during the end times. **Matthew 11:2-11** (Matthew 24:3-39)
Upon my house it will begin. Wrath-burning. **T&C 124:6-7** (D&C 112:23-28)
Last days perilous times shall come. **2 Timothy 1:8** (2 Timothy 3:1-7)
How often I called you by earthquakes, famines. **T&C 29:8** (D&C 43:24-25)
Testimony of thundering and earthquakes. **T&C 86:18** (D&C 88: 89-91)
Terror, famine, pestilence, required to remember Him. **Hel. 4:9** (Hel. 12:3)
Earth trembles. Moon bathed in blood. **T&C 86:17** (D&C 88:87)
Great hailstorm destroys crops of earth. **T&C 9:5** (D&C 29: 16)
Desolating scourge, sickness shall cover the land. **T&C 31:7** (D&C 45:31)
Hills and mountains quake. **Helaman 4:10** (Helaman 12:9)
People destroyed more wicked parts of the land. **Helaman 4:2** (Helaman 11:6)
God destroys/curses wicked for their sakes. **1 Nephi 5:20** (1 Nephi 17:36-38)
None to stop the shedding of blood. **Ether 6:6** (Ether 13:31)
Abominable church drunken with own blood. **1 Nephi 7:4** (1 Nephi 22:13)
Wicked destroy wicked. **Mormon 2:1** (Mormon 4:4-5)
Wicked slay wicked and are consumed with fire. **T&C 50:8** (D&C 63:33-34)
Saints shall hardly escape. **T&C 50:8** (D&C 63:33-34)
Prayers of righteous delay destruction. **Alma 8:5** (Alma 10:22)
Repent, prepare the way of the Lord, or be destroyed. **Ether 4:7** (Ether 9:28)
Fear shall come upon all people. **T&C 86:18** (D&C 88:91)
Gentiles will be destroyed. **Matthew 10:16** (JST Matthew 21:56)
Summer past, death overtake you, souls not saved. **T&C 31:1** (D&C 45:2)
Country desolate, except small remnant. **Isaiah 1:1** (Isaiah 1:7-9)
Who can abide His coming? Like refiner's fire. **Malachi 1:6** (Malachi 3:2-3)
Labor for Zion.If labor for money will perish. **2 Nephi 11:17** (2 Nephi 26:31)
Wise receive truth, shall abide the day. **T&C 31:12** (D&C 45:56-57)
Stand in holy places and be not moved. **T&C 85:4** (D&C 87:8)
Those who fight against Zion are destroyed. **1 Nephi 7:4** (1 Nephi 22:14-19)
End of all nations. Inhabitants of earth mourn. **T&C 85:3** (D&C 87:6)
Death is swallowed up in the victory of Christ. **Alma 15:9** (Alma 27:28)
Death swallowed up in victory. Lord wipes tears. **Isaiah 7:3** (Isaiah 25:8-9)
Return unto Jesus Christ and be healed. **3 Nephi 4:7** (3 Nephi 9:13-15)

CALAMITIES AND DESTRUCTION

Satan deceives, seeking to destroy souls of men. **JSH 10:11** (D&C 10:22-27)
If voice people chooses iniquity, ripe for destruction. **Alma 8:5** (Alma 10:19)
When righteous cast out, ripe for destruction. **Hel. 5:3** (Hel. 13:13-14)
When majority chooses evil = destruction. **Helaman 2:15** (Helaman 5:2)
Secret combinations oppress the people. **Alma 17:12** (Alma 37:21)
Secret combinations in more settled parts of the land. **Hel. 2:6** (Hel. 3:23)
Robbers administer old oaths to destroy kingdom. **Ether 4:16** (Ether 10:33)
Nations that uphold secret combinations destroyed. **Eth. 3:17-18** (Eth. 8:15-23)
More part of Nephites join Gaddiantons. **Helaman 2:30-31** (Helaman 6:18, 21)
Gaddiantons take sole management Government. **Hel. 2:35** (Hel. 6:39)
Foundation for destruction laid by lawyers. **Alma 8:5** (Alma 10:17)
People could not be governed by the rule of law. **Helaman 2:15** (Helaman 5:3)
Spirit will not always strive with man. **T&C 54:5** (D&C 1:33)
Speedy destruction when Spirit ceases with man. **2 Ne. 11:11** (2 Ne. 26:11)
Will not endure sound doctrine. **2 Timothy 1:10** (2 Timothy 4:2-4)
If you wrest scriptures, be to your destruction. **Alma 10:2** (Alma 13:20)
False security that U.S.A. can't fall. **Helaman 3:6** (Helaman 8:5-6)
This land choice land, serve God or be swept off. **Ether 1:7** (Ether 2:9-12)
Nephi mourns "how long God suffer this sin? **Hel. 3:16** (Hel. 9:21-22)
Prophets foretold of the very things now underway. **TSJ 2:4**

DIVINE PROTECTION

The Lord will gather the elect. **T&C 16:2** (D&C 33:6)
Gathering of elect into one place. **T&C 9:3** (D&C 29:8)
Lord is refuge and fortress. Angels bear us up. **Psalms 91:1-2** (Psalms 91:1-16)
God of Israel go before you, be rearward. **3 Nephi 9:10** (3 Nephi 20:42)
Friendship of the world is enmity with God. **James 1:16** (James 4:4)
God causes great division. His people spared. **2 Nephi 12:13** (2 Nephi 30:10)
Gentiles will be destroyed. **Matthew 10:16** (JST Matthew 21:56)
God will swallow up death in victory. **Isaiah 7:3** (Isaiah 25:8)
Vengeance is Lord's, not our role. **Mormon 1:11** (Mormon 3:15)
Defend only, no pre-emptive strikes. **Alma 21:34** (Alma 48:14)
Pre-emptive strikes bring destruction. **Mormon 2:1** (Mormon 4:4)
Permissible to defend family, rights, religion. **Alma 20:11** (Alma 43:47)
Few Humble Followers of Christ. **2 Nephi 12:2** (2 Nephi 28:14)
Overcome Satan through blood of lamb and testimony. **Rev. 4:4** (Rev.12:11)
Journey into the wilderness. **1 Nephi 5:3** (1 Nephi 16:9)
Lehi's family commanded into the wilderness. **1 Nephi 1:6** (1 Nephi 2:2)
Nephi warned to flee into the wilderness **2 Nephi 4:2** (2 Nephi 5:5-7)
Mosiah warned to flee into the wilderness. **Omni 1:6** (Omni 1:12-13)
People depart by night into wilderness. **Mosiah 10:2** (Mosiah 22:8-10)

Alma and people depart into wilderness. **Mosiah 11:10-12** (Mosiah 24:16-25)
Lord create dwelling place on Mount Zion a defense. **Isaiah 1:12** (Isaiah 4:5)
Zion escape for those who follow God's commands. **T&C 96:7** (D&C 97:25)
Zion is an escape from the destructions. **Genesis 4:22** (Moses 7:60-62)
Land of inheritance for your children. Jesus as King. **T&C 22:6** (D&C 38:20)
Zion a covert from the storm for those purged. **Isaiah 1:12** (Isaiah 4:5-6)
Zion defended with smoke by day, fire by night. **Isaiah 1:12** (Isaiah 4:5)
Those fight against Zion shall perish. **2 Nephi 7:2-3** (2 Ne. 10:11-14, 16-17)
Who can stand against God? Despisers perish. **Mormon 4:9** (Mormon 9:26)
Lord God is mighty in the midst of thee. **Zephaniah 1:12** (Zephaniah 3:17)
Those fight against Zion shall be as a night vision. **2 Ne. 11:18** (2 Ne. 27:3)
No weapon against will prosper. **3 Nephi 10:3** (3 Nephi 22:17)
Heritage of servants of the Lord. **3 Nephi 10:3** (3 Nephi 22:17)
If God be for us who can be against us. **Romans 1:37** (Romans 8:31)
Hope in a better world is anchor to soul. **Ether 5:1** (Ether 12:4)

A NEW HEAVEN AND A NEW EARTH
New Earth. **T&C Glossary: New Earth**
New Heaven. **T&C Glossary: New Heaven**
New Heaven/New Earth. New Jerusalem. **Ether 6:3** (Ether 13:1-12)
Jesus Christ comes in glory, dwells for thousand years. **T&C 9:3** (D&C 29:11)
Jesus Christ returns and Earth given to righteous. **T&C 31:12** (D&C 45:56-58)
Jesus Christ will reign personally upon earth. **T&C 146:30** (Article of Faith 10)
Jesus to reign on the earth. **Zechariah 1:39** (Zechariah 14:4–9)
Jesus to reign on the earth. **1 Nephi 7:5** (1 Nephi 22:24–25)
Lord will be in midst of people as King and lawgiver. **T&C 31:12** (D&C 45:59)
Ancient of days given dominion and glory. **Daniel 7:4** (Daniel 7:13-14)
Enoch and his city receive Zion-thousand years. **Genesis 4:22** (Moses 7:62-65)
Lord of Hosts reign in Mount Zion. **Isaiah 7:2** (Isaiah 24:23)
This is our God; we have waited for Him. **Isaiah 7:3** (Isaiah 25:8-12)
Those suffer persecution, death, partake of glory. **T&C 101:6** (D&C 101:35)
Fear not even unto death, in Christ joy is full. **T&C 101:6** (D&C 101:35-36)
He that overcomes shall inherit all things. **Revelations 8:9** (Revelations 21:7)
Martyrs for Christ reign thousand years. **Revelation 8:4-5** (Revelation 20:1-4)
Blessed are meek for they shall inherit the earth. **Matthew 3:8** (Matthew 5:5)
Kingdom given to saints of most high. **Daniel 7:8** (Daniel 7:27)
John sees new heaven and new earth. **Revelations 8:8** (Revelations 21:1-5)
Ocean driven back. All continents made one. **T&C 58:3** (D&C 133:20-25)
Righteousness and peace for 1,000 years. **T&C 86:1-28** (D&C 88:11-115)
Time is no longer. **T&C 86:27** (D&C 88:110)
Children grow up without sin unto salvation. **T&C 31:12** (D&C 45:58)
Enmity between man, beasts, all flesh shall cease. **T&C 101:5** (D&C 101:26)

Wolf and lamb to dwell together. **Isaiah 5:4** (Isaiah 11:6)
Desolate land like Garden of Eden. **Ezekiel 18:10-11** (Ezekiel 36:34-38)
During Millennium no sorrow because no death. **T&C 101:5** (D&C 101:29)
Changed twinkling of eye. **T&C 50:11-12** (D&C 63:49-53)
Infants live age of a tree. Changed in twinkling. **T&C 101:5** (D&C 101:30)
Islands become one land. **T&C 58:3** (D&C 133:17-25)
Lord will reveal all things. **T&C 101:5** (D&C 101:32) (D&C 101:32-34)
Saints filled with knowledge, sing a new song! **T&C 82:27** (D&C 84:98)
City of Enoch returns to New Jerusalem. **Genesis 4:22**. (Moses 7:62-63)
Satan overcome by blood of lamb, testimony. **Revelations 4:4** (Rev. 12:11)
Lucifer. **T&C Glossary: Lucifer**
Lucifer looked upon narrowly. **2 Nephi 10:6** (2 Nephi 24:12-17)
Satan shall be bound. **T&C 29:9** (D&C 43:31)
Satan is bound. **1 Nephi 7:5** (1 Nephi 22:26)
Satan will be bound. **Revelation 8:4** (Revelation 20:1-3).
Satan has no power to tempt. **T&C 101:4-5** (D&C 101:22–31)
Satan has no place in the hearts of children of men. **T&C 31:12** (D&C 45:55)
Satan loosed for little season. **T&C 29:9** (D&C 43:31)
Satan loosed little season end of Millennium. **T&C 86:28** (D&C 88:111-115)
Satan loosed, gathers to battle. **Revelation 8:6** (Revelations 20:7–10)
Armies of devil fight against hosts of heaven. **T&C 86:28** (D&C 88:111–115).
Satan and his followers defeated and cast out. **T&C 86:28** (D&C 88: 111-115)
Battle of Great God. Devil-his angels cast out. **T&C 86:28** (D&C 88:111-115)
Michael shall overcome him who seeks the throne. **T&C 86:28** (D&C 88:115)
End 1,000 years, new heaven and new earth. **T&C 9:7** (D&29:22-25)
Curtain of heaven unfolded. **T&C 86:20** (D&C 88:95)
Earth sanctified, immortal, eternal. **T&C 74:1** (D&C 77:1)
John sees earth like a sea of glass. **Revelation 2:2** (Revelations 4:6)
Sanctified earth like Urim and Thummim. **T&C Glossary** (D&C 130:8-11)
Celestial earth is home for righteous. **T&C 86:4** (D&C 88:25-26)
Church of the Firstborn. **T&C Glossary: Church of the Firstborn**
Church of the Firstborn caught up. **T&C 69:25** (D&C 76:94, 98-102)
Lord shall be King of whole earth. **Zechariah 1:39** (Zechariah 14:4-9)
Kingdom delivered unto the Father. **1 Cor. 1:63** (1 Cor. 15:23-28)
Lord's course is one eternal round. **T&C 18:1** (D&C 35:1)

FALL OF BABYLON

THE WHORE
Whore is Babylon. **T&C 84:1** (D&C 86:3)
Babylon is the Great Mother of Harlots. **Revelations 6:10** (Revelation 17:1-6)
Whore is among all nations and people. **1 Nephi 3:28** (1 Nephi 14:11)
Abominable church is whore of all earth. **1 Nephi 3:27** (1 Nephi 14:10)
Great and Abominable Church. **T&C Glossary: Great-Abominable Church**
Mother of abominations fights the Lamb. **1 Nephi 3:28** (1 Nephi 14:13)
Friendship of the world is enmity with God. **Jacob 1:16** (James 4:4)
Whole world in sin, possessions above another. **T&C 35:6** (D&C 49:20)
Political tyranny. Oppression we live under. **T&C 139:14** (D&C 123:7-11)
Whore of all the earth must tumble to the earth. **2 Nephi 12:4** (2 Nephi 28:18)
Whore of all earth will be drunk with own blood. **1 Nephi 7:4** (1 Nephi 22:13)
Those who fight against Zion are part of whore. **2 Nephi 7:3** (2 Nephi 10:16)
Church Lamb small due to wickedness of whore. **1 Nephi 3:28** (1 Nephi 14:12)
Great abominable church cast down by fire. **T&C 9:6** (D&C 29:21)
Great shall be the fall of the whore. **1 Nephi 7:4** (1 Nephi 22:14)

JUDGMENT UPON THE WORLD
Wrath. **T&C Glossary Wrath, Woe.**
Two Churches Only. Church Lamb, Church devil **1 Nephi 3:27** (1 Nephi 14:10)
Powers of darkness prevail upon earth. **T&C 22:4** (D&C 38:11)
Upon my house it will begin. Wrath-burning. **T&C 124:6-7** (D&C 112:23-28)
Parable of the wheat and tares. **Matthew 7:9** (Matthew 13:40-43)
Parable of the ten virgins. **Matthew 11:15** (Matthew 25:1-13)
Friendship of the world is enmity with God, **Jacob 1:16** (James 4:4)
Curse-judgment upon all nations that forget God. **T&C 58:1** (D&C 133:2)
Signs in heaven. Vengeance upon wicked. **T&C 9:5** (D&C 29:14-17)
Son to come-reward all according to their works. **Matt. 9:3** (Matt. 16:27)
The Lord cometh to execute judgement upon all. **Jude 1:3** (Jude 1:14:15)
Fear comes upon all people, men's hearts fail them. **T&C 86:18** (D&C 88:91)
Howl ye for the day of Lord is at hand. **Isaiah 6:2** (Isaiah 13:6)
World punished for evil. Haughtiness made low. **Isaiah 6:2** (Isaiah 13:11)
Wicked slay the wicked. Consumed with fire. **T&C 50:8** (D&C 63:33-34)
Fire will devour the great and abominable church. **T&C 9:6** (D&C 29:21)
All the proud, wicked, shall be as stubble. **Malachi 1:10** (Malachi 4:1-3)
Vengeance on disobedient at Christ's coming. **2 Thess. 1:2** (2 Thess. 1:7-10)
People destroyed in more wicked parts of land. **Helaman 4:2** (Helaman 11:6)
Lord empties Babylon with destroying wind. **Jeremiah 18:10** (Jeremiah 51:1-2)
Destruction in last days. **T&C 31:7-8** (D&C 45:32-35)
More settled parts land destroyed firsts. **Helaman 2:6** (Helaman 3:23)
Pit shall be filled by those who dug it. **1 Nephi 3:25** (1 Nephi 14:3)

Abominations shall not reign. **T&C 9:6** (D&C 29:21)
Destruction-calamities during end times. **Matthew 11:2-11** (Matthew 24:3-39)
Great hailstorm destroys crops. **T&C 9:5** (D&C 29:16)
Testimony of stars, thundering and earthquakes. **T&C 86:18** (D&C 88: 89-91)
Hills and mountains quake. **Helaman 4:10** (Helaman 12:9)
Moon shall turn to blood. Weeping-wailing. **Joel 1:12** (Joel 2:30-32)
Vengeance cometh speedily upon ungodly. **T&C 96:7** (D&C 97:22)
Nations mourn, those laughed shall see folly. **T&C 31:10** (D&C 45:49-50)
Lord holds destiny all armies and nations. **T&C 133:1** (D&C 117:6)
Great abominable church drunk with own blood. **1 Nephi 7:4** (1 Nephi 22:13)
Pit shall be filled by those who dug it. **1 Nephi 3:25** (1 Nephi 14:3)
Full end of all nations. Stand in holy places. **T&C 85:3-4** (D&C 87:6, 8)
Babylon suddenly fallen. Work of Lord in Zion. **Jer. 18:10-11** (Jer. 51:8-10)
Babylon the great is fallen. **Revelations 7:1** (Revelations 18:2)
Babylon the great shall fall. **T&C 54:3** (D&C 1:16)
Who can stand against God? **Mormon 4:9** (Mormon 9:26)

FLEE INTO THE WILDERNESS
Upon my house it shall begin. **T&C 124:6** (D&C 112:25-26)
Escape veil of darkness-destruction. **Genesis 4:22-23** (Moses 7:60-62, 66-67)
Flee out of Babylon for the nations are mad. **Jeremiah 18:10** (Jeremiah 51:6-7)
Flee Babylon and declare the work of Lord in Zion. **Jer. 18:10-11** (Jer. 51:6-10)
Gentiles shall be destroyed. **Matthew 10:16** (JST Mathew 21:56)
Go ye out from Babylon. Be clean. Gather. **T&C 58:1** (D&C 133:5-7)
The Lord will gather the elect. **T&C 16:2** (D&C 33:6)
Flee the land to escape enemies. **T&C 41:2** (D&C 54:7)
Lehi's family commanded into the wilderness. **1 Nephi 1:6** (1 Nephi 2:2)
Lord is merciful in warning Lehi to flee. **2 Nephi 1:1** (2 Nephi 1:3)
Sons of Lehi do not want Jews to know of flight. **1 Nephi 1:20** (1 Nephi 4:36)
Nephi warned to flee into the wilderness. **2 Nephi 4:2** (2 Nephi 5:5-7)
Mosiah warned to flee into the wilderness. **Omni 1:6** (Omni 1:12-13)
People depart by night into wilderness. **Mosiah 10:2-3** (Mosiah 22:8-13)
Alma - people depart into the wilderness. **Mosiah 11:10-12** (Mosiah 24:16-25)
Journey into the wilderness. **1 Nephi 5:3** (1 Nephi 16:9)
Let not your flight be in haste. **T&C 58:2** (D&C 133:15)
Shall not go out with haste nor go by flight. **3 Nephi 9:10** (3 Nephi 20:42)
Shall not go out with haste, Lord go before you. **Isaiah 18:8** (Isaiah 52:12)
Inhabitants of earth to flee wrath. **T&C 141:35** (D&C 124:106)
Those who will not fight, must flee unto Zion. **T&C 31:15** (D&C 45:68)
Let those among Gentiles flee unto Zion. **T&C 58:2** (D&C 133:12)
Hope in a better world is anchor to our soul. **Ether 5:1** (Ether 12:4

HOLY PRIESTHOOD

There is only one priesthood, *"after the order of my only Begotten Son."* (T&C 141:41). Conceptualizing priesthood in degrees is done for the purpose of considering role, influence, and progression. Personal affiliation with the Powers of Heaven determines degree of priesthood.

AARONIC
Priesthood. **T&C Glossary: Priesthood, Powers of Heaven.**
Aaronic Priesthood. **T&C Glossary: Aaronic Priesthood**
No man taketh this honor unto himself. **Hebrews 1:12** (Hebrews 5:4)
The Lord shall purify the sons of Levi. **Malachi 1:6** (Malachi 3:3)
Aaronic priesthood holds keys of ministering angels **T&C 82:14** (D&C 84:26)
Oath and Covenant of the priesthood. **T&C 82:17** (D&C 84:35-42)
Perfection does not come by Levitical Priesthood. **Heb. 1:19** (Heb. 7:11)
Many are called. Few are chosen. TC Reference **T&C 139:5** (D&C 121:34)
Hearts are set on world. Aspire to honors of me. **T&C 139:5** (D&C 121:35)
Unrighteous dominion = Amen to priesthood. **T&C 139:5** (D&C 121:37)
Priestcraft. **T&C Glossary: Priestcraft, Powers of Heaven.**
Keys. **T&C Glossary: Keys, Priesthood, Power in the.**
Fullness of Priesthood lost to church. **T&C 141:10** (D&C 124:28)
Faithful obtain priesthood to magnify calling. **T&C 82:16** (D&C 84:33)
If virtuous, priesthood distills upon your soul **T&C 139:6** (D&C 121:45)
Those called to bring Zion hold priesthood power. **T&C 129:4** (D&C 113:7-8)

MELCHIZEDEK
Priesthood. **T&C Glossary: Priesthood, Priesthood, Power in the.**
Melchizedek Priesthood. **T&C Glossary: Melchizedek Priesthood.**
Enoch's words-power to make mountains flee. **Gen. 4:2** (Moses 6: 31-34)
Melchizedek High Priest. Order Son of God. **Gen. 7:18** (JST Gen 14:26-29)
Fathers and children-welding link. **T&C 151:14** (D&C 128:18)
Abraham seeks for the blessings of the fathers. **Abr. 1:1** (Abr. 1:2)
Abraham seeks Priesthood, like the Fathers. **Abr. 1:1** (Abr. 1:4)
Abraham received priesthood through fathers. **T&C 82:10** (D&C 84:14-16)
Through Abraham's seed Priesthood to be in all nations. **Abr. 3:1** (Abr. 2:9-10)
Pharaoh tried imitate order from the Fathers. **Abraham 2:3** (Abraham 1:26)
Holy Order involves preaching repentance. **Alma 3:8-9** (Alma 5:44-49)
Holy Order correlates with entering rest of Lord. **Alma 10:1** (Alma 13:16)
Holy Order given to those who prove themselves. **Alma 9:10** (Alma 13:3-4)
Many choose to repent and be ordained in holy order. **Alma 10:1** (Alma 13:10)
Alma Holy Order. Pure testimony to end contention. **Alma 2:5** (Alma 4:19-20)

Alma consecrated to be High Priest over the church. **Alma 3:1 (**Alma 5:3)
Men ordained according to gifts and calling of God. **Moroni 3:1** (Moroni 3:4)
Ordained in manner people would take notice. **Alma 9:10** (Alma 13:2)
Power of word, mountains moved, roar of lions. **Genesis 4:13** (Moses 7:13)
Moroni leaves God's strength-blessings with freemen. **Alma 27:9** (Alma 60:25)
Power in Christ. Miracles among the people. **4 Nephi 1:6** (4 Nephi 1:30)
Lord's word smites earth. His power delivers. **3 Nephi 13:4** (3 Nephi 28:19-22)
Power in the Priesthood. **T&C Glossary: Priesthood, Power in the.**
Israel invited to covenant & become a nation of priests. **Exo 12:1** (Exo 19:1-5)
Priesthood revealed by Elijah before Lord comes. **JS History 3:4** (D&C 2:1)
Whoso is faithful obtaining these two priesthoods **T&C 82:16** (D&C 84:33)
Man must be called of God the way Aaron was. **Hebrews 1:12** (Hebrews 5:4)
Aaron was called of God by revelation. **Exodus 20:1** (Exodus 40:13)
Those who bring Zion hold priesthood power. **T&C 129:4** (D&C 113:7-8)
Priesthood needed for Zion. **T&C 129:4** (D&C 113:8)
Receive priesthood-become seed of Abraham. **T&C 82:16**(D&C 84:34)
Receive priesthood, receive Christ and Father. **T&C 82:17** (D&C 84:35-37)

PATRIARCHAL PRIESTHOOD
Priesthood. **T&C Glossary: Priesthood, Priesthood, Power in the.**
The Fathers. **T&C Glossary: Fathers, The; Powers of Heaven.**
Hearts turned to the Fathers. **T&C Glossary: Hearts turned to the Fathers**
Rights belonging to the Fathers. **T&C Glossary: Rights belonging to Fathers**
Blessings of the Fathers. **T&C Glossary: Blessings of the Fathers.**
Powers of Heaven. **T&C Glossary: Powers of Heaven, Priesthood.**
High Priesthood prepared from eternity to all eternity. **Alma 9:10** (Alma 13:7)
Order of Son of God has no beginning or end. **Heb. 1:17** (JST Heb. 7:3)
Jesus Christ has unchangeable priesthood. **Hebrews 1:20-21** (Hebrews 7:24-28)
Priesthood without beginning of days or end of years. **Alma 9:10** (Alma 13:7)
Adam given dominion over every living thing. **Gen. 2:8-9** (Gen. 1:26-28)
Adam first father given priesthood. **Abraham1:1** (Abraham 1:3)
Adam and Eve are after the order of God. **Gen. 4:10** (Moses 6:67)
Adam covenants through baptism **Gen. 4:10** (Moses 6:64)
All things confirmed unto Adam by holy ordinance. **Gen. 3:13** (Moses 5:59)
High and Holy Order of the High Priesthood. **Alma 9:10-10:2** (Alma 13:1-20)
Pure language of Adam associated with Priesthood. **Gen. 3:14** (Moses 6:5-6)
Lord confounds the language. **Genesis. 6:6** (Genesis 11:1-9)
T&C Glossary: Great Knowledge and Greater Knowledge
Lord gives Abraham His name, priesthood of his father. **Abr. 1:5** (Abr. 1:18)
Priesthood conferred by fathers from beginning of time. **Abr. 1:1** (Abr. 1:3)
Appointment unto priesthood from the Fathers. **Abraham 1:1** (Abraham 1:4)
Men ordained according gifts and calling of God. **Moroni 3:1** (Moroni 3:4)

By the power of word, mountains moved, roar of lions. **Gen 4:13** (Moses 7:13)
Powers of heaven in midst of this people. **3 Nephi 9:8** (3 Nephi 20:22)
In war Moroni leaves strength power blessing. **Alma 27:9** (Alma 60:25)
Power in Christ. Miracles among the people. **4 Nephi 1:6** (4 Nephi 1:30)
Nephi asks Lord to use famine instead of war. **Hel. 4:1-2** (Hel. 11:1-5)
Lord's word smites earth. His power delivers. **3 Nephi 13:4** (3 Nephi 28:19-22)
God gives power stronger than many waters to Moses. **Gen. 1:5** (Moses 1:25)
In name of Jesus, trees, mountains, waves obey us. **Jacob 3:2** (Jacob 4:6)
Israel invited to covenant & become nation of priests. **Exo. 12:1**(Exo. 19:1)
Those who give life for name of Christ-crowned. **T&C 101:3** (D&C 101:11)
Priesthood continues in church of God to generations. **T&C 82:10** (D&C 84:17)
Receive priesthood-become seed of Abraham. **T&C 82:16** (D&C 84:34)
Receive priesthood, receive Christ and Father. **T&C 82:17** (D&C 84:35-37)
Fullness of the Priesthood. **T&C Glossary: Fullness of the Priesthood**

NOTES:

COVENANT

NEW AND EVERLASTING COVENANT-ANCIENT
Lord's course is one eternal round. **1 Nephi 3:5** (1 Nephi 10:19)
Everlasting covenant existed in beginning. **T&C 35:3** (D&C 49:9)
Everlasting covenant sent as standard to prepare people. **T&C 31:3** (D&C 45:9)
Oath and Covenant. **T&C Glossary: Oath and Covenant**
The Lord gives pattern in all things. **T&C 39:4** (D&C 52:14)
God covenants with Adam and Eve. **Genesis 4:10** (Moses 6:64-66)
All things confirmed unto Adam by holy ordinance. **Genesis 3:13** (Moses 5:59)
Adam-Eve covenant through sacrifice, baptism. **Genesis 4:10** (Moses 6:64-66)
God covenants with Noah and his seed. **Genesis 5:22** (Genesis 9:8-17)
Abraham seeks for the blessings of the fathers. **Abraham 1:1** (Abraham 1:2)
Abrahamic covenant. **Genesis 7:29** (Genesis 17:2-7)
Abraham received priesthood through the fathers. **T&C 82:10** (D&C 84:14-16)
Abraham promised his posterity to be numerous. **Genesis 7:29** (Genesis 17:2-6)
Seed of Abraham blessed with Gospel, salvation. **Abr. 3:1** (Abr. 2:11)
Blessings of Abraham passed Isaac to Jacob. **Genesis 9:20** (Genesis 28:10-16)
God covenants Jacob/Israel. Given land-seed. **Gen. 9:55-56** (Gen. 35:10-15)
Covenant: Abram given land for seed forever. **Genesis 7:11** (Genesis 13:14-16)
Covenant: Abraham's posterity as sands of sea. **Genesis 8:7** (Genesis 22:17-18)
All invited enter gate, sit with Holy Fathers. **Helaman 2:7** (Helaman 3:27-30)
Israel invited keep covenant-be peculiar treasure. **Exodus 12:1** (Exodus 19:1-5)
Elijah keys seal hearts fathers to children. **JS History 3:4** (JS History 1:38-39)
Hearts fathers to children, children to fathers. **Malachi 1:11-12** (Malachi 4:4-6)
Fathers and children must be welded together. **T&C 151:14** (D&C 128:18)
Promises made to the fathers-in hearts of children. **JS History 3:4** (D&C 2:1-3)
Becoming heirs to Christ. (Abrahamic covenant) **Galatians 1:12** (Gal. 3:26-29)
Israel invited keep covenant-kingdom of priests. **Exodus 12:1** (Exodus 19:1-6)
Ordinances changed, broken everlasting covenant. **Isaiah 7:1** (Isaiah 24:5-6)
Blessings-cursings declared for Israel. **Leviticus 13:8-16** (Leviticus 26:1-46)
Gather together those make covenant by sacrifice. **Psalms 50:1** (Psalms 50:5)
Christ is the messenger of the covenant. **Malachi 1:6** (Malachi 3:1)
Christ is mediator of the new covenant. **Hebrews 1:22-23** (Hebrews 8:6-13)
Those hear Christ, children of the covenant. **3 Nephi 9:8.** (3 Nephi 20:21-26)
Lord sends his angels then and now. **Alma 19:3** (Alma 39:19)
Men are free to choose. **2 Nephi 1:10** (2 Nephi 2:27)
Come, Lord will make an everlasting covenant. **Isaiah 20:1** (Isaiah 55:3)
Cry out, Abba Father! Receive adoption. **Romans 1:34** (Romans 8:15-17)

NEW AND EVERLASTING COVENANT-MODERN

Great and marvelous work begins words Christ. **3 Nephi 9:12** (3 Nephi 21:9-10)
That mine everlasting covenant might be established. **T&C 54:4** (D&C 1:22)
New - Everlasting covenant from the beginning. **JS History 18:8** (D&C 22:1)
Oath and Covenant. **T&C Glossary: Oath and Covenant**
Old covenants done away, no entry law Moses. **JS History 18:8** (D&C 22:1-2)
Old things are done away, all becomes new. **3 Nephi 5:31** (3 Nephi 12: 47)
Without Christ, strangers from covenants. **Ephesians 1:6** (Ephesians 2:12)
Stand by my servant Joseph Smith faithfully. **JS History 13:9** (D&C 6:18)
Oath and covenant of the priesthood. **T&C 82:17** (D&C 84:33-40)
Church under condemnation, vanity-unbelief. **T&C 82:20** (D&C 84:54-55)
Satan lulls church away into carnal security, **2 Nephi 12:4** (2 Nephi 28:21)
Masses say "All is well in Zion" **2 Nephi 12:4** (2 Nephi 28:21)
Joseph identifies church as a Gentile Church. **T&C 123:18** (D&C 109:60)
Christ prophesies Gentile church loses fulness. **3 Nephi 7:5** (3 Nephi 16:10-11)
Gentiles receive not the fulness but reject it. **T&C 31:6-7** (D&C 45:28-30)
Wo unto the Gentiles…they will deny me **2 Nephi 12:7** (2 Nephi 28:32)
Ordinances changed, broken everlasting covenant. **Isaiah 7:1** (Isaiah 24:5-6)
House of God needs to be set in order. **T&C 83:4** (D&C 85:7)
Lord sets hand second time to restore people. **2 Nephi 11:6** (2 Nephi 25:17)
Lord offers hand second time to nourish and prune. **Jacob 4:1** (Jacob 6:2)
Covenant with His laws in their heart and mind. **Heb. 1:31** (Heb. 10:16)
Marvelous work has yet to occur. **JS History 11:2** (D&C 4:1)
The Lord brings forth His strange act. **T&C 101:20** (D&C 101:95)
Strange act to prune vineyard last time. **T&C 94:1** (D&C 95:4)
Several called to preach and testify of Christ. **3 Nephi 3:4** (3 Nephi 6:20)
When men covenant they are salt of the earth. **T&C 101:7** (D&C 101:39-40)
Gentiles who repent are covenant people. **2 Nephi 12:11** (2 Nephi 30:1-2)
Whosoever repents, comes unto me, my church. **JS History 10:19** (D&C 10:67)
Willing to enter covenant, be called name of Christ. **Mosiah 3:1** (Mosiah 5:5)
Baptism and re-baptism covenant. **Mosiah 9:7-8** (Mosiah 18:8-13)
If Gentiles repent, covenant established. **3 Nephi 10:1** (3 Nephi 21:22)
Few only that do not lift themselves in pride. **Mormon 4:5** (Mormon 8:36)
Few humble followers of Christ. **2 Nephi 12:2** (2 Nephi 28:14)
Humble overcome false precepts of men. **2 Nephi 12:2** (2 Nephi 28:14)
Scriptures wrested to their own destruction. **2 Peter 1:14** (2 Peter 3:16)
Scriptures given for salvation of elect. **T&C 18:6** (D&C 35:20–21)
Remnant of Israel receives revelation. **T&C 129:5** (D&C 113:9-10)
God makes new covenant with House of Israel. **Jer. 12:9** (Jer. 31:31-34)
Lord sends his angels then and now. **Alma 19:3** (Alma 39:19)
Angels prepare men for covenant work. **Moroni 7:6-7** (Moroni 7:31-38)
Lord has sent his angel to the people to cry repentance. **Alma 7:6** (Alma 9:25)
Everlasting Gospel comes from the angels. **T&C 86:24** (D&C 88:103)

Righteous Gentiles offered covenant in last days **3 Nephi 10:1** (3 Nephi 21:22-23)
Time Gentiles offered covenant, Christ in midst. **3 Nephi 10:1** (3 Nephi 21:25)
Lord is the messenger of the covenant. **Malachi 1:6** (Malachi 3:1)
Everlasting covenant given unto the people. **Isaiah 20:1** (Isaiah 55:3-4)
God has given David for a witness unto the people. **Isaiah 20:1** (Isaiah 55:3)
The new name of David given to Denver Snuffer. **T&C 162**
Prayer for Covenant through Denver Snuffer. **T&C 156**
Answer and Covenant through Denver Snuffer. **T&C 157**
Covenant of peace offered by servant David. **Ezek. 17:9-11** (Ezek. 34:22-27)
Blessings or cursing Israel? Repent-obey covenant. **Lev. 13:8-16** (Lev. 26:1-46)
Come-hear everlasting covenant, sure mercies David. **Isaiah 20:1** (Isaiah 55:3)
Incline your ear, Lord will make covenant with you. **Isaiah 20:1** (Isaiah 55:3)
One mighty and strong to set the House of God in order. **T&C 83:4** (D&C 85:7)
Those who will not believe what man declares. **3 Nephi 9:12** (3 Nephi 21:9)
Don't condemn things God, because of man. **Mor. 8:3-4** (Mor. 8:12-17)
Servant marred, but life of servant in God's hand. **3 Nephi 9:12** (3 Nephi 21:10)
Covenant of His peace not removed. **3 Nephi 10:2** (3 Nephi 22:10)
Need plates to preserve language of fathers. **1 Nephi 1:12** (1 Nephi 3:19)
Old things are done away, all things new. **3 Nephi 5:31** (3 Nephi 12: 47)
All invited heaven, to sit down Holy Fathers. **Helaman 2:7** (Helaman 3:27-30)
Seeking for the blessings of the Fathers. **Abraham 1:1** (Abraham 1:2-3)
Hearts fathers to children, children to fathers. **Malachi 1:11-12** (Malachi 4:4-6)
Elijah keys seal hearts fathers to children. **JS History 3:4** (JS History 1:38-39)
Fathers and children must be welded together. **T&C 151:14** (D&C 128:18)
Promises to fathers, in the hearts of children. **JS History 3:4** (D&C 2:1-3)
Covenants must be sealed by HSP. **Glossary Holy Spirit Promise** (D&C 132:7)
Watchmen cry let us go up to Zion. **Jeremiah 12:5-6** (Jeremiah 31:6-14)
Watchmen finally see eye to eye. **Isaiah 18:8** (Isaiah 52:8)
They will ask way to Zion-to make perpetual covenant. **Jer. 18:2** (Jer. 50:5)
Come let us join ourselves to Lord in perpetual covenant. **Jer. 18:2** (Jer. 50:5)
Because of covenant made, become children of Christ. **Mosiah 3:2** (Mosiah 5:7)
Gather together those make covenant by sacrifice. **Psalms 50:1** (Psalms 50:5)
Those willing to observe covenants are accepted. **T&C 96:3** (D&C 97:8)
Disbelieving cut off from covenant people. **3 Nephi 9:12** (3 Nephi 21:11)
Covenant people blessed-safe in wilderness. **Ezekiel 17:9-11** (Ezekiel 34:22-31)
Dispensation of the fullness of times. **T&C 151:14** (D&C 128:18)
Restitution of all things. **Acts 2:3** (Acts 3:21)
Redeemer will keep His word and come to Zion. **Isaiah 21:2** (Isaiah 59:20-21)
Dispensation fullness times. Glory-keys since Adam. **T&C 151:14** (D&C 128:18)
New Heaven/New Earth established for the pure. **Ether 6:1-3** (Ether 13:1-12)

MIRACLES AND SPIRITUAL GIFTS

MIRACLES AND SPIRITUAL GIFTS
Seek the best gifts to benefit those who love God. **T&C 32:4** (D&C 46:8-10)
Many signs and wonders wrought among the people. **Acts 3:4** (Acts 5:12-16)
Signs, healings, prophecies, all gifts of spirit. **1 Cor. 1: 48-50** (1 Cor. 12:4-31)
Desire spiritual gifts to prophecy. **1 Cor. 1:54** (1 Cor. 14:1-5)
Covet best gifts, shown a more excellent way. **1 Cor. 1:50** (1 Cor. 12:31)
Miracles by the power of word of God. **4 Nephi 1:6** (4 Nephi 1:30)
Armor of God and sword of Spirit. **Ephesians 1:25** (Ephesians 6:11-17)
Disciples enact miracles in name of Christ. **4 Nephi 1:2** (4 Nephi 1:5)
After the fire, Lord is in the still small voice. **1 Kings 4:26** (1 Kings 19:11-12)
Went forth as led by the Spirit of the Lord. **Alma 13:4** (Alma 21:16)
In name of Jesus, trees, mountains, waves obey us. **Jacob 3:2** (Jacob 4:6)
Spirit of prophecy, Spirit of revelation, Power of God. **Alma 12:1** (Alma 17:3)
Jesus calms the sea and the storm. **Mark 2:20** (Mark 4:36-40)
Jesus feeds the multitude. **Luke 7:3** (Luke 9:13-17)
Jesus walks on water. **Matt 8:6** (Matt 14:25-32)
Jesus heals all brought forth unto Him. **3 Nephi 8:2-3** (3 Nephi 17:7-10)
Jesus heals leper. **Mark 1:9** (Mark 1:40-45)
Jesus gives sight to the blind. **John 6:17-21** (John 9:1-34)
Jesus casts out devils. **Luke 6:7-9** (Luke 8:27-35)
Jesus heals the deaf. **Mark 4:14** (Mark 7:32-37)
Jesus raises the dead. **John 7:1-6** (John 11:1-44)
Jesus heals on the Sabbath. **John 5:2** (John 5:5-9)
Jesus heals by His Word. **John 4:12** (John 4:46-54)
Deny not the gifts of God, for there are many. **Moroni 10:3** (Moroni 10:8)
Wo unto those who deny revelations and miracles. **3 Nephi 13:8** (3 Nephi 29:6)
Miracles cease because unbelief. Signs follow. **Mormon 4:8** (Mormon 9:15-20)
Help thou my unbelief. **Mark 5:9** (Mark 9:23-24)
Believe in revelations, angels, speaking in tongues. **Omni 1:10** (Omni 1:25)
Day of Pentecost. Rushing mighty wind. Tongues. **Acts 1:7** (Acts 2:1-4)
Tongues for them that believe not. **1 Corinthians 1:57** (1 Corinthians 14:22-23)
Gift of speaking in tongues. **T&C 32:5** (D&C 46:24)
Gift of interpreting tongues. **T&C 32:5** (D&C 46:25)
Speaking in tongues, interpretation. **1 Cor. 1:54** (1 Corinthians 14:1-5)
Let tongues be poured out upon people. **T&C 123:10** (D&C 109:36)
Holy Ghost, speak tongues, prophesy. **Acts 11:2** (Acts 19:6)
Baptism of fire = speaking with tongue of angels. **2 Nephi 13:2** (2 Nephi 31:13)
Sons and daughters shall prophecy, dreams, visions. **Joel 1:12** (Joel 2:28)
Would to God all Lord's people prophets. **Numbers 7:19** (Numbers 11:26-29)

HEALING

All spirit is matter. **Glossary: Soul/Spirit/Body of Man** (D&C 131:7-8)
The whiteness of Jesus shed down on all. **3 Nephi 9:4** (3 Nephi 19:25)
Prayer of faith shall save the sick. **Jacob 1:23** (James 5:14-15)
Your faith is sufficient to be healed. **3 Nephi 8:2** (3 Nephi 17:8)
He knows how to succor us in our infirmities. **Alma 5:3** (Alma 7:12)
Jesus heals all brought forth unto Him. **3 Nephi 8:2-3** (3 Nephi 17:7-10)
Jesus heals leper. **Mark 1:9** (Mark 1:40-45)
Jesus gives sight to the blind. **John 6:17-21** (John 9:1-34)
Jesus casts out devils. **Luke 6:7-9** (Luke 8:27-35)
Jesus heals the deaf. **Mark 4:14** (Mark 7:32-37)
Jesus raises the dead. **John 7:1-6** (John 11:1-44)
Jesus heals on the Sabbath. **John 5:2** (John 5:5-9)
Jesus heals by His Word. **John 4:12** (John 4:46-54)
Woman touched His garment-made whole. **Matthew 4:11** (Matt 9:20-22)
Twelve ordained to heal sickness, cast out devils. **Mark 2:7** (Mark 3:14-15)
Disciples heal sick, raise the dead name Jesus. **4 Nephi 1:2** (4 Nephi 1:5)
Ananias heals Saul from blindness. **Acts 5:9** (Acts 9:17-18)
Paul lays hands on sick and heals. **Acts 13:9** (Acts 28:8-9)
Miracles, healing and casting out devils. **T&C 18:3** (D&C 35:8-9)
Zeezrom healed, leaped, baptized and preached. **Alma 10:12-14** (Alma 15:3-12)
Healing by faith and herbs. Some die in Christ. **T&C 26:11-15** (D&C 42:43-48)
Plants and roots are for diseases and fevers. **Alma 21:16** (Alma 46:40)
Music to heal, cast out evil spirits. **1 Samuel 7:19-21** (1 Samuel 16:16-23)
In name of Jesus Christ rise up and walk! **Acts 2:1** (Acts 3:1-8)

DREAMS

Lord speaks to prophets in dreams and visions. **Numbers 7:22** (Numbers 12:6)
Jacob dreams of ladder to heaven. **Genesis 9:20-21** (Genesis 28:12-16)
Word of Lord comes to Abram in vision. **Genesis 7:22** (Genesis 15:1-2)
Abraham filled with vision of Almighty. **Abraham 1:5** (Abraham 1:15)
God comes to Abimelech in a dream. **Genesis 7:46** (Genesis 20:3)
Daniel had understanding in all visions and dreams. **Daniel 1:4** (Daniel1:17)
Daniel interprets dream stone cut from mountain. **Daniel 2:4-8** (Daniel2:24-47)
Joseph dreams and brothers envy him. **Genesis 11:2-5** (Genesis 37:5-9)
Lord appears to Solomon in a dream. **1 Kings 2:17** (1 Kings 3:5)
Moses beholds all of the earth. **Moses 1:7** (Moses 1:37)
Joseph told in dream to take Mary as wife. **Matthew 1:5** (Matthew 1:20)
Mary and Joseph warned in dream flee to Egypt. **Matt. 1:10** (Matt. 2:13)
Joseph told in dream to return to Israel. **Matthew 1:12** (Matthew 2:19-20)
Pilot's wife warns him about a dream. **Matthew 12:21** (Matthew 27:19)
Lord speaks to Lehi in dream. **1 Nephi 1:6** (1 Nephi 2:1–2)

Lehi speaks words of dream. **1 Nephi 2:13** (1 Nephi 8:36)
Lehi writes many things he saw in dreams. **1 Nephi 1:4** (1 Nephi 1:16)
Lehi dreams that brothers are to return Jerusalem. **1 Nephi 1:10** (1 Nephi 3:2)
Our lives passed away as dream. **Jacob 5:9** (Jacob 7:26)
Lord warns Omer in a dream. **Ether 4:1** (Ether 9:3)
Alma in darkest abyss, beholds marvelous light. **Mosiah 11:28** (Mosiah 27:29)

VISIONS
Lord speaks to prophets in dreams and visions. **Numbers 7:22** (Numbers 12:6)
Thou speak in vision to thy Holy One. **Psalms 89:4** (Psalms 89:19)
Vision of Enoch. **Genesis 4:15-23** (Moses 7:21–67)
Enoch beholds all nations of the earth. **Genesis 4:15** (Moses 7:23)
Enoch sees things not visible to natural eye. **Genesis 4:3** (Moses 6:35-36)
Enoch beholds vision on journey from Cainan. **Genesis 4:5** (Moses 6:42)
Ezekiel sees visions of God. **Ezekiel 1:1** (Ezekiel 1:1)
Elisha prays servant will see more with them. **2 Kings 2:20-22** (2 Kings 6:8-17)
Daniel had understanding in all visions and dreams. **Daniel 1:4** (Daniel 1:17)
Moses beholds all of the earth. **Genesis 1:7** (Moses 1:37)
Zacharias is perceived to have had a vision. **Luke 1:4** (Luke 1:19-22)
Stephen sees Jesus son the right hand of Father. **Acts 4:10** (Acts 7:55)
Lord speaks to Paul in the night by vision. **Acts 10:17** (Acts 18:9)
John sees vision of the last days. **Revelations 2-8** (Revelations 4-21)
Brother of Jared is shown all inhabitants of earth. **Ether 1:15** (Ether 3:25)
Lehi is a visionary man. **1 Nephi 1:8** (1 Nephi 2:11)
Lehi sees pillar of fire. **1 Nephi 1:3** (1 Nephi 1:5-6)
Lehi carried away in vision. **1 Nephi 1:3** (1 Nephi 1:8)
Lehi's vision of the tree of life. **1 Nephi 2:8-9** (1 Nephi 8:11-14)
Lehi has visions, knows goodness of God. **1 Nephi 1:21** (1 Nephi 5:4)
Lehi sees destruction of Jerusalem. **2 Nephi 1:1** (2 Nephi 1:1,4)
Nephi obtains knowledge through visions. **2 Nephi 3:7** (2 Nephi 4:23)
Nephi desires to see vision of Tree of Life. **1 Nephi 3:5** (1 Nephi 10:17)
Nephi sees future and vision of tree of life. **1 Nephi 3:6-14** (1 Nephi 11:1-36)
Our lives passed away as dream. **Jacob 5:9** (Jacob 7:26)
Alma in darkest abyss, beholds marvelous light. **Mosiah 11:28** (Mosiah 27:29)
Angel in vision tells Amulek to receive Alma. **Alma 6:6** (Alma 8:20-21)
Abish converted by vision of father. **Alma 12:21** (Alma 19:16)
Moroni sees our doing and mourns. **Mormon 4:5** (Mormon 8:35-41)
Joseph Smith First Vision. **JSH 1:2-11, 2:1-9** (JSH 1:3-25)
Hiding place of plates is revealed in vision. **JSH 3:5** (JS History 1:42)
Joseph Smith sees Father, Son, Alvin in vision. **T&C 122:4** (D&C 137:3-5)
Joseph and Sidney converse with Son in vision. **T&C 69:3.** (D&C 76:14)
Vision received at dedication of Kirtland Temple. **T&C 157:26-30** (D&C 110)

Joseph Smith sees vision of Celestial Kingdom. **T&C 122:4-6** (D&C 137:1-10)
Joseph Smith vision of three degrees of glory. **T&C 69:3-28** (D&C 76:14-113)
Lord shows vision of kingdoms to many. **T&C 69:8** (D&C 76:47)
We believe in the gift of visions. **T&C 146:27** (Articles of Faith 1:7)
Denver Snuffer vision of the pass. **T&C 163**
Denver Snuffer vision of Gethsemane. **T&C 161**
Denver Snuffer vision of the train. **T&C 172**
Denver Snuffer vision of His return. **T&C 160**

PROPHECY

We believe in gift of prophecy. **T&C 146:27** (Aof 1:7)
Desire spiritual gifts to prophecy. **1 Corinthians 1:54** (1 Corinthians 14:1-3)
According to proportion faith, let us prophecy. **Romans 1:60** (Romans 12:3-6)
Prophecy provided for believers. **1 Cor. 1:57** (1 Cor. 14:22)
Spiritual gifts that you may prophecy. **1 Cor. 1:54** (1 Cor. 14:1-3)
Spirit of prophecy, Spirit of revelation, Power of God. **Alma 12:1** (Alma 17:3)
Man must be called of God by prophecy to preach. **T&C 146:25** (AoF 1:5)
Adam prophesies concerning all families of earth. **Genesis 3:4** (Moses 5:10)
Adam prophecies as moved upon by the Holy Ghost. **Genesis 3:14** (Moses 6:8)
Enoch prophesies as commanded by the Lord. **Genesis 4:12** (Moses 7:2, 7)
Noah prophesies and teaches things of God. **Genesis 5:6** (Moses 8:16)
Search prophecies of Isaiah. **Mormon 4:4** (Mormon 8:23)
Sons and daughters shall prophecy, dreams, visions. **Joel 1:12** (Joel 2:28)
Women prophets. **Acts 12:7** (Acts 21:8-9)
Eve is named the mother of all living. **Genesis 2:17-18** (3:13-20)
Sarah conceives Isaac in her old age. **Genesis 7:36-8:4** (Genesis 18-21)
Hannah prays for son, given to Eli for the Lord. **Samuel 1:1-7** (Samuel 1:2-28)
Rebekah at the well. **Genesis 8:12-16** (Genesis 24:13-28)
Debra a great judge in Israel. **Judges 2:4** (Judges 4:4)
Miriam the prophetess. **Exodus 9:9** (Exodus 15:20)
Mary is the servant of God. **Luke 1:6** (Luke 1:38)
Anna the Prophetess looks for Messiah. **Luke 2:7** (Luke 2:36-39)
Women who ministered to Jesus. **Luke 6:1** (Luke 8:2-3)
Woman anoints Jesus' head. **Matthew 12:1** (Matthew 26:6-13)
Sariah wife of Lehi. Goodly parents. **1 Nephi 1:1** (1 Nephi 1:1)
Nephi's wife and mother plead for him on ship. **1 Ne. 5:31** (1Ne. 18:18-20)
Nephi will prophesy with plainness. **2 Nephi 11:1** (2 Nephi 25:4)
Words of Isaiah plain with spirit of prophecy. **2 Nephi 11:1** (2 Nephi 25:4)
Nephi[1] proceeds with his own prophecy. **2 Nephi 11:3** (2 Nephi 25:7)
Nephites prophesy of Christ. **2 Nephi 11:8** (2 Nephi 25:26)
Nephites have many revelations and spirit of prophecy. **Jacob 3:2** (Jacob 4:6)
Prophesy to the understanding of men. **Jacob 3:4** (Jacob 4:13)

Lord sends Abinadi to prophesy against people. **Mosiah 7:17** (Mosiah 12:29)
Abish blessed for exceeding faith. **Alma 12:21-26** (Alma 19:16-36)
Alma testimony of word, according spirit prophecy. **Alma 2:5** (Alma 4:20)
Sons of Mosiah have spirit of prophecy. **Alma 12:1** (Alma 17:3)
People of Anti-Nephi-Lehi rely spirit of prophecy. **Alma 14:15** (Alma 25:16)
Nephites deny spirit of prophecy. **Helaman 2:14** (Helaman 4:23)
Ammonihahites will not believe prophesies destruction. **Alma 7:1** (Alma 9:4)
Ether prophesies great things, people don't believe. **Ether 5:1** (Ether 12:5)
Wo to him does not believe Lord works prophecy. **3 Nephi 13:8** (3 Nephi 29:6)
Prophecy will be fulfilled. **T&C 54:4** (D&C 1:18)
Believe so that prophecies may be fulfilled. **T&C 39:7** (D&C 52:36)
Deny not spirit of prophecy. **JSH 14:16** (D&C 11:25)
Prophesy, and it shall be given by the Holy Ghost. **T&C 17:3** (D&C 34:10)
Joseph Smith to prophesy. **T&C 18:6** (D&C 35:23)
Emma: sins are forgiven thee, and thou art an elect lady. **T&C 5:1** (D&C 25:3)
Hyrum is a prophet, seer, and patriarch. **T&C 141:32** (D&C 124:91-95)
Moroni quotes prophecy from OC to Joseph Smith. **JSH 3:4** (JSH 1:36)
Would to God all Lord's people were prophets. **Num. 7:19** (Num. 11:26-29)
Denver Snuffer revelation on the Lord coming in glory. **T&C 160**
Denver Snuffer revelation on the new name David. **T&C 162**
Denver Snuffer revelation on an end of authority. **T&C 166**
Denver Snuffer revelation on priesthood and seven women. **T&C 167**
Denver Snuffer prophecy of a sign in the heavens. **T&C 164**
John the Apostle to prophesy before nations. **JSH 13:18** (D&C 7:3)

ANGELS
Angel. **T&C Glossary: Angel**
God sends angels to converse with men. **Alma 9:7** (Alma 12:28-30)
Christ sends angels to minister. **Moroni 7:4** (Moroni 7:22)
Miracles, gifts, and angels come from Christ. **Moroni 10:3-4** (Moroni 10:8-19)
Ministry of angels involves faith and miracles. **Moroni 7:6-7** (Moroni 7:29-38)
Angels prepare people for Lord's word. **Alma 10:3** (Alma 13:22-24)
Angels speak words of Christ to those firm mind. **Moroni 7:6** (Moroni 7:29-30)
Angels speak by power of Holy Ghost. **2 Nephi 14:1** (2 Ne. 32:2-3)
Angels give words that confound the wise. **Alma 16:26** (Alma 32:22-23)
Angels belong to earth, live elsewhere. **T&C Glossary: Angel** (D&C 130:4-7)
Angels minister to man. **Moroni 7:6-7** (Moroni 7:29-38)
Angels are also God's messengers in flesh. **T&C Glossary: Angel**

ANGELS PROPHESY OF FUTURE
Voice of the Lord declared by angels. **Alma 10:3** (Alma 13:22, 24)
Angel prophesies Christ coming in 600 years. **1 Nephi 5:36** (1 Nephi 19:8-10)
Angels declare Christ. **Alma 10:3** (Alma 13:26)
Angels appear unto wise men among Nephites. **Helaman 5:20** (Helaman 16:14)
Many converse with angels. **Alma 12:26** (Alma 19:34)
Angel calls Gideon to deliver Israel. **Judges 3:2-3** (Judges 6:11-24)
Angel Gabriel promises Zacharias a son named John. **Luke 1:3** (Luke 1:11-13)
Angel Gabriel comes to Mary. **Luke 1:5-6** (Luke 1:26-38)
Angel reveals Christ's name to Jacob. **2 Nephi 7:1** (2 Nephi 10:3)
Angel appears unto shepherds, announce birth Christ. **Luke 2:2** (Luke 2:8-16)
Angel appears unto sons of Mosiah. **Mosiah 11:26** (Mosiah 27:11-17)
Angel appears unto Joseph Smith. **JSH 3:2-8** (JSH 30-47)
Everlasting Gospel comes with the Angels. **T&C 86:24** (D&C 88:103)
Angels state that Jesus will come the same way he left. **Acts 1:3** (Acts 1:9-11)

ANGELS CALL TO REPENTANCE
The voice of the Lord by mouth of Angels. **Alma 10:3** (Alma 13:22)
Angels declare Christ and repentance. **Helaman 2:17** (Helaman 5:11-12)
Lord sends angels to teach repentance. **Helaman 2:17** (Helaman 5:11)
Lord sent His angel, that they might cry repentance. **Alma 7:6** (Alma 9:25)
O that I were an angel, speak with trump of God! **Alma 15:12** (Alma 29:1-2)
God in mercy sends angels to teach plan of salvation. **Alma 14:8** (Alma 24:14)
God sends angels to commit everlasting Gospel. **T&C 58:4** (D&C 133:36-37)

ANGELS ANSWER PRAYER
Mighty prayer, night visions, angels minister. **2 Nephi 3:7** (2 Nephi 4:23-24)
God sends angels to teach, ordinances Adam. **Genesis 3:13** (Moses 5:58-59)
Angels minister to Nephi daily. **3 Nephi 3:10** (3 Nephi 7:18)
Angel comes to Alma the younger. **Mosiah 11:26** (Mosiah 27:14)
Angel tells King Benjamin tidings of great joy. **Mosiah 1:13** (Mosiah 3: 2-4)
Angel visits John, not to worship angel. **Revelation 7:10** (Revelations 19:10)
Angel comes and instructs Joseph Smith. **JSH 4:1** (JSH 1:54)
Satan can transform himself into angel of Light. **2 Cor. 1:37** (2 Cor. 11:14)
Some have entertained angels unaware. **Hebrews 1:58** (Hebrews 13:2)

ANGELS PROVIDE PROTECTION
Angels protect servants armed with power. **T&C 123:7** (D&C 109: 22)
Angel warns Joseph in dream to flee to Egypt. **Matthew 1:10** (Matthew 2:13)
Angel tells Joseph in dream return to Israel. **Matthew 1:12** (Matthew 2:19-20)
Two angels visit Lot in Sodom-save family. **Genesis 7:41-43** (Genesis 19:1-13)
Angels visit Abraham and foretell of Isaac. **Genesis 7:36-39** (Genesis 18:1-33)

Apostles delivered from prison by angels-told to teach. **Acts 3:5** (Acts 5:17-20)
Angel frees Peter from Prison. **Acts 7:4** (Acts 12:5-11)
Angel assures Paul no lives to be lost on the voyage. **Acts 13:4** (Acts 27:22-24)
Angel protects Nephi from Laman and Lemuel. **1 Nephi 1:14** (1 Nephi 3:28-31)
Nephi and Lehi ministered to by angels. **Helaman 2:20-26** (Helaman 5:23-52)
Elisha assures them that be with us are more. **2Kings 2:20-22** (2 Kings 6:8-17)

WOMEN OF WISDOM
Wisdom. **T&C Glossary: Wisdom**
Sons and daughters shall prophecy, dreams, visions. **Joel 1:12** (Joel 2:28)
Strong women, chief women not a few. **Acts 10:10** (Acts 17:4)
Would to God all people were prophets. **Numbers 7:19** (Numbers 11:26-29)
Women prophets. **Acts 12:7** (Acts 21:8-9)
Eve is named the mother of all living. **Genesis 2:18** (Genesis 3:13-20)
Sarah conceives Isaac in her old age. **Genesis 8:1** (Genesis 21:1-3)
Hannah prays and gives son Eli for Lord. **1 Samuel 1:2-7** (1 Samuel 1:2-28)
Rebekah at the well. **Genesis 8:12-16** (Genesis 24:13-28)
Debra a great judge in Israel. **Judges 2:4** (Judges 4:4)
Women of God, courageous midwives. **Exodus 1:3** (Exodus 1:15-21)
Widow woman sustains Elijah. **1 Kings 4:4-7** (1 Kings 17:11-24)
Ruth, your people will be my people. **Ruth 1:2** (Ruth 1:15-18)
Ruth: Thou art a virtuous woman. **Ruth 3:2** (Ruth 3:11)
Ruth lies at Boaz feet and he protects her. **Ruth 3:2-3** (Ruth 3:7-14)
Esther's courage. **Esther 1:15-22** (Esther 4-5)
Wise hearted women. **Exodus 19:5** (Exodus 35: 25-26)
Anna the Prophetess looks for Messiah. **Luke 2:7** (Luke 2:36-39)
Miriam the prophetess. **Exodus 9:9** (Exodus 15:20)
Huldah, the prophetess. **2 Kings 7:8** (2 Kings 22:14)
Huldah, the prophetess. **2 Chronicles 18:9** (2 Chronicles 34:22)
Elizabeth conceives John in her old age. **Luke 1:2-4** (Luke 1:5-25)
Mary is the servant of God. **Luke 1:6** (Luke 1:38)
Blessed art thou among women. **Luke 1:5** (Luke 1:28)
Women who ministered to Jesus. **Luke 6:1** (Luke 8:2-3)
Woman at the well. **John 4:2-10** (John 4:9-42)
Worship of Jesus. **Luke 5:21** (Luke 7:44-50)
Women came to the sepulcher. **Luke 14:1** (Luke 24:1)
Angels told the women to fear not. **Matthew 13:1** (Matthew 28:1-7)
Women prayed with apostles. **Acts 1:4** (Acts 1:13-14)
Jesus to Woman, where are your accusers. **John 6:10-11** (John 8:3-11)
Tabitha raised from the dead. **Acts 6:2** (Acts 9: 36-42)
Woman with issue of blood is healed. **Matthew 4:11** (Matthew 9:20-22)
Woman with issue of blood is healed. **Luke 6:11** (Luke 8:43-48)

Woman who washes the Lord's feet. **Luke 5:19-21** (Luke 7:36-50)
Woman anoints Jesus' head. **Matthew 12:1** (Matthew 26:6-13)
Lydia believes and is baptized. **Acts 10:5** (Acts 16:13-15)
Sariah wife of Lehi. Goodly parents. **1 Nephi 1:1** (1 Nephi 1:1)
Nephi's wife and mother plead for him on ship. **1 Ne. 5:31** (1Ne. 18:18-20)
Women were strong like unto the men. **1 Nephi 5:11** (1 Nephi 17:1-3)
Abish blessed for exceeding faith. **Alma 12:21-26** (Alma 19:16-36)
Abish and the King's wife. **Alma 12:21-26** (19:16-36)
Helaman's Sons. Their mothers taught them. **Alma 26:8** (Alma 56:46-48)
Emma: sins are forgiven thee, and thou art an elect lady. **T&C 5:1** (D&C 25:3)
Who can find a virtuous woman? **Proverbs 6:3** (Proverbs 31:10-31)
A gracious woman retaineth honor. **Proverbs 2:48** (Proverbs 11:16)
Whoso finds a wife, favored of the Lord. **Proverbs 2:267** (Proverbs 18:22)
Every wise woman buildeth her house. **Proverbs 2:117** (Proverbs 14:1)
Women have claim on their husbands. **T&C 79:1** (D&C 83:1-4)
Man and woman uniting is eternity. **Proverbs of Denver Snuffer 159:21**
Great symbol of woman in heaven. **Revelations 4:1-5** (Revelations 12:1-17)

NOTES:

ZION: THE PURE IN HEART

PURE IN HEART

Lord looks upon the heart. **1 Samuel 7:16** (1 Samuel 16:7)

Zion is pure in heart. **T&C 96:7** (D&C 97:7)

Garments washed white. **T&C Glossary: Garments washed white.**

Clean hands and pure heart ascends to the Lord. **Psalms 24:1** (Psalms 24:3-5)

Zion is one heart, one mind, no poor among them. **Gen 4:14** (Moses 7:16-18)

Believers were if one heart, one soul. **Acts 3:1** (Acts 4:32)

Believers had all things in common. **Acts 3:1** (Acts 4:32)

Be like-minded, of one accord, of one mind. **Philippians 1:6** (Philippians 2:2)

Be like-minded one toward another. **Rom 1:73** (Rom 15:5)

One mind, one mouth, glorify God. **Rom 1:73** (Rom 15:6)

Only upright in heart able to go to Zion upon waters, **T&C 48:3** (D&C 61:16)

Joined in same mind. No divisions. **1 Corinthians 1:3** (1 Corinthians 1:10)

Teach doctrine, avoid teachings causing division. **Rom. 1:80** (Rom. 16:17-18)

Esteem other as better than self. **Philippians 1:6** (Philippians 2:3)

Let the mind of Christ be in you. **Philippians 1:7** (Philippians 2:5)

Until we all come into unity of the faith. **Ephesians 1:13** (Ephesians 4:13)

Zion built up by law of Celestial kingdom. **T&C 107:1** (D&C 105:4-9)

Those come to city of living God are celestial heirs. **T&C 69:18 (**D&C 76:66)

Zion comes when men keep all commandments. **Gen. 5:22** (JST Gen. 9:2)

Lord bring to Zion one of a city, two of a family. **Jeremiah 2:3** (Jeremiah 3:14)

Ye shall be my people. I will be your God. **Jer. 4:3, 12:4** (Jer. 30:22)

Elect hear His voice. Gather the elect to one place. **T&C 9:3** (D&C 29:7)

Early Saints given five years to get to Zion. **T&C 51:6** (D&C 64:21-22)

After Lord purges and washes with spirit of burning. **Isaiah 1:13** (Isaiah 4:4)

Zion a city of solemnities. **Isaiah 11:5** (Isaiah 33:20-22)

From Zion shall come law, Jerusalem the word. **Isaiah 1:6** (Isaiah 2:2-3)

Watchmen cry out: arise, let us go up to Zion. **Jeremiah 12:5** (Jeremiah 31:6-9)

Watchmen shall see eye to eye. **Isaiah 18:7** (Isaiah 52:8)

Watchman see eye to eye in Zion. **Mosiah 7:17** (Mosiah 12:21-22)

See eye to eye even with differences. **T&C 82:27-28** (D&C 84:98,106-109)

Zion must arise and be equal. **T&C 78:3** (D&C 82:14-19)

Equality in earthly and heavenly things. **T&C 70:2** (D&C 78:3-8)

Consecration, one heart, one soul. **Acts 3:1** (Acts 4:32-37)

Apostles and believers lived the law of consecration. **Acts 1:13** (Acts 2:44-45)

Zion requires consecration and equality. **Alma 1:5** (Alma 1:26-27)

We should not possess that which is above another. **T&C 35:6** (D&C 49: 19-20)

Be equal in temporal things with no grudges. **T&C 61:4** (D&C 70:14)

Whole world in sin because possess above another. **T&C 35:6** (D&C 49:20)

Plead for the pure love of Christ- to be like Him. **Moroni 7:9** (Moroni 7:48)

To see Him and be pure, even as He is pure. **Moroni 7:9** (Moroni 7:48)

THE FEW

Noble and great intelligences before world. **Abraham 6:1** (Abraham 3:22-23)
Whom shall I send? Son of Man: Here am I, send me. **Abr. 6:3** (Abr. 3:27)
Whom shall I send? Isaiah: Here am I, send me. **Isaiah 2:2** (Isaiah 6:8)
Here am I. Joseph answers. **Genesis 11:3** (Genesis 37:13)
Satan: Here am I send me. Give me thine honor. **Genesis 2:15** (Moses 4:1-4)
Many called. Few are chosen. **T&C 139:5** (D&C 121:34-35)
Those called bring Zion and redemption of Israel. **T&C 129:4** (D&C 113:7-8)
Lord looks upon the heart. **Samuel 7:16** (1 Samuel 16:7)
Zion is the pure in heart. **T&C 96:7** (D&C 97:21)
Clean hands-pure heart to ascend into hill of Lord. **Psalm 24:1** (Psalms 24:3-5)
Mine elect hear my voice and harden not hearts. **T&C 9:3** (D&C 29:7)
Few humble followers of Christ. **2 Nephi 12:2** (2 Nephi 28:14)
Become joint heirs with Christ. **Romans 1:34** (Romans 8:16-17)
Let the mind of Christ be in you. **Philippians 1:7** (Philippians 2:5)
Commanded my sanctified ones. Called mighty ones. **Isaiah 6:1** (Isaiah 13:3)
Covenant offered to Gentile who repent. **3 Ne. 10:1** (3 Ne. 21:22)
Gentiles numbered among Jacob if they repent. **3 Ne. 7:5** (3 Ne. 16:13)
Savior resides with His people, Israel - Ephraim **T&C 58:3** (D&C 133:25-34)
Ephraim is God's firstborn. **Jeremiah 12:5** (Jeremiah 31:9)
New Heaven/New Earth involves seed of Joseph. **Ether 6:1-3** (Ether 13:1-12)
Remnant of Joseph inherit land, build a holy city. **Ether 6:3** (Ether 13:8)
Ephraim crowns those from north country. **T&C 58:3** (D&C 133:25-33)
Rich blessings upon the head of Ephraim. **T&C 58:3** (D&C 133:34)
Seed of Joseph dwell within the New Jerusalem. **Ether 6:3** (Ether 13:10)
Gather mine elect from the four quarters of earth. **T&C 16:2** (D&C 33:6)
Elect. **T&C Glossary: Elect, Calling and Election, Chosen Vessel.**
Elect hear His voice. Gather the elect to one place. **T&C 9:3** (D&C 29:7)
Outcasts gathered to the Holy Mountain. **Isaiah 20:3** (Isaiah 56:7-8)
Israel builds New Jerusalem. Gentiles assist. **3 Ne. 9:12-10:1** (3 Ne. 21:21-29)
Lord bring to Zion one of a city, two of a family. **Jeremiah 2:3** (Jeremiah 3:14)
Ye shall be my people. I will be your God. **Jer. 4:3, 12:4,** (Jer. 11:4, 30:22)
Only a few not prideful. **Mormon 4:5** (Mormon 8:35-36)
Weak things called to thrash nations. **T&C 18:4** (D&C 35:13-14)
Waxing Strong. **T&C Glossary: Waxing Strong, Elect.**
Magnify priesthood to become elect of God. **T&C 82:16** (D&C 84:33–34)
They who minister will have power to seal. **T&C 54:2** (D&C 1:8)
Scriptures given for salvation of elect. **T&C 18:6** (D&C 35:20–21)
I am not ashamed of Gospel of Christ. **Romans 1:3** (Romans 1:16)
Behold, I am a disciple of Jesus Christ. **3 Nephi 2:17** (3 Nephi 5:13)
Called to declare His word. **3 Nephi 2:17** (3 Nephi 5:13)
Disciples continue in Lord's word. **John 6:14** (John 8:31)

I will boast of my God. In Him can do all things. **Alma 14:17** (Alma 26:11-12)
I Moroni will not deny the Christ. **Moroni 1:1** (Moroni 1:3)
For the elect, days of tribulation shortened. **Matthew 11:5** (JS Matthew 24:20)
Blessed those die in Lord, will receive Holy City. **T&C 50:11** (D&C 63:49)
Martyrs for Christ reign with Him. **Revelation 8:4** (Rev. 20:1-4)
Resurrected saints sing song of Lamb on mount Zion. **T&C 58:6** (D&C 133:56)
Lamb overcomes with those called and chosen. **Revelation 6:12** (Rev. 17:14)

HOUSE OF THE LORD

Adam-Eve call on Lord and make sacrifice. **Genesis 3:2-3** (Moses 5:5-8)
Make a sanctuary that I may dwell among them. **Exo. 14:1** (Exo. 25:8-9)
Moses-Aaron washed feet tent congregation. **Exo. 20:2** (Exo. 40:17-33)
Lord to Moses, Moses to people. Blessings. **Exo. 19:27** (Exo. 39:32-43)
Tabernacle of the congregation finished. **Exodus 19:27** (Exodus 39:32).
Putting on the temple garments. **Ezekiel 21:25** (Ezekiel 42:14).
Solomon builds temple 1005 B.C. **2 Chronicles 2:24** (2 Chronicles 7:11)
Zerubbabel builds altar. Temple stands centuries. **Ezra 1:15** (Ezra 3:1-7)
Mary and Joseph bring Jesus to temple. **Luke 2:4** (Luke 2:22)
Jesus in temple hearing, asking questions. **Luke 3:2** (Luke 2:46)
Jesus casts money changers out of temple. **Mark 5:34-35** (Mark 11:15-26)
Temple to be destroyed, not one stone. **Matt. 11:1** (Matt. 24:1-2)
Paul purifying self enters temple. **Acts 12:10-12** (Acts 21:26-30)
Paul purified in the temple. **Acts 12:30** (Acts 24:17-18)
Nephites separate Lamanites, build temple. **2 Nephi 4:3** (2 Nephi 5:15-16)
Jacob teaches in the temple. **Jacob 1:4** (Jacob 1:17)
People to the temple to hear King Benjamin. **Mosiah 1:4** (Mosiah 1:18)
Temple in land Bountiful. Christ appears. **3 Nephi 5:1-4** (3 Nephi 11:1-11)
Lord accepts and visits Kirtland temple. **T&C 157:28** (D&C 110: 7-8)
City of Zion to be built beginning at temple lot. **T&C 82:1** (D&C 84:2-3)
God's will a house is built in Zion unto Lord. **T&C 96:4** (D&C 97:10-14)
Lord commands His house be built. **T&C 141:13-17** (D&C 124:40-55)
Temple is to be built in this generation. **T&C 82:2-3** (D&C 84:4-5)
Temple is to be built with tithing. **T&C 96:4** (D&C 97:11)
Better to purchase land than obtain by blood. **T&C 50:7** (D&C 63:25-31)
Prophet shown where to build Temple. **T&C 141:13** (D&C 124:40-45)
Joseph Smith shown where to build temple. **T&C 141:13** (D&C 124:40-45)
Do not be idle in building the temple. **T&C 26:10** (D&C 42:42)
He that is idle, not wear garments of the laborer. **T&C 26:10** (D&C 42:42)
Let all things be prepared in order. **T&C 101:15** (D&C 101:68-71)
Work not to be in haste, nor by flight. **T&C 101:16** (D&C 101:68-69)
Prepare every needful thing for a house of God. **T&C 86:29** (D&C 88:119)
If labor in might, Lord consecrate land holy. **T&C 141:13** (D&C 124:44)

Nauvoo temple needed to restore Priesthood. **T&C 141:10** (D&C 124:28)
Temple needed for baptisms-washings. **T&C 141:11-12** (D&C 124:29-37)
Temple needed, avoid rejection-cursing. **T&C 141:11-14** (D&C 124:32-48).
If temple undefiled. God's glory shall rest upon it. **T&C 96:5** (D&C 97:15)
Pure in heart come into temple and see God! **T&C 96:5** (D&C 97:16)
Higher ordinances needed for crown. **T&C 141:17** (D&C 124:55)
Fullness of the priesthood lost. **T&C 141:10** (D&C 124:28)
Temple to restore fullness of ordinances. **T&C 141:11-13** (D&C 124:28-41)
House of prayer, fasting, faith, learning, glory. **T&C 86:29** (D&C 109:8-9)
Temple instruction for those called to ministry. **T&C 96:4** (D&C 97:13-14)
Temple with angels, books, and power. **T&C 123:6-8** (D&C 109:14-25)
All shall know Lord. Filled with knowledge. **T&C 82:27** (D&C 84:98)
Like Pentecost:, filled glory-rushing wind. **T&C 123:10** (D&C 109:36-37)
Sons filled glory in Lords house Mount Zion. **T&C 82:16.** (D&C 84:32)
Outcasts gathered, joy in House of the Lord. **Isaiah 20:3** (Isaiah 56:7-8)
Build house and Lord will come to his temple. **T&C 123:1** (D&C 109:1-5)
Lord suddenly come to His temple, who shall abide? **Mal. 1:6** (Mal. 3:1-6)

NEW JERUSALEM
Seek to establish the cause of **JSH 13:6**(D&C 6:6)
Flee Babylon, declare work of Lord in Zion. **Jer. 18:10-11** (Jeremiah 51:6-10)
Go ye out from Babylon. Be clean. **T&C 58:1-2** (D&C 133:5-7)
Enoch and his people walked with God. **Genesis 4:23** (Moses 7:69)
ZION city of holiness taken up to heaven. **Genesis 4:14-15** (Moses 7:18-23)
Enoch's Zion is FLED. **Genesis 4:23** (Moses 7:69)
New Jerusalem will come out heaven. **Revelations 1:18** (Revelations 3:12)
Posterity looks upward, Zion looks downward. **Gen. 5:22** (JST Gen. 9:21-23)
Kingdom of Zion is kingdom of our God. **T&C 107:7** (D&C 105:32)
New Jerusalem built upon land of America. **Ether 6:2** (Ether 13:5-6)
New Jerusalem will be in this land. **3 Nephi 9:8** (3 Nephi 20:22)
New Jerusalem built on this land unto seed Joseph. **Ether 6:2-3** (Ether 13:1-12)
Remnant of Joseph build a Holy City on this land. **Ether 6:3** (Ether 13:8-10)
Lost ten tribes return from North. **Jeremiah 2:3** (Jeremiah 3:18)
Zion and Jerusalem turned back own place. **T&C 58:3** (D&C 133:23-24)
Two places. From Zion law, Jerusalem the word. **Isaiah 1:5** (Isaiah 2:2-3)
Two places. Lords voice in Zion and Jerusalem. **T&C 58:3** (D&C 133:21-22)
Two places. Those in Zion, those remain Jerusalem. **Isaiah 1:12** (Isaiah 4:2-4)
Two places. Zion is wilderness. Jerusalem desolation. **Isa. 24:5** (Isa. 64:10)
Zion invitation to mountains. To walk in light Lord. **Isaiah 1:5-6** (Isaiah 2:2-5)
Purchase land for Zion. **T&C 50:7** (D&C 63:25-27)
Zion in the Lords hand. Better to purchase land. **T&C 50:7** (D&C 63:25-30)
No curse upon the land when Lord comes. **T&C 22:6** (D&C 38:18)

Prepare all things and do not gather in haste. **T&C 101:15** (D&C 101:68-69)
Do not gather in haste, brings confusion, pestilence. **T&C 50:6** (D&C 63:24)
When city prepared, gather in one to be His people. **T&C 26:2** (D&C 42:9)
Lord performs His work upon Mount Zion. **2 Nephi 9:17** (2 Nephi 20:12)
Powers of heaven in midst this people. Zion. **3 Nephi 9:8** (3 Nephi 20: 22)
Zion flourish in hills, rejoice at place in mountains. **T&C 35:8** (D&C 49:25)
Zion gather in Holy places, kings crowned. **T&C 101:3** (D&C 101:11-22)
Lord's house established in tops mountains. **Isaiah 1:5** (Isaiah 2:2)
Lord will come to His temple, bring judgement. **T&C 58:1** (D&C 133:2-3)
How blessed they seek Zion. Beautiful on mount. **1 Nephi 3:23** (1 Nephi13: 37)
New Jerusalem: land to flee for peace-safety. **T&C 31:13-15** (D&C 45:62-71)
Stand Mount Zion! Sing Songs of Joy. **T&C 58:6** (D&C 133:55-56)
Zion is with me. **Genesis 4:19** (Moses 7:47)
Lamb will stand on Mount Zion with 144,000. **T&C 58:3** (D&C 133:18-23)
Praise! For the Lord has brought again Zion. **T&C 82:27** (D&C 84:98-102)
Lord shall appear in glory and build up Zion. **Psalms 102:2** (Psalms 102:16)
God Reigns in Zion. **Mosiah 7:17** (Mosiah 12:21)
New Heaven and New Earth. The New Jerusalem. **Ether 6:1-3** (Ether 13:1-12)

ZION PROTECTION

Lord God is mighty in the midst of thee. **Zephaniah 1:12** (Zephaniah 3:17)
Gathering of elect into one place. **T&C 9:3** (D&C 29:7-8)
Zion is an escape from the destructions. **Genesis 4:22** (Moses 7:60-62)
Land of inheritance for your children. Lord is King! **T&C 22:6-7.** (D&C 38:20-21)
New Jerusalem: a land to flee to peace and safety. **T&C 31:13-15** (D&C 45:62-71)
Zion a covert from the storm for those purged. **Isaiah 1:12** (Isaiah 4:5-6)
Zion defended with smoke by day, fire by night. **Isaiah 1:12** (Isaiah 4:5)
Who can abide day His coming, like refiner's fire. **Malachi 1:6** (Malachi 3:2-3)
Depart. God will go before you, be rearward. **3 Nephi 9:10** (3 Nephi 20:40-42)
Remnant gathered. Receive Jesus in power-glory. **T&C 31:9** (D&C 45:43-44)
Saints gather to stand upon Mount Zion. **T&C 82:1** (D&C 84:2)
Hope in a better world is anchor to our soul. **Ether 5:1** (Ether 12:4)
God will swallow up death in victory. **Isaiah 7:3** (Isaiah 25:8-9)
Those fight against Zion shall perish. **2 Nephi 7:2** (2 Ne. 10:11-14, 16-17)
Those fight against Zion shall be as night vision. **2 Nephi 11:18** (2 Nephi 27:3)
No weapon against will prosper. **3 Nephi 10:3** (3 Nephi 22:17)
Elisha prays servant eyes open-see more with us. **2 Kings 2:20-22** (2 Kings 6:8-17)
Heritage of the servants of the Lord. **3 Nephi 10:3** (3 Nephi 22:17)
If God is for us, who can prevail against us? **Romans 1:37** (Romans 8:31)

NOTES:

RESTORATION OF THE ANCIENT RELIGION

RESTORATION OF THE ANCIENT RELIGION

All things created spiritually before physical. **Genesis 2:11** (Moses 3:5)
All things bear record of Creator. **Genesis 4:9** (Moses 6:63)
Commanded to multiply-replenish earth. **Genesis 2:8-9** (Genesis 1:28)
Commanded not eat tree of knowledge. **Genesis 2:13** (Genesis 2:17)
Adam and Eve partake of fruit. **Genesis 2:16** (Genesis 3:6)
Adam and Eve shut out Lord's presence. **Genesis 3:2** (Moses 5:4)
Adam and Eve called upon name of Lord. **Genesis 3:2** (Moses 5:4)
Commanded to worship God. **Genesis 3:2** (Moses 5:5)
Commanded sacrifice firstlings of flock. **Genesis 3:2** (Moses 5:5)
God to Adam: Return, repent, baptized, Holy Ghost, **Genesis 4:7** (Moses 6:52)
Angel appears unto Adam. **Genesis 3:3** (Moses 5:6)
God sends angels to Adam, teaching-ordinances. **Gen. 3:13** (Moses 5:58-59)
Gospel, angels, holy ordinances, in world until end. **Gen. 3:13** (Moses 5: 57-59)
Gospel of Adam taught by angels sent from God. **Genesis 3:13** (Moses 5:58)
Commanded to do *all* in the name of the Son. **Genesis 3:3** (Moses 5:8)
Repent and call on God in the name of the Son. **Genesis 3:3** (Moses 5:8)
Holy Ghost falls upon Adam. **Genesis 3:4** (Moses 5:9)
Adam prophecies concerning all families of the earth. **Genesis 3:4** (Moses 5:10)
Adam prophecies and keeps genealogy. **Genesis 3:14** (Moses 6:8)
Writings done by spirit of inspiration. **Genesis 3:14** (Moses 6:5)
Book of Generations. **Genesis 3:14** (Moses 6:8)
Children taught to read-write with pure language. **Genesis 3:14** (Moses 6:5-6)
Pure language correlates with Priesthood. **Genesis 3:14** (Moses 6:6-7)
In language of Adam, Man of Holiness God's name. **Genesis 4:9** (Moses 6:57)
Lord confounds the language. **Genesis 6:6** (Genesis 11:1-9)
Book of Remembrance. **Genesis 3:14** (Moses 6:5)
Book of Remembrance-powerful language. **Genesis 4:5** (Moses 6:46)
Everlasting Covenant. **Genesis 5:21-22** (JST Genesis 9:21-23)
Record of the Fathers. **Abraham 2:4** (Abraham 1:31)
The Fathers. **T&C Glossary: The Fathers.**
Rights belonging to the Fathers. **T&C Glossary: Rights belonging to Fathers**
Blessings of the Fathers. **T&C Glossary: Blessings of the Fathers**
Powers of Heaven. **T&C Glossary: Powers of Heaven, Power in Priesthood.**
Adams gospel survived unto Noah. **Genesis 5:9-10** (Moses 8:22-23)
Same priesthood in the beginning, shall be in the end. **Genesis 3:14** (Moses 6:7)
Covenants-tokens between God, man, earth. **Genesis 5:22-24** (Genesis 9:8-23)
Holy garments and Holiness to the Lord. **Exodus 19:23, 26** (Exodus 39:1, 30)
Sabbath day, holy convocation, feasts. **Leviticus 11:1-12** (Leviticus 23:1-44)
Sabbath year, Jubilee. **Leviticus 13:1-2** (Leviticus 25:1-1)

100

Melchizedek: High Priest Order of Son of God. **Gen. 7:18** (JST Gen. 14:26-29)
Melchizedek King of Salem, Abraham blessed. **Gen. 7:14-15** (Gen. 14:18-20)
Abraham promised priesthood continue seed. **Abraham 3:1** (Abraham 2:9-11)
Abraham builds altar, offers sacrifice-blessed. **Abr. 4:2** (Abr. 2:17-20)
Lord appears Isaac-builds altar and covenant. **Gen. 9:9-10** (Gen. 26: 24-28)
All families of earth blessed though Jacob. **Genesis 9:20-21** (Genesis 28:13-16)

RESTITUTION OF ALL THINGS
Until the times for the restitution of All Things. **Acts 2:3** (Acts 3:21)
Need plates to preserve language of fathers. **1 Nephi 1:12** (1 Nephi 3:19)
Scriptures given for salvation of elect. **T&C 18:6** (D&C 35:20–21)
Because of fall we partake of misery and woe. **Genesis 4:7** (Moses 6:48)
Men are carnal and shut out from presence of God. **Genesis 4:7** (Moses 6:49)
Real plan of salvation, sanctified by blood. **Genesis 4:9** (Moses 6:57-62)
Must be born again into the kingdom of heaven. **Genesis 4:9** (Moses 6:59)
Record of heaven to abide in you. **Genesis 4:9** (Moses 6:61)
Jacobs ladder. **Genesis 9:20** (Genesis 28:12)
Lord sends his angels then and now. **Alma 19:3** (Alma 39:19)
Everlasting Gospel comes with the Angels. **T&C 86:24** (D&C 88:103)
Blessings or cursing for Israel? Obey covenant. **Lev. 13:8-16** (Lev. 26:1-46)
All invited gate heaven - sit with holy fathers. **Helaman 2:7** (Helaman 3:27-30)
Abraham sought for the blessings of the Fathers. **Abr. 1:1** (Abr. 1:2-3)
Promises made to fathers, hearts of children. **JS-History 3:4** (D&C 2:1-3)
Fathers and children must be welded together. **T&C 151:14** (D&C 128:18)
Elijah hearts fathers to children, children to fathers. **Mal. 1:11-12** (Mal. 4:4-6)
Pharaoh tried to imitate order of the Fathers. **Abraham 2:3** (Abraham 1:26)
Appointment unto priesthood from the Fathers. **Abraham 1:1** (Abraham 1:4)
Same priesthood as in beginning, shall be in end. **Genesis 3:14** (Moses 6:7)
Dispensation fullness. Glory and keys since Adam. **T&C 151:14** (D&C 128:18)
I will bring forth a marvelous work and a wonder. **Isaiah 9:5** (Isaiah 29:13-14)
A marvelous work and a wonder is about to come forth. **JSH 11:2** (D&C 4:1-2)
Gospel of the kingdom preached all the world. **Matthew 11:7** (Matthew 24:14)
Prophecy occurring after the death of Jesus. **Acts 11:2** (Acts 19:6)
According to proportion of faith, let us prophecy. **Romans 1:60** (Romans 12:6)
Prophecy helps those that will believe. **1 Cor. 1:57** (1 Cor. 14:22)
The times of the restitution of all things. **Acts 2:3** (Acts 3:19-24)
Everlasting gospel preached unto those on earth. **Revelation 5:2** (Rev. 14:6-7)
Lord will reestablish Ephraim in last days. **Jeremiah 12:5-10** (Jeremiah 31)
Lord create new covenant with Judah. **Jeremiah 5-10** (Jeremiah 31)
I will make an everlasting covenant with you. **Isaiah 20:1** (Isaiah 55:3-5)
I will make an everlasting covenant in the last days. **Isaiah 23** (Isaiah 61:8)
Shall we not go on in so great cause! **T&C 151:15, 18-20** (D&C 128: 19, 22-23)

PATRIARCHAL PRIESTHOOD

Priesthood. **T&C Glossary: Priesthood, Priesthood, Power in the.**
The Fathers. **T&C Glossary: Fathers, The; Powers of Heaven.**
Hearts turned to the Fathers. **T&C Glossary: Hearts turned to the Fathers**
Rights belonging to the Fathers. **T&C Glossary: Rights belonging to Fathers**
Blessings of the Fathers. **T&C Glossary: Blessings of the Fathers.**
Powers of Heaven. **T&C Glossary: Powers of Heaven, Priesthood.**
High Priesthood prepared from eternity to all eternity. **Alma 9:10** (Alma 13:7)
Order of Son of God has no beginning or end. **Heb. 1:17** (JST Heb. 7:3)
Jesus Christ has unchangeable priesthood. **Hebrews 1:20-21** (Hebrews 7:24-28)
Priesthood without beginning of days or end of years. **Alma 9:10** (Alma 13:7)
Adam given dominion over every living thing. **Gen. 2:8-9** (Gen. 1:26-28)
Adam first father given priesthood. **Abraham1:1** (Abraham 1:3)
Adam and Eve are after the order of God. **Gen. 4:10** (Moses 6:67)
Adam covenants through baptism **Gen. 4:10** (Moses 6:64)
All things confirmed unto Adam by holy ordinance. **Gen. 3:13** (Moses 5:59)
High and Holy Order of the High Priesthood. **Alma 9:10-10:2** (Alma 13:1-20)
Pure language of Adam associated with Priesthood. **Gen. 3:14** (Moses 6:5-6)
Lord confounds the language. **Genesis. 6:6** (Genesis 11:1-9)
T&C Glossary: Great Knowledge and Greater Knowledge
Lord gives Abraham His name, priesthood of his father. **Abr. 1:5** (Abr. 1:18)
Priesthood conferred by fathers from beginning of time. **Abr. 1:1** (Abr. 1:3)
Appointment unto priesthood from the Fathers. **Abraham 1:1** (Abraham 1:4)
Men ordained according gifts and calling of God. **Moroni 3:1** (Moroni 3:4)
By the power of word, mountains moved, roar of lions. **Gen 4:13** (Moses 7:13)
Powers of heaven in midst of this people. **3 Nephi 9:8** (3 Nephi 20:22)
In war Moroni leaves strength power blessing. **Alma 27:9** (Alma 60:25)
Power in Christ. Miracles among the people. **4 Nephi 1:6** (4 Nephi 1:30)
Nephi asks Lord to use famine instead of war. **Hel. 4:1-2** (Hel. 11:1-5)
Lord's word smites earth. His power delivers. **3 Nephi 13:4** (3 Nephi 28:19-22)
God gives power stronger than many waters to Moses. **Gen. 1:5** (Moses 1:25)
In name of Jesus, trees, mountains, waves obey us. **Jacob 3:2** (Jacob 4:6)
Israel invited to covenant & become nation of priests. **Exo. 12:1**(Exo. 19:1)
Those who give life for name of Christ-crowned. **T&C 101:3** (D&C 101:11)
Priesthood continues in church of God to generations. **T&C 82:10** (D&C 84:17)
Receive priesthood-become seed of Abraham. **T&C 82:16** (D&C 84:34)
Receive priesthood, receive Christ and Father. **T&C 82:17** (D&C 84:35-37)
Fullness of the Priesthood. **T&C Glossary: Fullness of the Priesthood**

HOLY ORDER

Holy Order. **T&C Glossary: Holy Order, Priesthood.**
T&C Glossary: Great Knowledge and Greater Knowledge
High and Holy Order of the High Priesthood. **Alma 9:10-10:2** (Alma 13:1-20)
Order of Son of God without beginning-end. **Hebrews 1:17** (JST Hebrews 7:3)
Adam given dominion over every living thing. **Gen. 2:8-9** (Genesis 1:26-28)
Adam and Eve are after the order of God. **Gen. 4:10** (Moses 6:67)
All things confirmed unto Adam by holy ordinance. **Gen. 3:13** (Moses 5:59)
Adam baptized into order, Him without beginning. **Gen. 4:10** (Moses 6:67)
Adam/Eve in covenant through sacrifice-baptism. **Gen. 4:10** (Moses 6:64-66)
Adam given priesthood before foundation of earth. **Abr. 1:1** (Abr. 1:3)
Priesthood without beginning of days or end of years. **Alma 9:10** (Alma 13:7)
Priesthood in church of God in all generations. **T&C 82:10** (D&C 84:17)
Priesthood of thy Fathers. **Abraham 1:5** (Abraham 1:18)
Priesthood conferred by fathers from beginning. **Abraham 1:1** (Abraham 1:3)
Melchizedek High Priest. Order Son of God. **Gen. 7:18** (JST Gen. 14:26-29)
Fathers and children-welding link. **T&C 151:14** (D&C 128:18)
Abraham seeks for the blessings of the fathers. **Abraham 1:1** (Abraham 1:2)
Abraham seeks Priesthood, like the Fathers. **Abraham 1:1** (Abraham 1:4)
Abraham priesthood through lineage fathers. **D&C 82:10** (D&C 84:14-16)
Abraham's seed bear Priesthood all nations. **Abraham 3:1** (Abraham 2:9-10)
Receive priesthood, become seed of Abraham. **T&C 82:16-17** (D&C 84:34-35)
Israel invited covenant-become kingdom of priests. **Ex. 12:1** (Ex. 19:1-5)
Holy Order given only to those who prove themselves. **Alma 9:10** (Alma 13:3)
Alma in Holy Order. Pure testimony ends contention. **Alma 2:5** (Alma 4:19-20)
Many choose to repent and be ordained in holy order. **Alma 10:1** (Alma 13:10)
Holy Order involves preaching repentance. **Alma 3:8-9** (Alma 5:48-49)
Holy order correlates with entering rest of Lord. **Alma 10:1** (Alma 13:16)
Receive Jesus Christ and the Father. **T&C 82:17** (D&C 84:35-37)

NOTES

SEALED TO THE FATHERS

Sealing Power. **T&C Glossary: Sealing Power**
Priesthood. **T&C Glossary: Priesthood, Priesthood Power.**
Fullness of the Priesthood. **T&C Glossary: Fullness of the Priesthood**
The Fathers. **T&C Glossary: Fathers, The; Powers of Heaven.**
Hearts turned to the Fathers. **T&C Glossary: Hearts turned to the Fathers**
Rights belonging to the Fathers. **T&C Glossary: Rights belonging to Fathers**
Blessings of the Fathers. **T&C Glossary: Blessings of the Fathers.**
Powers of Heaven. **T&C Glossary: Powers of Heaven, Priesthood.**
All invited heaven, to sit down Holy Fathers. **Helaman 2:6**9 (Helaman 3:27-30)
Seeking for the blessings of the Fathers. **Abraham 1:1** (Abraham 1:2-3)
Adam given dominion over every living thing. **Gen. 2:8-9** (Gen. 1:26-28)
God covenants with Adam and Eve. **Genesis 4:10** (Moses 6:64-66)
Adam first father given priesthood. **Abraham1:1** (Abraham 1:3)
Adam and Eve are after the order of God. **Gen. 4:10** (Moses 6:67)
All things confirmed unto Adam by holy ordinance. **Genesis 3:13** (Moses 5:59)
Abraham promised his posterity to be numerous. **Genesis 7:29** (Genesis 17:2-6)
Seed of Abraham blessed with Gospel, salvation. **Abr. 3:1** (Abr. 2:11)
Blessings of Abraham passed Isaac to Jacob. **Genesis 9:20** (Genesis 28:10-16)
God covenants Jacob/Israel. Given land-seed. **Gen. 9:55-56** (Gen. 35:10-15)
Covenant: Abram given land for seed forever. **Genesis 7:11** (Genesis 13:14-16)
Covenant: Abraham's posterity as sands of sea. **Genesis 8:7** (Genesis 22:17-18)
Elijah keys seal hearts fathers to children. **JS History 3:4** (JS History 1:38-39)
Hearts fathers to children, children to fathers. **Malachi 1:11-12 (**Malachi 4:4-6)
Fathers and children must be welded together. **T&C 151:14** (D&C 128:18)
Promises made to the fathers-in hearts of children. **JS History 3:4** (D&C 2:1-3)
Becoming heirs to Christ. (Abrahamic covenant) **Galatians 1:12** (Gal. 3:26-29)
Israel invited keep covenant-kingdom of priests. **Exodus 12:1 (**Exodus 19:1-6)
Receive priesthood-become seed of Abraham. **T&C 82:16** (D&C 84:34)
Receive priesthood, receive Christ and Father. **T&C 82:17** (D&C 84:35-37)
Promises made to fathers, in the hearts of children. **JSH 3:4** (D&C 2:1-3)
Hearts of fathers to children, children to fathers. **Mal. 1:11-12** (Mal. 4:4-6)
Fathers and children must be welded together. **T&C 151:14** (D&C 128:18)
Men are free to choose. **2 Nephi 1:10** (2 Nephi 2:27)
Cry out, Abba Father! Receive adoption. **Romans 1:34** (Romans 8:15-17)

NOTES:

ETERNAL PROGRESSION

<u>MILLLENNIUM</u>
The first shall be last and the last first **Jacob 3:25** (Jacob 5:63)
Old things are done away, all things new. **3 Nephi 5:31** (3 Nephi 12: 47)
New Heaven/New Earth. New Jerusalem. **Ether 6:1-3** (Ether 13:1-12)
Jesus Christ comes in glory, dwells for thousand years. **T&C 9:3** (D&C 29:11)
Jesus Christ returns and Earth given to righteous. **T&C 31:12** (D&C 45:56-58)
Jesus Christ will reign personally upon earth. **T&C 146:30** (Article of Faith 10)
Jesus to reign on the earth. **Zechariah 1:38-39** (Zechariah 14:4–9)
Jesus to reign on the earth. **1 Nephi 7:5** (1 Nephi 22:24–25)
Lord will be in midst of people as King and lawgiver. **T&C 31:12** (D&C 45:59)
Ancient of days given dominion and glory. **Luke 12:16** (Luke 21:20)
Enoch and his city receive Zion-thousand years. **Gen. 4:22-23** (Moses 7:60-66)
Lord of Hosts reign in Mount Zion. **Isaiah 7:2** (Isaiah 24:23)
This is our God; we have waited for Him. **Isaiah 7:3** (Isaiah 25:8-12)
Those suffer persecution, death, partake of glory. **T&C 101:6** (D&C 101:35-36)
Fear not even unto death, in Christ joy is full. **T&C 101:6** (D&C 101: 35-36)
He that overcomes shall inherit all things. **Revelations 8:6** (Revelations 20:7-8)
Martyrs for Christ live-reign 1000 years. **Revelation 8:4-5** (Revelation 20:1-4)
Blessed are meek for they shall inherit the earth. **Matthew 3:8** (Matthew 5:5)
Kingdom given to saints of most high. **Daniel 7:7-8** (Daniel 7:27)
John sees new heaven and new earth. **Revelations 8:8-9** (Revelations 21:1-5)
Ocean driven back. All continents made one. **T&C 58:3** (D&C 133:20-25)
Righteousness and peace for a 1,000 years. **T&C 86:1-28** (D&C 88: 11-115)
Time is no longer. **T&C 86:27-28** (D&C 88:110)
Children grow up without sin unto salvation. **T&C 31:12** (D&C 45:58)
Enmity between man, beasts, all flesh, shall cease. **T&C 101:5** (D&C 101:26)
Enmity between man, beasts, all flesh shall cease. **Isaiah 5:4** (Isaiah 11:6–9)
Wolf and lamb to dwell together. **Isaiah 5:4** (Isaiah 11:1–9)
Desolate land like Garden of Eden. **Ezekiel 18:10-11** (Ezekiel 36:34-38)
During Millennium no sorrow because no death. **T&C 101:5** (D&C 101:29)
Changed twinkling of eye. **T&C 50:11-12** (D&C 63:49-53)
Infants live age of a tree. Changed in twinkling. **T&C 101:5** (D&C 101:30)
Islands become one land. **T&C 58:3** (D&C 133: 17-25)
Lord will reveal all things. **T&C 101:5** (D&C 101:32)
Saints filled with knowledge, sing a new song! **T&C 82:27-28** (D&C 84:98-99)
City of Enoch returns to New Jerusalem. **Genesis 4:2-23** (Moses 7:60-66)
Satan overcome by blood of lamb and testimony. **Rev. 4:4** (Rev. 12:11)
Lucifer. **T&C Glossary: Lucifer**
Lucifer looked upon narrowly. **2 Nephi 10:6** (2 Nephi 24:12-16)
Satan shall be bound. **T&C 29:9** (D&C 43:31)

Satan is bound. **1 Nephi 7:5** (1 Nephi 22:26)
Satan will be bound. **Revelation 8:4** (Revelation 20:1–3).
Satan has no power to tempt. **T&C 101:4-5** (D&C 101:22–31)
Satan has no place in the hearts of children of men. **T&C 31:12** (D&C 45:55)
Satan loosed for little season. **T&C 29:9** (D&C 43:31)
Satan loosed little season end of Millennium. **T&C 86:28** (D&C 88: 111-115)
Satan loosed, gathers to battle. **Revelation 8:6** (Revelations 20:7–10)
Armies of devil fight against hosts of heaven. **T&C 86:28** (D&C 88:111–115.)
Satan and his followers defeated and cast out. **T&C 86:28** (D&C 88: 111-115)
Battle of Great God,Devil, his angels cast away.**T&C 86:28** (D&C 88:111-114)
Michael shall overcome him who seeks the throne. **T&C 86:28** (D&C 88:115)
End 1,000 years, new heaven and new earth. **T&C 9:7** (D&29:22-24)
Curtain of heaven unfolded. **T&C 86:20** (D&C 88:95)
Earth sanctified, immortal, eternal. **T&C 74:1** (D&C 77:1)
John sees earth like a sea of glass. **Revelations 2:2** (Revelations 4:6)
Sanctified earth like Urim and Thummin. **T&C Glossary** (D&C 130:8-11)
Celestial earth is home for righteous. **T&C 86:4** (D&C 88:25-26)
Church of the Firstborn. **T&C Glossary: Church of the Firstborn**
Church of the Firstborn caught up. **T&C 69:25-27** (D&C 76: 94, 98-102)
Lord shall be King of whole earth. **Zechariah 1:39** (Zechariah 14:4-9)
Kingdom delivered unto the Father. **1 Cor. 1:63** (1 Cor. 15:23-28)
Lord's course is one eternal round. **T&C 18:1** (D&C 35:1)

EXALTATION

There are many Gods, many Lords. **1 Corinthians 1:32** (1 Corinthians 8:5-6)
In my Father's house are many mansions. **John 9:6** (John 14:2)
Today thou shalt be with me in paradise. **Luke 13:22** (Luke 23:43)
Christ preached to the spirits in prison. **1 Peter 1:14** (1 Peter 3:18-20)
Ye are god's; and all are children Most High. **Psalms 82:2** (Psalms 82:6)
Is it not written in you law, I said ye are gods? **John 6:30** (John 10:34-36)
The kingdom of God is within you. **Luke 10:2** (Luke 17:20-21)
Cry out, Abba Father! Receive spirit adoption. **Romans 1:34** (Romans 8:15-17)
We are children God - joint heirs with Christ. **Romans 1:34** (Romans 8:14-18)
Jesus Christ: not robbery to be equal God. **Philippians 1:7** (Philippians 2:5-6)
God's work and glory is eternal life of man. **Genesis 1:7** (Moses 1:39)
Be ye therefore perfect as your father in Heaven. **Matthew 3:26** (Matthew 5:48)
Man is become as one of us, to know good - evil. **Genesis 2:19** (Genesis 3:22)
As many obtain authority gain right to ascend **TSJ 1:4**
If you want to ascend to Heavenly Council, you must heed messengers. **TSJ 2:3**
Whoever drinks from living water…shall live from eternity to eternity. **TSJ 4:3**
Anyone who helps me with harvesting souls will save their own. **TSJ 4:8**
Son of Man comes to save the lost. **Luke 10:7** (Luke 18:10)

We are engraved upon His Hands. **1 Nephi 6:8** (1 Nephi 21:16)
Those blinded by falseness, can see or remain blind. **TSJ 7:8**
Those who believe and follow His Son will escape limitations of sin. **TSJ 2:4**
Disciple not above Master, those perfect are as Master. **Luke 5:5** (Luke 6:40)
Advance to be like Him. **TSJ 1:12**
Knowledge to become like Him. **TSJ 1:3**
Teaching every man to be perfect in Christ. **1 Col. 1:5** (1 Col. 1:28)
He that overcomes shall inherit all things. **Revelation 8:6** (Revelations 20:7-8)
Followers will also finish the path...at the place my Father dwells. **TSJ 10:10**
Be steadfast, Christ may seal you His. **Mosiah 3:3** (Mosiah 5:15)
Eternal purposes of the Lord roll on. **Mormon 4:3** (Mormon 8:22)
Lord brings about his eternal purposes. **2 Nephi 1:8** (2 Nephi 2:15)
Lord's purposes fail not. **T&C 69:1** (D&C 76:3)
For ever. **T&C Glossary: For Ever, Eternity, Eternal Life.**
Exaltation. **T&C Glossary: Exaltation, Eternity, Eternal Life.**

ETERNITY TO ETERNITY
God is unchangeable from all Eternity to all Eternity. **Mor. 8:4** (Mor. 8:18)
Lord is the same today as yesterday, and forever. **T&C 18:1** (D&C 35:1)
High Priesthood prepared from eternity to all eternity. **Alma 9:10** (Alma 13:7)
Sons of God shouted for joy. **Job 12:2** (Job 38:7)
The works and purposes of God cannot be frustrated. **JSH 10:2** (D&C 3:1-3)
His purposes fail not. He is same eternity to eternity. **T&C 69:1** (D&C 76:3-4)
Father's work and glory immortality of man. **Genesis 1:7** (Moses 1:39)
Jacobs ladder. **Genesis 9:20** (Genesis 28:12)
You are from a lower estate. You are stuck in this world. **TSJ 6:15**
Principalities. **T&C Glossary: Principalities, Powers of Heaven.**
Eternity is our covering and rock and salvation. **Abraham 4:1** (Abraham 2:16)
There be gods many and lords many. **1 Corinthians 1:32** (1 Corinthians 8:5-6)
As many obtain authority gain right to ascend. **TSJ 1:4**
In my Father's house are many mansions. **John 9:6** (John 14:2)
Father's realms there are many stages with temporary abodes. **TSJ 10:9**
If you want to ascend to Heavenly Council, you must heed messengers. **TSJ 2:3**
Whoever drinks from living water...shall live from eternity to eternity. **TSJ 4:3**
He that overcomes shall inherit all things. **Revelations 8:9** (Revelations 21:7)
Saints filled with glory-made equal with Him. **T&C 86:26** (D&C 88:107)
Follow Jesus: generate endless lives, worlds without end. **TSJ 5:16**
Followers will also finish the path...at the place my Father dwells. **TSJ 10:10**
Riches of eternity are mine to give. **T&C 56:1** (D&C 67:2)
Wonders of eternity. **T&C 69:2** (D&C 76:8-10)
His right hand spans heavens, stand up together. **1 Nephi 6:3** (1 Nephi 20:13)
His command God can roll the earth as a scroll. **Mormon 2:7** (Mormon 5:23)

His command heavens open. My word last day. **Ether 1:18** (Ether 4:8-10)
God moving in His majesty and power. **T&C 86:7-8** (D&C 88:43-47)
Curtain of heaven unfolded. **T&C 86:20** (D&C 88:95)
Church of the Firstborn caught up. **T&C 69:25-27** (D&C 76:94-102)
Wide expanse of eternity. **T&C 22:1** (D&C 38:1)
Account of stewardship in time and eternity. **T&C 63:1** (D&C 72:3)
Men to be judged by their works. **1 Nephi 4:6** (1 Nephi 15:30-36)
Dead, small and great, stand before God. **Revelation 8:7** (Revelation 20:12-13)
Resurrection in the flesh. **Job 7:9** (Job 19:26)
Righteous to receive glory; wicked misery. **Romans 1:8** (Romans 2:3-8)
Degrees of glory explained. **T&C 69:9-28** (D&C 76:50-113)
Characteristics, qualifications celestial glory. **T&C 69:9-22** (D&C 76:50-70)
Celestial, and terrestrial bodies. **1 Corinthians 1:65** (1 Corinthians 15:40)
Man…caught up to the third heaven. **2 Corinthians 1:41** (2 Corinthians 12:1-4)
Sons of Perdition fate. **T&C 69:6-7** (D&C 76:30-40)
Sin and rebellion = horror and the pains of hell. **Alma 17:3** (Alma 36:12-15)
Silence reigns. All eternity pained. **T&C 22:4** (D&C 38:11-12)
Remember all judgments not given unto man. **T&C 9:9** (D&C 29:30)
Endless is my name. **T&C 4:2** (D&C 19:10)
Punishment given is endless punishment. **T&C 4:4** (D&C 19:12)
Written eternal damnation to work upon hearts. **T&C 4:2** (D&C 19:7)
Light fills the immensity space. **T&C 86:1** (D&C 88:11-13)
Enoch's heart swells wide as eternity. **Genesis 4:18** (Moses 7:41)
I am Messiah, Rock of Heaven, broad as eternity. **Genesis 4:20** (Moses 7:53)
Lord reigns eternity to all eternity. **Mosiah 1:14** (Mosiah 3:5)
Lord brings about his eternal purposes. **2 Nephi 1:8** (2 Nephi 2:15)
Eternal purposes of the Lord roll on. **Mormon 4:3** (Mormon 8:22)
Lord's course is one eternal round. **T&C 18:1** (D&C 35:1)
Endure to the End. **T&C Glossary: Endure to the end**
Powers of Heaven. **T&C Glossary: Powers of Heaven, Principalities.**
For ever. **T&C Glossary: For ever, Eternity.**
Eternity. **T&C Glossary: Eternity, Eternal Life**

NOTES:

CANON ORGANIZATION

OLD TESTAMENT
RECORDED IN OLD COVENANT

NEW TESTAMENT
RECORDED IN NEW COVENANT

BOOK OF MORMON
RECORDED IN NEW COVENANT

DOCTRINE AND COVENANTS
RECORDED IN TEACHINGS & COMMANDMENTS

PEARL OF GREAT PRICE:
RECORDED IN OLD COVENANT AND TEACHINGS

OLD TESTAMENT
Correlation with
OLD COVENANT

LDS	Restoration	Theme-Event
Genesis 1-2:5	**Genesis 2:1-11**	The Creation
Genesis 2	**Genesis 2:12-14**	Garden of Eden
Genesis 3	**Genesis 2:16-20**	The Fall
Genesis 4	**Genesis 3:6-10**	Cain kills Abel
Genesis 5	**Genesis 3:14-25, 5:1-4**	From Adam to Noah
Moses 7	**Genesis 4**	Enoch
Genesis 6	**Genesis 5:11-20**	Noah and the flood
Genesis 11	**Genesis 6:6**	Tower of Babel
Genesis 12	**Genesis 7:1-3**	Abraham called
Genesis 14	**Genesis 7:12-21**	Aspects of Ancient Gospel
Genesis 17	**Genesis 7:22-24**	Abrahamic Covenant
Genesis 18	**Genesis 7:43-45**	Destruction Sodom-Gomorrah
Genesis 22	**Genesis 8:5-7**	Abraham sacrificing Isaac
Genesis 28	**Genesis 9:20**	Jacob's Ladder
Genesis 32:24-30	**Genesis 9:44**	Jacob sees God. New Name.
Genesis 37	**Genesis 11:1**	Joseph's coat of many colors.
Genesis 49	**Genesis 12:19-32**	Israel blesses 12 Sons. Dies.
Exodus 1	**Exodus 1:2**	Israel in slavery
Exodus 2	**Exodus 1:4-5**	Birth of Moses
Exodus 3:13-14	**Exodus 2:5**	I AM THAT I AM
Exodus 7-11	**Exodus 4-8**	The Ten Plagues
Exodus 12	**Exodus 8:2-3**	Passover. God rescues Israel.
Exodus 14	**Exodus 9:4**	Parting the Red Sea
Exodus 32	**Exodus 17:2**	Golden Calf
Exodus 33:11	**Exodus 18:2**	Moses sees God face to face
Exodus 39:30	**Exodus 19:26**	HOLINESS TO THE LORD
Leviticus 25:1-22	**Leviticus 13:1-3**	Sabbath years and jubilee
Numbers 11:29	**Numbers 7:19**	Would to God all were prophets
Numbers 12:2-8	**Numbers 7:22**	Dreams and Visions
Joshua 6:1-21	**Joshua 2:1-3**	Jericho
Joshua 24:15	**Joshua 5:5**	Choose ye this day to serve Lord

LDS	Restoration	Theme-Event
Judges 16	**Judges 6:9-16**	Samson and Delilah
Ruth 1-4	**Ruth 1-3**	Ruth
1 Samuel 3:1-14	**1 Samuel 2:8-11**	Lord Calls. Here am I.
1 Samuel 8	**1 Samuel 4:1-4**	Samuel Principle. Rejecting God
1 Samuel 16:7	**1 Samuel 7:16**	Lord judges the heart.
1 Samuel 17	**1 Samuel 8:1-18**	David and Goliath
2 Samuel 2:1-7	**2 Samuel 1:8-9**	David Anointed King
2 Samuel 5:1-5	**2 Samuel 1:32-33**	David reigns over all Israel
2 Samuel 6:1-12	**2 Samuel 2:7-10**	The ark is brought to Jerusalem
2 Samuel 11-12	**2 Samuel 4**	David and Bathsheba
1 Kings 1-2:11	**1 Kings 1:1-2:4**	David's last days
1 Kings 1:39	**1 Kings 1:9**	Solomon anointed King
1 Kings 3:5-15	**1 Kings 2:17-19**	God's appearance to Solomon
1 Kings 9:1-9	**1 Kings 2:70-71**	Second appearance to Solomon
1 Kings 11:1-13	**1 Kings 2:85-86**	Solomon's wives and idolatry
1 Kings 12	**1 Kings 3:1-10**	Kingdom Divided
1 Kings 13	**1 Kings 3:11-21**	Followed a prophet over God
1 Kings 17	**1 Kings 4:1-7**	Elijah raises child from dead.
1 Kings 18	**1 Kings 4:8-22**	Elijah and the prophets of Baal
1 Kings 19:4-13	**1 Kings 4:23-26**	Still small voice
2 Kings 2:1-11	**2 Kings 1:7-11**	Elijah taken to heaven
2 Kings 6:11-17	**2 Kings 2:21-22**	Them that be with us are more.
2 Kings 25	**2 Kings 8:5-10**	Fall of Jerusalem
Ezra 1	**Ezra 1:1-2**	Israel rebuilding land and temple
Ezra 6	**Ezra 1:27-30**	Completion of new temple
Esther 2-4	**Esther 1:5-19**	Esther saving her people
Job 1-4	**Job 1-3:3**	Job - sacrifice and faith
Job 38:1-7	**Job 12:1-2**	Sons of God shouted for joy!
Psalms 9	**Psalms 9**	Cry unto the Lord
Psalms 23	**Psalms 23**	Valley of shadow of death
Psalms 46	**Psalms 46**	Be still and know that I am God.
Proverbs 3:5-6	**Proverbs 1:8**	Trust in the Lord. He will direct
Proverbs 8:1-21	**Proverbs 1:34-36**	Wisdom
Ecclesiastes 3	**Ecclesiastes 1:10-14**	Time for all things
Isaiah 2	**Isaiah 1:5**	Mountain of Lords House
Isaiah 3-4:1	**Isaiah 1:9-11**	Daughters of Zion cursed
Isaiah 4:2-5:7	**Isaiah 1:12-13**	Zion as a defense and a refuge.
Isaiah 6	**Isaiah 2**	Altar-Here I am. Send me.
Isaiah 8	**Isaiah 3:5-7**	Wizards that peep and mutter

LDS	Restoration	Theme-Event
Isaiah 9:6	**Isaiah 4:1**	Wonderful Counselor! Mighty God!
Isaiah 9:16-17	**Isaiah 4:3**	Leaders cause people to error.
Isaiah 13:3	**Isaiah 6:1**	Called my mighty ones.
Isaiah 14:9-20	**Isaiah 6:5-6**	Look narrowly at Lucifer.
Isaiah 24	**Isaiah 7:1-2**	Broken covenant-defiles earth.
Isaiah 28:1-22	**Isaiah 8:1-5**	Drunkards of Ephraim
Isaiah 29	**Isaiah 9:1-6**	Marvelous work and a book
Isaiah 30:8-26	**Isaiah 9:9-10**	False prophets speak smooth things
Isaiah 53	**Isaiah 19:2**	Man of sorrows, acquainted grief.
Isaiah 55	**Isaiah 20:1-2**	God thoughts higher than mans.
Isaiah 56	**Isaiah 20:3-4**	Gather outcasts to Holy Mountain
Isaiah 58	**Isaiah 20:3-7**	Sabbath day
Jeremiah 4	**Jeremiah 2:5-3:2**	Zion standard and fall of Babylon
Jeremiah 5	**Jeremiah 3:3-7**	False prophets
Jeremiah 11-12	**Jeremiah 5:1-7**	Jeremiah proclaims Gods Covenant
Jeremiah 23	**Jeremiah 8:16-20**	False prophets
Jeremiah 31:31-34	**Jeremiah 12:9**	New covenant-all know the Lord.
Jeremiah 50	**Jeremiah 18:2-9**	Jeremiah prophecies against Babylon
Jeremiah 51	**Jer. 18:10-19:1**	Babylon destroyed
Ezekiel 14	**Ezekiel 5:8-11**	Deceiving prophets
Ezekiel 34	**Ezekiel 17:5-11**	Shepherd s feed selves-flock lost
Ezekiel 34:23-24	**Ezekiel 17:10**	Covenant of peace through David
Ezekiel 36:24-32	**Ezekiel 18:9**	New spirit, new heart.
Ezekiel 37:1-14	**Ezekiel 19:1-3**	Dry bones resurrected.
Ezekiel 37:15-20	**Ezekiel 19:4**	Stick of Judah, Stick of Joseph
Ezekiel 38	**Ezekiel 20:1-6**	Battle of God and Magog
Daniel 2	**Daniel 2**	Dream of stone cut out mountain
Daniel 3	**Daniel 3**	Shadrach, Meshach, Abednego.
Daniel 6	**Daniel 6**	Daniel and lion's den
Joel 1	**Joel 1:1-5**	Word of Lord to Joel
Joel 2	**Joel 1:6-12**	Dreams, visions, prophecies
Amos 8:11	**Amos 1:27**	Famine in the land of hearing word.
Jonah 1-4	**Jonah 1**	Great fish, repentance of Nineveh
Malachi 3:8-12	**Malachi 1:7**	Tithes
Malachi 4:5-6	**Malachi 1:12**	Hearts of children unto the fathers

NEW TESTAMENT
Correlation with
NEW COVENANT

LDS	Restoration	Theme-Event
Matthew 1	Matthew 1:5	Jesus is Born
Matthew 3	Matthew 2:1-3	John the Baptist prepares the way
Matthew 3	Matthew 2:4	Baptism of Jesus
Matthew 5	Matthew 3:4-26	Sermon on the Mount
Matthew 7	Matthew 3: 40	Judge not, that ye be not judged.
Matthew 7	Matthew 3: 46	Know a false prophet by fruit.
Matthew 10	Matthew 4:15	Lord gives apostles divine power
Matthew 10	Matthew 5:2	Lord sends apostles out.
Matthew 10	Matthew 5:7	Must love God more than family.
Matthew 11	Matthew 6:8	In Jesus our burden is light
Matthew 12	Matthew 6:9	Jesus Lord of Sabbath
Matthew 13	Matthew 7:5	Parable of sower, wheat and tares
Matthew 14	Matthew 8:6	Peter walks on water
Matthew 16	Matthew 9:1	Peter declares the Christ
Matthew 16	Matthew 9:3	Whosoever lose life in Christ will save life
Matthew 17	Matthew 9:4	Transfiguration
Matthew 19	Matthew 9:22-24	Consecrate all to Lord
Matthew 20	Matthew 10:1-6	Final Journey to Jerusalem
Matthew 21	Matthew 10:5	Triumphal Jerusalem entry
Matthew 21	Matthew 10:7	Cleansing the Temple
Matthew 22	Matthew 10:23	Two great commandments
Matthew 24	Matthew 11:2-13	Destruction and signs of the times.
Matthew 24	Matthew 11:3,6	False prophets.
Matthew 25	Matthew 11:15	Parable of ten virgins, sheep and goats,
Matthew 25	Matthew 11:22-23	Done unto least of these, done unto me.
Matthew 26	Matthew 12:3-6	Last Supper
Matthew 26	Matthew 12:7-11	Gethsemane
Matthew 27	Matthew 12:22-31	Crucifixion
Matthew 28	Matthew 13	Resurrection
Matthew 28	Matthew 13:4	Go and teach and baptize all nations
Mark 1	Mark 1:1	John the Baptist prepares the way
Mark 3	Mark 2:4	Jesus Lord of Sabbath
Mark 4	Mark 2:12-14	Parable of the sower.
Mark 4	Mark 2:20	Jesus calms the storm

LDS	Restoration	Theme-Event
Mark 6	**Mark 3:6**	Prophet not accepted in own country
Mark 6	**Mark 3:8-11**	John the Baptist Beheaded
Mark 9	**Mark 5:8-10**	Help thou my unbelief
Mark 9	**Mark 5:5-6**	Transfiguration
Mark 11	**Mark 5:34**	Jesus casts out moneychangers.
Mark 12	**Mark 5:48**	Widows mite
Luke 2	**Luke 2:1-3**	Birth of Jesus Christ
Luke 2	**Luke 3:1-2**	Jesus teaching in the temple
Luke 3	**Luke 3:3-7**	John the Baptist prepares the way
Luke 5	**Luke 4:8-12**	Jesus calls His first disciples
Luke 8	**Luke 6:12**	Jesus raises girl from the dead
Luke 9	**Luke7:3**	Jesus feeds the 5,000
Luke 10	**Luke 8:8**	Good Samaritan,
Luke 10	**Luke 8:9**	Mary and Martha
Luke 15	**Luke 9:14**	Prodigal Son
Luke 16	**Luke 9:16**	Rich man and his steward
Luke 16	**Luke 9:20**	Rich Man and Lazarus the beggar
Luke 18:1-9	**Luke 10:6**	Parable of unjust judge
Luke 22	**Luke 13:12**	Peter denies Christ three times.
Luke 23	**Luke 13:21**	Forgive them, know not what they do.
Luke 24	**Luke 14:2**	Road to Emmaus
John 1	**John 1:1**	THE WORD
John 3	**John 2:2**	Born of the Water and of Spirit
John 3	**John 2:2**	For God so loved the world
John 4	**John 4:3**	Women at well - Everlasting waters
John 6	**John 5:9-10**	Jesus feeds the 5,000
John 8	**John 6:10**	Woman taken in adultery. Cast first stone?
John 7:10	**John 6:2-5**	Jesus teaches at Feast of Tabernacles
John 10	**John 6:26**	Other sheep
John 11	**John 7:6**	Lazarus Raised
John 13:34	**John 9:5**	Love one another
John 14:6	**John 9:7**	The Way, the Truth, and the Life
John 14	**John 9:9**	Holy Ghost teaches all. Comforter peace.
John 15	**John 9:13**	Comforter is spirit of truth.
John 16	**John 9:14**	Holy Ghost guides into all truth
John 17:1-26	**John 9:19-21**	Intercessory prayer
John 17:3	**John 9:19**	Eternal life is to know God and Jesus Christ.
Acts 1	**Acts 1:3**	Ascension to right hand of God
Acts 2	**Acts 1:9**	Women prophets

114

LDS	Restoration	Theme-Event
Acts 2	**Acts 1:7**	Day of Pentecost
Acts 3	**Acts 2:3**	Restitution of all things
Acts 5	**Acts 3:7**	Apostles choose to obey God over men.
Acts 7	**Acts 4:10**	Stephen martyrdom
Acts 9	**Acts 5:8**	Saul sees Christ and is converted.
Acts 9	**Acts 6:2**	Peter raises Tabitha from the dead.
Acts 10	**Acts 6:4**	Peter commanded take gospel to the Gentiles
Acts 13:9	**Acts 8:2**	Saul now named Paul.
Acts 15	**Acts 10:1**	Paul and Barnabas divide over differences
Acts 17	**Acts 10:14**	Paul: we are children of a knowable God
Acts 27	**Acts 13:7**	Paul shipwrecked.
Acts 28	**Acts 13:9**	Paul stayed barbarous people three months
Romans 1	**Romans 1:4-6**	Homosexuality is an abomination
Romans 8	**Romans 1:35**	All things work together for good love God.
Romans 8	**Romans 1:34,38**	Spirit of adoption.
Romans 8	**Romans 1:34**	Children of God, joint heirs with Christ
Romans 16	**Romans 1:80**	Teach correct doctrine. Avoid divisions.
1 Cor. 3	**1 Cor. 1:9**	Milk and meat.
1 Cor. 3	**1 Cor. 1:12**	Ye are the temple of God.
1 Cor. 12	**1 Cor. 1:54**	Spiritual gifts.
1 Cor. 13	**1 Cor. 1:53**	See through a glass darkly.
2 Cor. 3	**2 Cor. 1:9**	Letter kills, but the Spirit giveth life.
2 Cor. 4	**2 Cor. 1:12**	God of this world blinds the minds.
2 Cor, 6	**2 Cor. 1:21**	Unequally yoked.
2 Cor. 12	**2 Cor. 1:43**	Paul's thorn. Glories in Lord-tribulation.
Galatians 5	**Galatians 1:22**	Fruit of the Spirit.
Ephesians 4	**Ephesians 1:12**	Unity of the faith.
Ephesians 4	**Ephesians 1:13**	Tossed every wind of Doctrine.
Ephesians 6	**Ephesians 1:25**	Spiritual wickedness high places.
Ephesians 6	**Ephesians 1:25**	Armor of God.
Phil. 2	**Phil. 1:8**	Work out salvation with fear-trembling.
Phil. 2:5	**Phil. 1:7**	Let the mind of Christ be in you.
Phil. 2:6	**Phil. 1:7**	Not robbery to be equal with God.
Phil. 4	**Phil. 1:16**	Can do all things through Christ Jesus.
2 Thess. 2	**2 Thess. 1:4**	Falling away before coming of Lord.
2 Timothy 3	**2 Timothy 1:8**	Last days are perilous times.
2 Timothy 4	**2 Timothy 1:10**	Will not endure sound doctrine.
2 Timothy 4	**2 Timothy 1:10**	Paul fought good fight
Hebrews 8	**Hebrews 1:23**	New Covenant with Israel-House Judah

LDS	Restoration	Theme-Event
Hebrews 11	**Hebrews 1:36**	Faith: substance things hoped for, not seen.
Hebrews 11	**Hebrews 1:42**	Strangers and Pilgrims upon the Earth
Hebrews 13	**Hebrews 1:58**	Entertain angels unaware.
James 1	**Jacob 1:2**	If any lack wisdom let him ask of God.
James 1	**Jacob 1:7**	Pure religion: visit widows- be unspotted.
James 2	**Jacob 1:11**	Faith without works is dead.
James 5	**Jacob 1:23**	Prayer of faith will heal the sick.
2 Peter 1	**2 Peter 1:3**	Calling and Election. Divine nature
Rev. 1	**Revelations 1:4**	John exiled to island of Patmos
Rev. 2	**Revelations 1:12**	White Stone and a new name
Rev. 3	**Revelations 8:8**	New Jerusalem comes out of Heaven
Rev. 7	**Revelations 2:16**	No Pre-Tribulation Rapture.
Rev. 11	**Revelations 3:17**	Jerusalem prophets killed-resurrected.
Rev. 12	**Revelations 4:3-7**	War in Heaven.
Rev. 12	**Revelations 4:3**	Satan deceives the whole world.
Rev. 14	**Revelations 5:1**	Lamb will stand on Mount Zion.
Rev. 17	**Revelations 6:12**	Lamb overcomes with the chosen.
Rev. 19	**Revelations 7:10**	Testimony of Jesus = spirit of prophecy.
Rev. 20	**Revelations 8:5**	Martyrs for Jesus refuse mark of beast.
Rev. 20	**Revelations 8:7**	Book of Life.
Rev. 21	**Revelations 8:8**	New Heaven and a new earth.
Rev. 22	**Revelations 8:15**	The Lord: I come quickly.

BOOK OF MORMON
Correlation with
BOOK OF MORMON

LDS	Restoration	Theme-Event
1 Nephi 1:5-15	**1 Nephi 1:3**	Lehi's Vision.
1 Nephi 2:1-3	**1 Nephi 1:6**	Lehi commanded to leave Jerusalem.
1 Nephi 4:10-18	**1 Nephi 1:16-17**	Nephi slays Laban, obtains plates.
1 Nephi 6:3-6	**1 Nephi 2:1**	Nephi writes only what **is** pleasing to God.
1 Nephi 7:1-5	**1 Nephi 2:2**	Ishmael's family joins Lehi.
1 Nephi 8:2-18	**1 Nephi 2:7-13**	Lehi's Tree of Life Dream.
1 Nephi 9:2-6	**1 Nephi 2:14**	Plates of Nephi created.
1 Nephi 10:2-6	**1 Nephi 3:2**	Lehi prophesies destruction of Jerusalem.
1 Nephi 11:1-25	**1 Nephi 3:6-31**	Nephi's vision of Tree of Life.
1 Nephi 11:7	**1 Nephi 3:6**	Vision of Christ.
1 Nephi 13:1-20	**1 Nephi 3:19**	Great and abominable church.
1 Nephi 13:3	**1 Nephi 3:19-26**	Prophecy of the Gentiles.
1 Nephi 14:10	**1 Nephi 3:27**	Two Churches Only.
1 Nephi 15:19-20	**1 Nephi 4:4**	Restoration House of Israel in Last Days.
1 Nephi 16:10	**1 Nephi 5:3**	Liahona.
1 Nephi 17:8-18	**1 Nephi 5:15-16**	Nephi commanded to build **a** ship.
1 Nephi 18:8-23	**1 Nephi 5:27-32**	Voyage to Promised Land.
1 Nephi 19	**1 Nephi 5:37-38**	Jews scattered but Israel gathered in.
1 Nephi 20	**1 Nephi 6:2-5**	Israel chosen furnace affliction.
1 Nephi 21	**1 Nephi 6:6-10**	Israel gathered in the last days.
1 Nephi 22:13-14	**1 Nephi 7:4**	Fate of great and abominable church.
1 Nephi 22	**1 Nephi 7:3**	Gentiles nourish Israel with Gospel.
2 Nephi 1:1-27	**2 Nephi 1:1**	Lehi prophecies of descendant-covenant.
2 Nephi 2	**2 Nephi 1:7**	There must be opposition in all things.
2 Nephi 3:1-21	**2 Nephi 2:1-7**	Joseph as a title and calling.
2 Nephi 4:17-33	**2 Nephi 3:7-8**	O wretched man that I am!
2 Nephi 4:34-35	**2 Nephi 3:8**	Trust not in the arm of flesh.
2 Nephi 5:16-25	**2 Nephi 4:3-4**	Build temple; covenantal cursing.
2 Nephi 5:26	**2 Nephi 4:5**	Jacob and Joseph consecrated.
2 Nephi 6:11	**2 Nephi 5:4**	Lord will gather people again .
2 Nephi 7:8	**2 Nephi 5:7**	Let us stand together.
2 Nephi 8	**2 Nephi 5:8-11**	Lord gathers Israel. Redeemed to Zion.
2 Nephi 9:7-23	**2 Nephi 6:2-7**	Infinite Atonement, all men to repent.
2 Nephi 9:41	**2 Nephi 6:11**	Christ employs no servant at gate.

LDS	Restoration	Theme-Event
2 Nephi 11:2-3	**2 Nephi 8:2**	Nephi, Jacob, Isaiah all saw the Lord.
2 Nephi 12	**2 Nephi 8:4-6**	Lord's house top of mountains.
2 Nephi 12	**2 Nephi 8:4-6**	House of God. Learn of His ways.
2 Nephi 13	**2 Nephi 8:7-8**	Leaders cause Lord's people to err.
2 Nephi 14	**2 Nephi 8:9-10**	Glory of Zion shall be a defense.
2 Nephi 15	**2 Nephi 8:11:18**	Ensign lifted. Israel gathered.
2 Nephi 16	**2 Nephi 9:1-2**	Wo unto me! Altar of purification.
2 Nephi 17	**2 Nephi 9:3-6**	Birth of Jesus Christ to a virgin.
2 Nephi 18	**2 Nephi 9:7-10**	Seek God, not wizards peep and mutter.
2 Nephi 19	**2 Nephi 9:11-14**	Wonderful, Counselor, Mighty God!
2 Nephi 20	**2 Nephi 9:15-20**	Wicked destroyed at Second Coming.
2 Nephi 21	**2 Nephi 9:21-22**	Outcasts of Israel assembled.
2 Nephi 22	**2 Nephi 9:23**	Cry out-shout. Great is the Holy One!
2 Nephi 23	**2 Nephi 10:1-3**	Babylon shall fall forever. (Isaiah 13)
2 Nephi 24	**2 Nephi 10:4-9**	Lucifer looked upon narrowly.
2 Nephi 25:4	**2 Nephi 11:1**	Isaiah's words plain with prophecy.
2 Nephi 25:17	**2 Nephi 11:6**	A marvelous work and wonder.
2 Nephi 25:26	**2 Nephi 11:8**	We talk, preach, prophecy: CHRIST!
2 Nephi 26:29	**2 Nephi 11:17**	Priestcrafts forbidden, false churches
2 Nephi 28:1-25	**2 Nephi 12:1-5**	False Religion. Pride; all is well in Zion.
2 Nephi 28:32	**2 Nephi 12:7**	Woe unto gentiles, they reject Christ.
2 Nephi 29	**2 Nephi 12:8-10**	A Bible a Bible! 2 nations, 2 books.
2 Nephi 30	**2 Nephi 12:11-13**	After Gentiles, Jews-remnant believes.
2 Nephi 31	**2 Nephi 13**	Doctrine of Christ.
2 Nephi 32	**2 Nephi 14:1**	Feast upon the words of Christ.
Jacob 1:17-19	**Jacob 1:4**	Errand from the Lord.
Jacob 2:18-19	**Jacob 2:5**	Seek riches to do good.
Jacob 2:10-33	**Jacob 2:2-8**	Abominations.
Jacob 3:2	**Jacob 2:11**	Pleasing word of God.
Jacob 4:14	**Jacob 3:5**	Looking beyond the mark.
Jacob 5	**Jacob 3:7-28**	Parable of the Vineyard.
Jacob 7	**Jacob 5**	Sherem - Anti Christ.
Enos 1:1-8	**Enos 1:1**	Enos received a remission of his sins.
Mosiah 1:10-17	**Mosiah 1:2-3**	King Benjamin gathers people.
Mosiah 2:9	**Mosiah 1:7**	King Benjamin desires unfold mysteries.
Mosiah 2:21-26	**Mosiah 1:8-9**	All are unprofitable servants.
Mosiah 3:17	**Mosiah 1:16**	No other name can save but Jesus Christ.
Mosiah 4:19	**Mosiah 2:4**	King Benjamin - Are we not all beggars?
Mosiah 5:2	**Mosiah 3:1**	Mighty change of heart, new name.

LDS	Restoration	Theme-Event
Mosiah 7:29	**Mosiah 5:10**	No prosperity in wickedness.
Mosiah 8:15	**Mosiah 5:13**	Seer greater than a prophet.
Mosiah 11:20	**Mosiah 7:8**	Abinadi the Prophet.
Mosiah 12:29	**Mosiah 7:17**	Hearts upon riches?
Mosiah 15:1	**Mosiah 8:5**	God Himself shall come down.
Mosiah 17	**Mosiah 9:1-5**	Abinadi martyred. Alma Believes.
Mosiah 18:8-11	**Mosiah 9:7**	Baptism covenant.
Mosiah 19:20	**Mosiah 9:17**	King Noah dies by fire.
Mosiah 21:22	**Mosiah 9:32**	People of Limhi in bondage.
Mosiah 22:11-16	**Mosiah 10:3**	Ammon leads Limhi people - Zarahemla.
Mosiah 24:13	**Mosiah 11:9**	Lord honors covenants made with Him.
Mosiah 26:15-32	**Mosiah 11:20-22**	Lord speaks to Alma and blesses him.
Mosiah 27:4-5	**Mosiah 11:24**	Equality among all men, all labor.
Mosiah 27:13	**Mosiah 11:26**	Transgression can overthrow a church.
Mosiah 27:24	**Mosiah 11:28**	Alma the younger is born again.
Mosiah 28:1-8	**Mosiah 12:1-3**	Sons of Mosiah go on missions
Mosiah 29:41	**Mosiah 13:9**	Judges appointed to succeed Mosiah.
Alma 1:1-15	**Alma 1:1-3**	Nehor is Anti-Christ.
Alma 1:26	**Alma 1:5**	Church of Christ- priests all labor.
Alma 4:6	**Alma 2:3**	Pride-contention in church-hearts riches.
Alma 5:14	**Alma 3:3**	Born of God?
Alma 6:6	**Alma 4:1**	Commanded meet, fast, pray, often.
Alma 7:14	**Alma 5:4**	Born again to enter heaven.
Alma 10:14	**Alma 8:5**	Corrupt lawyers and judges.
Alma 12:9	**Alma 9:3**	Many know mysteries, forbear sharing.
Alma 13:1-9	**Alma 9:10**	Holy Order of God.
Alma 14:11	**Alma 10:7**	Believers thrown fire, Alma constrained.
Alma 15:6-13	**Alma 10:14**	Zeezrom converted, healed, preached.
Alma 16:2	**Alma 11:1**	City of Ammonihah destroyed.
Alma 17:18-27	**Alma 12:5-6**	Ammon and the flocks of the King.
Alma 18-19	**Alma 12:11-26**	King Lamoni and household converted.
Alma 22:15	**Alma 13:9**	King willing give kingdom for joy
Alma 24:19	**Alma 14:9**	Anti-Nephi-Lehi bury weapons, covenant
Alma 26:1	**Alma 14:16**	Alma boasts in His God.
Alma 29	**Alma 15:12-14**	O that I were an angel! Voice of thunder.
Alma 30:12	**Alma 16:3**	Korihor- Anti Christ.
Alma 31:21	**Alma 16:19**	Zoromite Rameumptom.
Alma 31:22	**Alma 16:19**	Zoromites believe they are chosen people.
Alma 31:29	**Alma 16:20**	Zoromites say there will be no Christ.

LDS	Restoration	Theme-Event
Alma 32:6	**Alma 16:24**	Alma preaches to humble cast out poor.
Alma 32:28	**Alma 16:28**	Seed of faith. Experiment on Word.
Alma 34:18	**Alma 16:35**	Cry unto Him, poor out your souls.
Alma 37:6	**Alma 17:8**	Small and simple things.
Alma 38	**Alma 18**	Christ is the light and life of the world.
Alma 39	**Alma 19:1-3**	Sexual sin is an abomination.
Alma 41	**Alma 19:9-11**	Nature of men not changed after death.
Alma 42	**Alma 19:12-17**	Mercy cannot rob justice.
Alma 43-44	**Alma 20:1-19**	Captain Moroni defeats Zoramites.
Alma 45:16	**Alma 21:3**	Cursed is this land if people do wickedly.
Alma 46	**Alma 21:6-16**	Title of Liberty.
Alma 48	**Alma 21:31-35**	Moroni and the cause of Christians.
Alma 51	**Alma 23:2-5**	King men; secret combinations.
Alma 53	**Alma 24:15-22**	Helaman's 2,000 stripling warriors.
Alma 57	**Alma 26:13-22**	2,000 stripling warriors.
Alma 61	**Alma 28**	Kingmen attempt to take Government.
Alma 63:5	**Alma 30:3**	Hagoth sails ships to the north.
Helaman 1	**Helaman 1**	Politics and secret combinations.
Helaman 3:24	**Helaman 2:7**	Great prosperity-pride within church.
Helaman 4	**Helaman 2:9-14**	Dissensions in the church.
Helaman 5:12	**Helaman 2:17**	Rock of Christ foundation.
Helaman 6	**Helaman 2:27-35**	Lamanites more righteous than Nephites.
Helaman 6:38	**Helaman 2:35**	Gaddianton robbers control government.
Helaman 7:11	**Helaman 3:2**	Nephi prays on tower for people.
Helaman 8	**Helaman 3:6-10**	Nephi prophesies murder of chief judge.
Helaman 10	**Helaman 3:19-21**	Nephi receives sealing power.
Helaman 12	**Helaman 4:9-11**	Except afflicted, Lord's people forget.
Helaman 13	**Helaman 5:1-9**	Samuel False prophets popular.
Helaman 16	**Helaman 5:17-21**	Samuel persecuted but escapes.
3 Nephi 1	**3 Nephi 1:1-7**	Signs of Savior's birth.
3 Nephi 2	**3 Nephi 1:8-12**	People forget signs and wonders.
3 Nephi 2-6	**3 Nephi 1:8-3:5**	Wickedness and abominations.
3 Nephi 7	**3 Nephi 3:6-12**	Chief Judge killed, people break tribes.
3 Nephi 7:18	**3 Nephi 3:10**	Nephi preaches in power of God.
3 Nephi 8:23	**3 Nephi 4:5**	Signs Christ's death. Destruction, 3 days.
3 Nephi 9	**3 Nephi 4:6-7**	Jesus appears in Bountiful.
3 Nephi 11	**3 Nephi 5:1-9**	Jesus teaches the Doctrine of Christ.
3 Nephi 12	**3 Nephi 5:10-31**	Twelve Apostles commissioned.
3 Nephi 13-14	**3 Nephi 5:32-6:6**	Sermon on the mount teachings.

LDS	Restoration	Theme-Event
3 Nephi 15	**3 Nephi 7:1-3**	Law of Moses fulfilled in Christ.
3 Nephi 16	**3 Nephi 7:3-6**	Jesus to visit the Lost tribes of Israel.
3 Nephi 16	**3 Nephi 7:3-6**	Gospel to be taken to House of Israel.
3 Nephi 17	**3 Nephi: 8:1-5**	Jesus blesses little children.
3 Nephi 18	**3 Nephi: 8:6-10**	Instructions regarding sacrament.
3 Nephi 19	**3 Nephi 9:1-5**	Christ's intercessory prayer.
3 Nephi 20	**3 Nephi 9:6-10**	Christ prophesies fate of Gentiles.
3 Nephi 21	**3 Nephi 9:11-12**	Covenant of Israel-Great work coming..
3 Nephi 21	**3 Nephi 9:11-12**	Marred Servant,
3 Nephi 21	**3 Nephi 9:11-12**	Gentiles repent or be cut off.
3 Nephi 22	**3 Nephi 10:1**	Gentiles humbled. Israel gathered.
3 Nephi 22	**3 Nephi 10:2-3**	Zion established.
3 Nephi 24	**3 Nephi 11:1-4**	Malachi: not kept My ordinances.
3 Nephi 26	**3 Nephi 11:6-12:3**	Reveals history of earth.
3 Nephi 26	**3 Nephi 11:6-12:3**	Greater things revealed if faithful.
3 Nephi 27	**3 Nephi 12:4-13:2**	Repent, baptized to be sanctified.
3 Nephi 27:21	**3 Nephi 12:5**	Gospel of Christ.
3 Nephi 28	**3 Nephi 13:3-6**	Three Nephites, Apostles to heaven.
3 Nephi 29	**3 Nephi 13:7-8**	Covenant to Gentiles-children of Israel.
3 Nephi 30	**3 Nephi 14**	Warning to the Gentiles, repent.
4 Nephi 1	**4 Nephi 1**	Law of consecration. Unity and peace.
Mormon 1	**Mormon 1:1-4**	War and wickedness among Nephites.
Mormon 1:16-17	**Mormon 1:4**	Mormon forbidden to preach.
Mormon 3	**Mormon 1:9-12**	Mormon preaches one last time.
Mormon 3	**Mormon 1:9-12**	Mormon writes to the Gentiles.
Mormon 4	**Mormon 2:1-3**	Nephites take offensive.
Mormon 4	**Mormon 2:1-3**	Wicked punish the wicked.
Mormon 5	**Mormon 2:4-7**	Gentiles repent or earn fate of Nephites.
Mormon 6	**Mormon 3:1-4**	Nation Destroyed. Plates go to Moroni.
Mormon 8	**Mormon 4:1-5**	God will remember covenant.
Mormon 8	**Mormon 4:1-5**	Gentile practices condemned.
Ether 1	**Ether 1:1-4**	Tower of Babel.
Ether 1	**Ether 1:1-4**	Jaredites language not confounded.
Ether 2	**Ether 1:5-10**	America must serve God or swept off.
Ether 3	**Ether 1:11-16**	Brother Jared sees Lord. Redeem fall.
Ether 4:7	**Ether 1:17**	Have faith like brother of Jared.
Ether 4:13	**Ether 1:19**	Come unto me, receive greater things.
Ether 8	**Ether 3:13-19**	Secret combination, political corruption.
Ether 12:3	**Ether 4:17**	Faith all things are possible.

LDS	Restoration	Theme-Event
Ether 12:23-25	**Ether 5:4**	Moroni concerned Gentiles will mock.
Ether 12:27	**Ether 5:5**	Weak things become strong.
Ether 12:39	**Ether 5:8**	Moroni saw the Lord face to face.
Ether 13:9-10	**Ether 6:3**	Zion. New Jerusalem.
Ether 13:9-10	**Ether 6:3**	New Heaven/New Earth. Zion.
Ether 14-15	**Ether 6:7-20**	Final destruction of the Jaredites
Moroni 1	**Moroni 1**	Moroni will not deny The Christ.
Moroni 4	**Moroni 4**	Sacrament prayer for bread.
Moroni 5	**Moroni 5**	Sacrament prayer for wine.
Moroni 7:13-19	**Moroni 7:2-3**	Judging good from evil.
Moroni 7:47	**Moroni 7:9**	Pure love of Christ.
Moroni 8	**Moroni 8**	Infant baptism rejected.
Moroni 10:4-5	**Moroni 10:2**	Testing for truth of all things.
Moroni 10:8-18	**Moroni 10:3**	Gifts of the Spirit.

DOCTRINE AND COVENANTS
Correlation with
TEACHINGS AND COMMANDMENTS

LDS	Restoration	Theme-Event
D&C 1	T&C 54	Warning voice proclaimed by weak and simple.
D&C 2	JSH 3:4	Coming of Elijah the Prophet
D&C 3	T&C 2	Joseph Smith chastised for losing transcript.
D&C 4	T&C 11:2-3	Marvelous work and wonder-called to serve
D&C 5	T&C 12:2-7	Greater worksif accept words Joseph Smith
D&C 6	T&C 13:3-15	Inquire to know the mysteries
D&C 7	T&C 13:18-19	John the Beloved ministers to heirs of salvation.
D&C 8	T&C 3	Revelation in your mind and heart.
D&C 9	T&C 13:24-28	How to discern answer to prayers
D&C 10	T&C 10:8-21	Repent and come into Church of Christ.
D&C 10	T&C 10:8-21	True doctrine decreases contention
D&C 11	JSH 14:7-16	Seek first to obtain my word.
D&C 12	T&C 14:20	Love, faith, hope, and charity to do the work.
D&C 13	T&C 14:1	John Baptist confers the priesthood of Aaron
D&C 14	T&C 15:3-7	Seek to bring forth My Zion. Ask Holy Ghost.
D&C 15	T&C 15:8-9	Most worth declare repentance unto this people.
D&C 16	T&C 15:10-11	Bringing souls unto Christ is of most worth.
D&C 17	T&C 15:18	Three witnesses promised they can see plates.
D&C 18	JSH 15:27-38	Worth of soul. Great joy in soul that repents!
D&C 18	JSH:27-38	Calling of twelve apostles.
D&C 19	T&C 4	Eternal and Endless punishment.
D&C 19	T&C 4	God suffered that we might not suffer.
D&C 20	T&C16:2-28	Revelation on Church Organization
D&C 21	T&C 18:3-5	Joseph seer and revelator. Receive him.
D&C 22	T&C 18:8	Baptism: New and Everlasting covenant.
D&C 23	T&C 18:10-14	Hyrum, Joseph calling to strengthen church.
D&C 23	T&C 18:10-14	Beware of pride.
D&C 23	T&C 18:10-14	Pray vocally before the world and in secret.
D&C 24	T&C 7	Attend to thy calling and you will have strength.
D&C 25	T&C 5	Emma is an elect lady.
D&C 26	T&C 6	Law of common consent.
D&C 27	T&C 8	Does not matter what eat-drink for sacrament.
D&C 28	T&C 10	Only Joseph will receive revelations for church.
D&C 28	T&C 10	Oliver called to the Lamanites.

LDS	Restoration	Theme-Event
D&C 29	T&C 9	Destruction foretold. New Heaven and Earth.
D&C 30:1	T&C 11	David Whitmer feared men and not God.
D&C 30:5	T&C 12	Peter Whitmer called with Oliver to Lamanites.
D&C 30:9	T&C 13	John Whitmer called to preach.
D&C 31	T&C 14	Thomas M. called to preach. Patient in affliction.
D&C 32	T&C 15	Parley Pratt called to preach to Lamanites.
D&C 33	T&C 16	Voice-Trump, gather elect, Bridegroom comes!
D&C 34	T&C 17	Lift up thy voice and spare not.
D&C 35	T&C 18	Great work to do among the Gentiles.
D&C 36	T&C 19	Edward Partridge called to preach the gospel.
D&C 37	T&C 20	Joseph and Sydney travel to serve.
D&C 38:8	T&C 22:3	Be pure and live to see Christ.
D&C 38:20	T&C 22:6	Covenant land set aside
D&C 38:12	T&C 22:4	Enemy is Combined
D&C 39	T&C 23	Receive Lord, become His sons. The comforter.
D&C 40	T&C 24	Cares world, fear persecution, rejection of word.
D&C 41	T&C 25	Assemble yourselves together to agree.
D&C 42	T&C 26	Missionary instructions. New Jerusalem revealed
D&C 42:30	T&C 26:7	Consecrate all property to Lord for support poor
D&C 42:74	T&C 28	Murder and Adultery addressed
D&C 42:78	N/A	NOT IN T&C
D&C 43	T&C 29	Revelations received from those appointed
D&C 44	T&C 30	Conference called. Administer to the poor.
D&C 45	T&C 31	Everlasting covenant for Gentiles. Signs last days.
D&C 45:29	T&C 31:6	Times of Gentiles fulfilled. Reject Fullness
D&C 45:56	T&C 31:12	Righteous shall be gathered, parable of 10 virgins.
D&C 45:66	T&C 31:14	New Jerusalem and Zion described.
D&C 46	T&C 32	Gifts of the Spirit enumerated.
D&C 47	T&C 33	John Whitmer appointed historian.
D&C 48	T&C 34	Instruction to the church in New York.
D&C 49:15	T&C 35:5	Marriage is of God, meat made for man.
D&C 49:24	T&C 35:8	Lamanites will blossom.
D&C 50	T&C 36	Discerning the word of truth.
D&C 51	T&C 38	Lord's economy established.
D&C 52	T&C 39	Pattern is given in all things-not deceived.
D&C 53	T&C 40	Sidney Gilbert given a calling.
D&C 54	T&C 41	Blessed when keep covenant. Patient tribulation.
D&C 55	T&C 42	William Phelps to assist Oliver Cowdery.
D&C 56	T&C 43	Selfishness-covetousness leads broken covenant.
D&C 56	T&C 43	Poor in heart see God.

LDS	RE	Theme-Event
D&C 57	T&C 44	Missouri designated as center place for gathering.
D&C 58	T&C 45	Land of Zion. Be anxiously engaged in a good cause.
D&C 59	T&C 46	Thank the Lord thy God in all things.
D&C 59	T&C 46	Honor the Sabbath Day, Fulness of the earth is yours
D&C 60	T&C 47	Be not idle, neither bury thy talent.
D&C 61	T&C 48	Destroyer controls the waters.
D&C 62	T&C 49	Instructions to Elders on their journey to Missouri.
D&C 63	T&C 50	Faith not by signs, signs follow those that believe.
D&C 63	T&C 50	This is a day of warning and not a day of many words
D&C 64	T&C 51	Forgive all men and repent.
D&C 64	T&C 51	Today is a day of sacrifice.
D&C 65	T&C 53	Keys & the gospel will roll forth to ends of the earth.
D&C 66	T&C 52	William McLellin is clean but not all.
D&C 67	T&C 56	Elders challenged to create revelation.
D&C 68	T&C 55	Words spoken-moved by the Holy Ghost are scripture.
D&C 69	T&C 60	Instructions to preserve historical records.
D&C 70	T&C 61	Must be equal in temporal things.
D&C 71	T&C 62	Now is the time to proclaim My gospel.
D&C 72	T&C 63-65	Bishop appointed to the church.
D&C 72	T&C 63-65	Duties of the Bishop.
D&C 72	T&C 63-65	Certificate required of those going to Zion
D&C 73	T&C 66	Elders to continue preaching in Ohio
D&C 74	T&C 21	Children are holy
D&C 75	T&C 66-67	Elders called to preach, Comforter teaches all things.
D&C 75	T&C 66-67	Duty to care for families of men called on missions.
D&C 76	T&C 69	Vision of the kingdoms of glory.
D&C 76	T&C 69	Requirements Celestial Glory. Church of Firstborn.
D&C 77	T&C 74	Questions from Book of Revelation answered.
D&C 78	T&C 70	Command to create a Zion economy. All equal.
D&C 79	T&C 72	Lord will bless his faithful servants.
D&C 80	T&C 71	Revelation to Stephen Burnett and Eden Smith
D&C 81	T&C 73	Frederick Williams called to be councilor
D&C 82	T&C 78	Unto him much is given, much is required.
D&C 82	T&C 78	Lord is bound. Bind yourselves with new covenant
D&C 82	T&C 78	Zion equality.
D&C 83	T&C 79	Widows come under the church for support
D&C 84	T&C 82	Revelation on priesthood
D&C 84	T&C 82	Oath and covenant of the priesthood.
D&C 84	T&C 82	Church under condemnation.
D&C 85	T&C 83:3-5	Instructions on inheritance & consecration

LDS	RE	Theme-Event
D&C 86	T&C 84	Parable of wheat and tares.
D&C 87	T&C 85	War and end of all nations. Starts in South Carolina
D&C 88	T&C 86-87	Olive Leaf Revelation
D&C 88	T&C 86-87	Nature of light; parable of kingdoms.
D&C 88	T&C 87-87	Order of School of Prophets
D&C 89	T&C 89	Word of Wisdom.
D&C 90	T&C 90	Oracles of God are not to be taken from Joseph Smith
D&C 90	T&C 90	Word taken to Gentiles first. All nations hear gospel.
D&C 91	T&C 91	Apocrypha beneficial, no need to translate.
D&C 92	T&C 92	Frederick Williams into the United Order
D&C 93	T&C 93	Every soul can see the face of God.
D&C 93	T&C 93	John's testimony of Christ.
D&C 93	T&C 93	Nature of God and man.
D&C 93	T&C 93	Glory of God is intelligence.
D&C 94	T&C 97	Building a house dedicated to Lord's work.
D&C 95	T&C 94	Lord's house that His strange work may proceed.
D&C 96	T&C 95	Newell Whitney to take charge of property.
D&C 97	T&C 96	Instruction School of Prophets and House of the Lord
D&C 98	T&C 98	Laws of land good. Live by every word of God.
D&C 98	T&C 98	I will prove your faithfulness to the covenant.
D&C 98	T&C 98	Law of vengeance and righteous war.
D&C 99	T&C 81	Mission calling to John Murdock.
D&C 100	T&C 100	Sidney and Joseph sent to East Coast to proselyte.
D&C 101	T&C 101	Reaction to persecution. Zion shall be redeemed.
D&C 101	T&C 101	Saints should gather and lands be purchased.
D&C 102	T&C 103	Stake high council-stake organized, rules of conduct.
D&C 103	T&C 104	Saints driven from Jackson County.
D&C 103	T&C 104	United Order is dissolved in Zion
D&C 104	T&C 105	Rules of conduct for United Order.
D&C 105	T&C 107	Revelation Zion's camp. Redemption of Zion later.
D&C 105	T&C 107	Zion must be built principles of celestial kingdom.
D&C 106	T&C 108	Gird up loins that you might be children of light.
D&C 107	T&C 154	Dispensation Head has right to organize dispensation
D&C 108	T&C 121	Be careful with vows. Obedience brings blessings.
D&C 109	T&C 123	Kirtland temple prayer dedication
D&C 110	T&C 157:26-30	Lord appears in the Kirtland Temple
D&C 111	N/A	Not included in T&C
D&C 112	T&C 124	Wrath shall begin upon My house.
D&C 113	T&C 129	Stem and rod of Jesse.
D&C 114	T&C 130	Revelation to David Patton.

LDS	RE	Theme-Event
D&C 115	T&C 131	Far West a holy place for gathering of saints.
D&C 116	T&C 132	Adam-Ondi-Ahman.
D&C 117	T&C 133	Business in Kirtland, disposition of properties.
D&C 118	T&C 134:2-3	Frederick Williams, William Phelps transgressed.
D&C 119	T&C 135	Law of Tithing.
D&C 120	T&C 136	Disposition of Tithed properties.
D&C 121	T&C 138	Oh, God, where art Thou?
D&C 121	T&C 138	Testimony against persecutors.
D&C 121	T&C 138	Things of God are of deep import.
D&C 121	T&C 138	Unrighteous dominion; many called, few chosen.
D&C 122	T&C 139:7-9	All things for they good. Art thou greater than He?
D&C 123	T&C 139:13-16	Many blinded, not knowing where to find truth.
D&C 124	T&C 141	Write a proclamation to kings.
D&C 124	T&C 141	Temple to restore lost fullness-church rejected.
D&C 125	T&C 143	Establish city of Zarahemla opposite Nauvoo.
D&C 126	N/A	Not included in T&C
D&C 127	T&C 150	Instructions on baptisms for dead
D&C 128	T&C 151	Further instructions on baptisms for the dead
D&C 129	N/A	Not included in T&C
D&C 130	N/A	Not included in T&C
D&C 131	N/A	Not included in T&C
D&C 132	N/A	Not included in T&C, see T&C 157
D&C 133	T&C 58	Go out of Babylon, flee unto Zion.
D&C 133	T&C 58	Testimony of Christ's coming.
D&C 137	T&C 122:4-6	Josephs vision of Alvin and Heaven.

PEARL OF GREAT PRICE-MOSES
Correlated with
OLD COVENANT

LDS	Restoration	Theme-Event
Moses 1	**Genesis 1:3-5**	Moses redeemed from Satan.
Moses 1	**Genesis 1:6-7**	God's work and His glory.
Moses 2	**Genesis 2:2-11**	Creation.
Moses 3	**Genesis 2:11**	All things created spiritually.
Moses 4	**Genesis 2:16-20**	The Fall.
Moses 5	**Genesis 3:1-5**	Sacrifice and the Redemption of Adam and Eve.
Moses 5	**Genesis 3:6-10**	Cain and Able.
Moses 6	**Genesis 3:14**	Book of Remembrance.
Moses 6	**Genesis 4:4**	Enoch is a wild man come among us.
Moses 6	**Genesis 4:9**	Plan of Salvation.
Moses 7	**Genesis 4:12**	Enoch sees Lord face to face and prophecies.
Moses 7	**Genesis 4:14**	Zion is New Jerusalem. One Heart, One Mind.
Moses 7	**Genesis 4:22**	Tribulation, God's people preserved.
Moses 7	**Genesis 4:22**	Return of City of Enoch. Kissed upon neck.
Moses 8	**Genesis 3:5-25**	Genealogy Adam to Noah. Ancient Gospel.
Moses 8	**Genesis 5:5-20**	Great Flood. Altar and Sacrifice.

PEARL OF GREAT PRICE-ABRAHAM
Correlated with
TEACHINGS AND COMMANDMENTS

LDS	Restoration	Theme-Event
Abraham 1	**T&C 145:1:5**	The Lord saves Abraham from Sacrifice.
Abraham 2	**T&C 145:2:5**	God sends Abram to land of Canaan.
Abraham 3	**T&C 145:5:3**	Abraham sees Lord face to face. Descendants.
Abraham 3	**T&C 145:6:1**	Great and Noble Intelligences.
Abraham 3	**T&C 145: 6:3**	Redeemer is chosen. Here I am. Send me.
Abraham 4	**T&C 145:7:1-11**	Creation, Garden of Eden, Adam and Eve.

Missing Revelations previously excluded from the D&C now included in the Teachings and Commandments.

Section	Theme or Event
T&C 37	Ezra Thayer
T&C 57	Testimony of Book of Commandments
T&C 75	Names of God, Son, man, Angels in pure language.
T&C 76	Questions asked and answered by the Lord
T&C 80	1832 History of Joseph Smith
T&C 88	Instruction to FG Williams to consecrate his farm
T&C 99	Letter to Uncle Silas
T&C 102	Letter to Elders and those abroad
T&C 106	Close out the United Firm
T&C 109	Rebuke to leaders of the church
T&C 110	Lectures on Faith
T&C 111	Some council to FG Williams
T&C 112	Revelations to Reynolds Cahoon
T&C 113	Condemnation of 12 Apostles
T&C 114	Isaac Morley
T&C 115	W.W. Phelps
T&C 116	Coming forth of Book of Mormon
T&C 117	Words to 12 on washing of feet and endowment
T&C 118	Warren Parrish
T&C 119	Harvey Whitlock
T&C 120	Erastus Holmes
T&C 125	John Whitmer and WW Phelps warned
T&C 126	Procedures for trying 1st presidency.
T&C 127	Stakes must acknowledge authority of 1st presidency.
T&C 128	First presidency to remove to Missouri as fast as able.
T&C 137	John Whitmer, William Phelps removed standing.
T&C 140	Discourse on the priesthood
T&C 142	William Allred
T&C 144	Accommodations for Nancy Hyde
T&C 145	Book of Abraham
T&C 146	Wentworth Letter
T&C 147	Try the spirits
T&C 148	Hyrum Kimball must repent or be accursed.
T&C 149	Member not leave nonmember spouse
T&C 152	Letter from Hyrum Smith against polygamy
T&C 153	Dream of Joseph Smith night before martyrdom
T&C 155	Proverbs of Joseph Smith

Additional Revelations added to T&C

MINISTRY

"Go ye therefore, and teach all nations,
baptizing them in the name of the Father,
and of the Son, and of the Holy Ghost:
Teaching them to observe all things
whatsoever I have commanded you:
and, lo, I am with you always,
even unto the end of the world."
Matthew 14:3

Those who accept the Lord's covenant are required to *"seek to recover the lost sheep remnant of this land and of Israel and no longer forsake them."* And *"bring them unto me and teach them of my ways, to walk in them."*[5]

This ministry section has been organized to assist the Lord in His last day gathering, (T&C 9:3), and support all who desire to fulfill His prophecies.

In harmony with God's Covenant, it is anticipated the time will arrive when those qualified, called, and ordained, are sent forth to provide direct ministry unto the world.

Scriptures within the Ministry section have been selected and compiled to assist in the sacred process of gathering the wheat.

When possible, a "notes section" has been placed at the end of each topic for personal revelation, referencing, and insight.

Ministry Unto All The World

"And it came to pass that the Lord of the vineyard sent his servant; and the servant went and did as the Lord had commanded him, and brought other servants; and they were few. And the Lord of the vineyard said unto them: Go to, and labor in the vineyard, with your might. For behold, this is the last time that I shall nourish my vineyard; for the end is nigh at hand, and the season speedily cometh; and if ye labor with your might with me ye shall have joy in the fruit which I shall lay up unto myself against the time which will soon come. And it came to pass that the servants did go and labor with their mights; and the Lord of the vineyard labored also with them; and they did obey the commandments of the Lord of the vineyard in all things."
Jacob 3:26

When the prophet Alma ministered among his people, he faced political corruption and religious apostasy. Alma responded by committing his life to the Lord Jesus Christ and the preaching of repentance.

As a disciple of the Lord, Alma knew the only real solution to spiritual deception, political contention, and social sicknesses, was to proclaim the Holy Word of God. (Alma 2:4)

At this sacred time, Alma's choice is our choice. The solution is the same and all who desire to serve God are called to the work. (Joseph Smith History 11:2).

DOCTRINE OF CHRIST

DOCTRINE OF CHRIST
Must be born of water and of spirit. **John 2:2** (John 3:5)
Doctrine of Christ. **2 Nephi 14:1-3** (2 Nephi 32:1-9)
Doctrine of Christ. **3 Nephi 5:9** (3 Nephi 11:35-41)
Gospel of Christ. **3 Nephi 12:5** (3 Nephi 27:19-21)
Faith, Repentance, Baptism, Holy Ghost. **Moroni 8:5** (Moroni 8:25)
Repent, be baptized and receive Holy Ghost. **Moroni 6:1** (Moroni 6:1-9)
Repent, be baptized and receive Holy Ghost. **Acts 1:12** (Acts 2:37-38)
Result: conversion, consecration, peace, miracles. **4 Ne. 1:1-2** (4 Nephi 1:1-5)
Teach all, baptizing name Father, Son, Holy Ghost. **Matt 13:4** (Matt. 28:19-20)

FAITH
Faith substance of things hoped for. **Hebrews 1:36** (Hebrews 11:1)
the seed of Developing faith. **Alma 16:27-30** (Alma 32:26-43)
All things possible to him that believes. **Mark 5:9** (Mark 9:23)
Faith is not only the principle of action, but of power too. **LoF, First: 13**
Prayer of faith will shall save the sick. **Jacob 1:23** (James 5:14-15)
Faith will move mountains. **Matthew 9:7** (Matthew 17:20)
We walk by faith, not by sight. **2 Corinthians 1:15** (2 Corinthians 5:7)
By grace saved through faith, not yourselves. **Ephesians 1:5** (Ephesians 2:8-9)
Elements required for exercising real faith. **Lecture Third.** (Lecture Third)
Faith is to hope for unseen things that are true. **Alma 16:26** (Alma 32:21)
Greater things for those who exercise faith. **3 Nephi 12:1** (3 Nephi 26:8-10)
Without faith, impossible to please God. **Hebrews 1:38** (Hebrews 11:6)
The just shall live by faith. **Romans 1:3** (Romans 1:17)
Jew and Gentiles must believe or be cut off. **2 Nephi 12:11** (2 Nephi 30:1-2)
If lack wisdom, ask of God and it shall be given you. **Jacob 1:2** (James 1:5-6)
All things denote there is a God. **Alma 16:9** (Alma 30:44)
Receive end of your faith, even salvation of your souls. **1 Peter 1:2** (1 Peter 1:9)
Faith. **T&C Glossary: Faith**

REPENTANCE
Repent, for the kingdom of God is at hand. **Matthew 3:1** (Matthew 4:17)
Parable of the lost sheep. **Luke 9:11** (Luke 15:3-7)
Life is time for men to prepare to meet God. **Alma 16:37** (Alma 34:32-35)
Days of men prolonged that they might repent. **2 Nephi 1:9** (2 Nephi 2:19-21)
Repent and bring forth fruit of repentance **Mathew 2:2** (Mathew 3:8)
Lord desires all to come unto repentance. **2 Peter 1:12** (2 Peter 3:9)
Christ came to call sinners to repentance. **Matthew 4:8** (Matthew 9:10-13)
Repent, be baptized and receive Holy Ghost. **Moroni 6** (Moroni 6:1-9)

Repent, be baptized and receive Holy Ghost. **Acts 1:12** (Acts 2:37-38)
Come unto Christ, broken heart, contrite spirit. **3 Nephi 4:7** (3 Nephi 9:19-22)
Repentance and baptism for those accountable. **Moroni 8:3** (Moroni 8:10-11)
Repentance and baptism as a witness unto God. **3 Nephi 3:12** (3 Nephi 7:24-25)
Repent, come unto Christ and be in His church. **JSH 10:18-19** (D&C 10:62-67)
Godly sorrow worketh repentance. **2 Corinthians 1:24** (2 Corinthians 7:10)
Repent, Lord suffered so others do not. **T&C 17:5** (D&C 19:15-20)
Justice demands suffering if no repentance. **Alma 19:15-16** (Alma 42:22-25)
Christ sacrifice for those broken heart-contrite spirit. **2 Nephi 1:6** (2 Nephi 2:7)
Having these promises, let us cleanse ourselves. **2 Cor. 1:22** (2 Cor. 7:1)
The Lord remembers sins no more. **T&C 45:9** (D&C 58:42)
Parable of the lost coin. Joy over soul that repents. **Luke 9:12** (Luke 15:8-10)
Except ye repent, ye shall all perish. **Luke 8:30** (Luke 13:1-5)
Devils recognize and believe on Christ. Not saved. **Jacob 1:12** (James 2:19)
Devils recognize and believe on Christ. Not saved. **Mark 2:6** (Mark 3:11-12)
Repent, to avoid the fullness of God's wrath. **Ether 1:7** (Ether 2: 11-12)
Repent or receive testimony of destruction. **T&C 29:6-8** (D&C 43:18-25)
Brought to repentance often means driven out land. **Alma 16:44** (Alma 35:14)
This land choice land, serve God or be swept off. **Ether 1:7** (Ether 2:9-12)
Inhabitants of earth repent or be scourged. **JSH 12:4** (D&C 5:19-20)
If Gentiles repent it will be well with them. **1 Nephi 3:26** (1 Nephi 14:5-7)
The goodness of God leads to repentance. **Romans 1:8** (Romans 2:4)
Worth of souls is great. Joy in those who repent. **JSH 15:31** (D&C 18:10-16)
Most worth to teach repentance. **JSH 15:11** (D&C 16:6)
Whatsoever a man soweth, that shall he reap. **Galatians 1:24** (Galatians 6:7-10)
Through Christ all might be saved by obedience. **T&C 146:23** (D&C 138:4).
Lord redeems men from sin, not in their sins. **Helaman 2:17** (Helaman 5:10)
Repent and endure to end. **2 Nephi 13:2-3** (2 Nephi 31:10-16)
Endure to the end to be saved. **Matthew 11:3** (Matthew 24:13)
Repent quickly for the hour is close at hand. **Alma 3:5-6** (Alma 5:27-35)
Hearken unto my voice lest death overtake you. **T&C 31:1-3** (D&C 45: 2-10)
Repentance. **T&C Glossary: Repentance**

BAPTISM AND RE-BAPTISM
Jesus baptized to fulfill all righteousness. **2 Nephi 13:2** (2 Nephi 31:6-12)
Jesus baptized as an example for all. **Matthew 2:4** (Matthew 3:13-17)
He that believeth on me, the works I do he shall do also. **John 9:7** (John 14:12)
Follow me, do the things ye have seen me do. **2 Nephi 13:2** (2 Nephi 31:12)
Gate to enter is repentance-baptism. **2 Nephi 13:3-5** (2 Nephi 31:17-21)
Baptism is the first fruits of repentance. **Moroni 8:5** (Moroni 8:25)
Baptism doth also now save us. **1 Peter 1:14** (1 Peter 3:21)
He that believeth and is baptized shall be saved. **Mark 8:6** (Mark 16:15-16)

Must be born of water and spirit to enter kingdom. **John 2:1-2** (John 3:3-7)
All must be baptized to be saved in kingdom. **2 Nephi 6:7** (2 Nephi 9:23-24)
Must be baptized to ascend into God's presence. **TSJ 2:2**
We have great need of being baptized. **2 Nephi 13:2** (2 Nephi 31:5-7)
Be baptized and forsake sin to ascend into God's presence. **TSJ 2:2**
Baptized in my name, Father gives Holy Ghost. **2 Nephi 13:2** (2 Nephi 31:12)
Commanded to baptize-lay hands for Holy Ghost. **T&C 18:2** (D&C 35:6)
Baptized unto repentance, cleansed unrighteousness. **Alma 5:4** (Alma 7:14-16)
Garments must be washed white, cleansed all stain. **Alma 3:3-5** (Alma 5:21-27)
Old man of sin crucified, body of sin destroyed. **Romans 1:25** (Romans 6:6)
Buried in baptism-death, raised resurrection life. **Romans 1:25** (Romans 6:4)
Buried in baptism, risen in faith from dead. **Colossians 1:7** (Colossians 2:12)
Walk in newness of life. **Romans 1:25** (Romans 6:4)
Those baptized in Christ, have put on Christ. **Galatians 1:12** (Gal 3:27)
Believe and be baptized. **Mark 8:6** (Mark 16-15-16)
Arise and be baptized, and wash away thy sins. **Acts 12:16** (Acts 22:16)
Adam is baptized. **Genesis 4:7** (Moses 6:51-58)
Adam and Eve baptized and born of Spirit. **Genesis 4:10** (Moses 6:65-66)
John baptizes those confessing sin. **Matthew 2:1** (Matthew 3:1-2)
Jesus baptized of John. **Matthew 2:4** (Matthew 3:13-17)
Peter cries repentance and baptizes thousands. **Acts 1:12-13** (Acts 2:37-41)
Paul is baptized. **Acts 11:5** (Acts 19:17-18)
Cornelius vision, Holy Ghost, Gentile baptism **Acts 6:3-8** (Acts 10:1-48)
King Limhi and his people desire baptism. **Mosiah 9:34** (Mosiah 21:33-35)
Alma re-baptizes those coming out of apostasy. **Mos. 9:7-8** (Mos. 18: 8-17)
Ordained in ministry, baptized unto repentance. **3 Nephi 3:12** (3 Nephi 7:23-26)
Paul re-baptizes disciples. **Acts 11:2** (Acts 19:1-5)
Philip runs to chariot, baptizes eunuch. **Acts 5:7** (Acts 8:35-39)
Samuel protected. Many believe and baptized. **Hel. 5:18** (Hel. 16:3-5)
Twelve desire Holy Ghost, re-baptized, fire. **3 Nephi 9:2** (3 Nephi 19:9-13)
Sign given, people again baptized unto repentance. **3 Nephi 1:6** (3 Nephi 1:23)
All who repented were baptized. **3 Nephi 3:12** (3 Nephi 7:23-26)
Righteous previously baptized survive. **3 Nephi 4:10** (3 Nephi 10:12)
Lord gives Nephi power to baptize, re-baptize. **3 Nephi 5:8** (3 Nephi 11:18-21)
Nephi is re-baptized. **3 Nephi 9:2** (3 Nephi 19:11-12)
Elders, priests, teachers, repent and are rebaptized. **Moroni 6:1** (Moroni 6:1-4)
Alma invites church members to repent, be baptized. **Alma 3:12** (Alma 5:62)
Priesthood of Aaron restored for baptism. **JSH 14:1** (D&C 13:1)
Apostles commissioned to go and baptize. **T&C 55:2** (D&C 68:8-12)
Blessed are those baptized without being stubborn. **Alma 16:25.** (Alma 32:16)
Come all ye Gentiles, repent and be baptized. **3 Nephi 14** (3 Nephi 30:1-2)

HOLY GHOST
Holy Ghost. **T&C Glossary: Holy Ghost**
Baptizing name of Father, Son, Holy Ghost. **Matthew 13:4** (Matthew 28:19)
Faith, repentance, baptism, and then Holy Ghost. **T&C 35:4** (D&C 49: 11-14)
He shall baptize you with Holy Ghost and fire. **Matthew 2:3** (Matthew 3:11)
Adam baptized with fire and the Holy Ghost. **Genesis 4:10** (Moses 6:66)
Repent, baptized, then remission of sins by fire. **2 Nephi 13:3** (2 Nephi 31:17)
Must be born of water and spirit to enter the kingdom. **John 2:2** (John 3:5)
Christ to go away, that Comforter will come unto us. **John 9:13** (John 16:7)
Another comforter to abide with you forever. **John 9:8** (John 14:16)
When the comforter is come, he will testify of me. **John 9:13** (John 15:26)
I will send Comforter, promise of eternal life. **T&C 86:1** (D&C 88:3-4)
Comforter teaches all things, restores memory of all truth. **TSJ 10:15**
Knowledge by unspeakable gift of Holy Ghost. **T&C 138:21** (D&C 121:26).
Comforter will bring all things to remembrance. **John 9:9** (John 14:26)
Spirit guides you into all truth. **John 9:14** (John 16:13-16)
Truth of all things - by power of Holy Ghost. **Moroni 10:2-4** (Moroni 10:4-19)
Holy Ghost given to those who obey. **Acts 3:7** (Acts 5:32)
Holy Ghost comes upon Gentiles. God no respecter. **Acts 6:6-8** (Acts 10:28-48)
Holy Ghost came, tongues, prophesy. **Acts 11:2** (Acts 19:6)
Meetings are to be led by the Holy Ghost. **Moroni 6:2** (Moroni 6:9)
Fruit of Spirit: love, joy, peace, faith. **Galatians 1:22** (Galatians 5:22-26)
Apostles baptized with Holy Ghost. **Acts 1:7** (Acts 2:1-4)
Paul laid hands-Holy Ghost received. Prophecy. **Acts 11:2** (Acts 19:1-6)
Men ordained by power of Holy Ghost. **Moroni 3** (Moroni 3:4)
Receive the Holy Ghost. **Moroni 2** (Moroni 2:1-3)

SACRAMENT
Lord's Supper. Take, eat, this is my body. **Matthew 12:5-7** (Matthew 26:26-30)
This is my body. Remember me. **Luke 13:3-4** (Luke 22:15-20)
Partake of His flesh and blood to have eternal life. **John 5:17** (John 6:54)
Sacrament a testimony we remember the Son. **3 Nephi 8:6** (3 Nephi 18:7)
Sacrament observed by early Christians. **Acts 1:13** (Acts 2: 46-47)
Disciples break bread on first day of week. **Acts 12:1** (Acts 20:7)
Lord establishes sacrament among Nephites. **3 Nephi 8: 6-7** (3 Nephi 18:1-12)
Jesus breaks bread and blesses it often. **3 Nephi 12:**1 (3 Nephi 26:13)
Partake of sacrament with eye single to glory of God. **T&C 8:1** (D&C 27:2)
Offer up sacraments to stay unspotted from the world. **T&C 46:3** (D&C 59:9)
Offer sacraments in house of prayer on holy day. **T&C 46:3** (D&C 59:9)
Rejoice together-offer sacrament unto Most High. **T&C 49:2** (D&C 62:4)
Does not matter what is used to eat and drink. **TC 8:1** (D&C 27:2)
Wine-strong drink not good except for sacraments. **T&C 89:2** (D&C 89:5)

Wine should be pure wine of grape, of own make. **T&C 89:2** (D&C 89:6)
Be worthy when take sacrament. **1 Corinthians 1:46** (1 Corinthians 11:27-30)
Do not take sacrament of Christ unworthily. **Mormon 4:10** (Mormon 9:29)
Make reconciliation before taking sacrament. **T&C 32:2** (D&C 46:4-5)
Church meets often to fast, pray, take sacrament. **Moroni 6:2** (Moroni 6:5-6)
Prayer for the bread. **Moroni 4** (Moroni 4:3)
Prayer for the wine. **Moroni 5** (Moroni 5:2)

NOTES:

MINISTRY AMONG THE LAMANITES

And thus commandeth the Father that I should say unto you:
At that day when the Gentiles shall sin against my gospel,
and shall reject the fulness of my gospel, and shall be lifted up
in the pride of their hearts above all nations, and above all the
people of the whole earth, and shall be filled with all manner
of lyings, and of deceits, and of mischiefs, and all manner of
hypocrisy, and murders, and priestcrafts, and whoredoms,
and of secret abominations; and if they shall do all those
things, and shall reject the fulness of my gospel, behold, saith
the Father, I will bring the fulness of my gospel from among
them. And then will I remember my covenant which I have
made unto my people, O house of Israel, and I will bring my
gospel unto them. And I will show unto thee, O house of
Israel, that the Gentiles shall not have power over you; but I
will remember my covenant unto you, O house of Israel, and
ye shall come unto the knowledge of the fulness of my gospel.
3 Nephi 7:5

The terms "Jew," "Gentile," "House of Israel," and "Remnant," are utilized in scripture with diverse application and overlapping meaning. Scriptures listed here can be interpreted and applied on numerous levels.

LOSING FOCUS ON THE REMNANT

"Six months after publication of the Book of Mormon, the first missionary assignment was given by revelation. The Lord commanded, "And now behold, I say unto you that thou shall go unto the Lamanites and preach my gospel unto them and cause my church to be established among them. And thou shall have revelations…" (September 1830) The purpose of the first missionary work was to announce the fullness of the gospel to the scattered remnants, and the first remnant of Israel to be sent the invitation was the Lamanites. That mission failed to produce any Lamanite converts. Instead, gentile, Campbellite disciples of Sidney Rigdon in Kirtland, Ohio joined by the hundreds. The focus quickly changed from recovering remnants of Israel, to successfully growing a large gentile church. This was not a temporary change. Its lasting effect has skewed the entire gentile effort. While some limited gestures have been made, recovering the remnants of Israel has been secondary. Once the focus left the Lamanites, all subsequent Mormon sects have likewise failed to fulfill the covenant in the Book of Mormon to seek to reclaim the remnants of Israel. They have remained intent on converting gentiles." (Denver Snuffer, Scripture, Prophecy, and Covenant, pg. 2)

CHALLENGES
Lamanites taught false traditions. **Mosiah 6:12** (Mosiah 10:12)
Lamanites dwindle in unbelief. **1 Nephi 3:18** (1 Nephi 12:20-23)
Keep the commandments and prosper or be cut off. **2 Nephi 1:4** (2 Nephi 1:20)
Lamanites who will not repent will be cut off. **2 Nephi 12:11** (2 Nephi 30:2)
Lamanites keep not commandments, have been cut off. **Alma 7:3** (Alma 9:14)
Lord's vineyard, Israel scattered and desolate. **Isaiah 1:13** (Isaiah 5:1-7)
Lord's vineyard, Israel is dried up land of waste. **Isaiah 1:13-15** (Isaiah 5:1-13)
House of Israel scattered among all nations. **1 Nephi 7:1-2** (1 Nephi 22:3-5)
Lamanites scattered, eventually be gathered. **1 Nephi 7:1-3** (1 Nephi 22:3-12)
Remnant. **T&C Glossary**

PROMISES
Covenant unto House of Israel. **3 Nephi 9:11 (**3 Nephi 21:7)
Many promises unto the Lamanites. **Alma 7:3** (Alma 9:16)
Lamanites smitten but not forgotten. **2 Nephi 11:13** (2 Nephi 26:14-15)
Lamanites will scourge Gentiles. **3 Nephi 9:7-8** (3 Nephi 20:13-29)
Lamanites given the land of their fathers. **3 Nephi 9:8** (3 Nephi 20:29)
God will fulfill all promises made to the Fathers. **Alma 17:10** (Alma 37:17)
Lord will keep covenant to House of Israel. **3 Nephi 13:7-8** (3 Nephi 29:1-9)
Lord will remember covenant of his people. **Mormon 4:3-4** (Mormon 8:22-24)
Lord will remember prayers for Israel. **Mormon 2:6** (Mormon 5:20-21)
Isaiah's words fulfilled, remnant gathered. **3 Nephi 9:7** (3 Nephi 20:11-13)
Land of liberty and safety for those who obey. **2 Nephi 1:1-2** (2 Nephi 1:5-9)
Covenant to the native inhabitants of America.**1 Nephi 3:22** (1 Nephi 13:30)

AWAKENING
Time when Lamanites believe and are saved. **Alma 7:3** (Alma 9:16-17)
Future generation of Lamanites receive truth. **Alma 17:10-11** (Alma 37:18-19)
BOM shows God's power-future generations. **Alma 17:10** (Alma 37:18)
BOM to know Jesus Christ and covenants. **Dedication** (BoM title page)
Records unto house of Jacob. Promises fulfilled. **4 Nephi 1:9** (4 Nephi 1:49)
Record written that all of Israel might believe. **Mormon 2:6** (Mormon 5:12-14)
Remnant urged to receive Bible and BOM. **Mormon 3:5** (Mormon 7:8-10)
Turn hearts Jews unto prophets, prophets unto Jews. **TC 98:3** (D&C 98:17)
Gospel from Gentiles to the House of Israel. **Mormon 2:6** (Mormon 5:15)
Record for ancient covenant people of the Lord. **Mormon 4:3** (Mormon 8:15)
Remnant knows they are descendants of Jews. **2 Nephi 12:12** (2 Nephi 30:4-6)
Role and title of Joseph among the Lamanites. **2 Nephi 2:1-7** (2 Nephi 3:2-25)
Righteous branch shall come forth. **2 Nephi 2:2** (2 Nephi 3:4-5)
Messiah brings righteous branch out in last days. **2 Nephi 2:2** (2 Nephi 3:5)
Gods condescension results in righteous branch **2 Nephi 6:13** (2 Nephi 9:53)
God merciful in restoring a righteous branch. **2 Nephi 7:1** (2 Nephi 10:1-2)
Remnant believes, restored lands of inheritance. **2 Nephi 7:2** (2 Nephi 10:7)
Gentiles receive choice land if part of remnant. **2 Nephi 7:4** (2 Nephi 10:19)
Gentiles don't repent, Jacob tread them down. **3 Nephi 9:7** (3 Nephi 20:15-16)
Remnant of Jacob tears Gentiles as a Lion. **3 Nephi 9:12** (3 Nephi 21:11-12)

TRANSITIONS
Times of the Gentiles. **T&C Glossary**
Remnant. **T&C Glossary**
Repentant Gentiles bring the gospel to remnant. **2 Nephi 12:11** (2 Nephi 30:3)
Gentiles bring many books to remnant. **1 Nephi 3:24** (1 Nephi 13:38-39)
Book of Mormon to go forth to the Israel. **TC 4:8** (D&C 19:26-27)
Gentiles bring gospel, sign Father begun His work. **3 Ne. 9:11** (3 Ne. 21:1-7)
Covenant House of Israel restored to fold of God. **2 Nephi 6:1** (2 Nephi 9:1-2)
God's people gather to land inheritance. **3 Nephi 9:7-8** (3 Nephi 20:13-29)
Gather all people home to their inheritance. **3 Nephi 10:1** (3 Nephi 21:26-28)
Remnant shall be grafted into true olive tree. **1 Nephi 4:3** (1 Nephi 15:16)
God restores Jacob, gathers from four quarters. **3 Nephi 2:18** (3 Nephi 5:21-26)
Remnant gathered. Receive Christ in glory. **TC 31:9** (D&C 45:43-44)
House of Israel. **T&C Glossary**

FULFILLMENT

Lord remembers prayers for House of Israel. **Mormon 2:6** (Mormon 5:21)
Pray for House of Israel, remember covenant. **Mormon 2:6** (Mormon 5:20-21)
Seed of Joseph not forgotten, shall never parish. **2 Nephi 11:7** (2 Nephi 25:21)
Gentiles will not destroy seed of Lehi. **1 Nephi 3:22-23** (1 Nephi 13:30-37)
Gentiles heart softened-like a father to Remnant. **2 Nephi 7:4** (2 Nephi 10:18)
Lord set hand second time. **2 Nephi 12:8** (2 Nephi 29:1-2)
Fullness of Gospel from the Gentiles to Remnant1 **Nephi 4:3** (1 Nephi 15:13)
Remnant invited to believe, repent, be baptized. **Mormon 3:5** (Mormon 7:1-8)
Gospel declared, come to know Jesus-Fathers. **2 Nephi 12:12** (2 Nephi 30:4-6)
Called to labor, preach fullness of gospel to Israel. **TC 23:3-4** (D&C 39:11-13)
God's record will come to Lamanites. **Enos 1:2-4** (Enos 1:11-12, 16)
BOM is meant to restore all House of Israel. **Mormon 2:6** (Mormon 5:13-20)
Bible and other books convince of the truth. **1 Nephi 3:24** (1 Nephi 13:38-39)
BOM revealed, Lamanites know Jewish ancestry. **2 Nephi 12:8.** (2 Nephi 29:4)
Lamanite remnant to know they are Israel. **1 Nephi 4:3** (1 Nephi 15:13-14)
Preach Gospel by borders of the Lamanites. **TC 10:2-3** (D&C 28:8-10)
Lord will go with servants among Lamanites. **TC 15:1-2** (D&C 32:1-4)
Journey to Lamanites, declare gospel rejoicing. **TC 10:4-5** (D&C 28:14-16)
Prayer for mercy and conversion of Jacob. **TC 123:18** (D&C 109:62-67)
Lamanites taught, become His sheep. **Helaman 5:16** (Helaman 15:11-14)
Lamanites blossom, Jacob flourishes in wilderness. **TC 35:8.** (D&C 49:24-25)
House of Jacob restored knowledge of covenant. **3 Ne. 2:18** (3 Ne. 5:25-26)
Remnant of Joseph come to knowledge of Lord. **3 Nephi 2:18** (3 Nephi 5:23)
Covenant of Abraham fulfilled in last days. **1 Nephi 4:3** (1 Nephi 15:18)
Marvelous work among children of men. **2 Nephi 11:6** (2 Nephi:25:17)
Lord does marvelous work and wonder. **2 Nephi11:21** (2 Nephi 27:26)
Marvelous work, Gentiles nourish House Israel. **1 Nephi 7:3** (1 Nephi 22:7-12)
Gospel returned to House of Israel. **3 Nephi 7:5** (3 Nephi 16:10)
Gentiles bring gospel, sign Father begun His work. **3 Ne. 9:11** (3 Ne. 21:1-7)
Lamanites will blossom as a rose. **TC 35:8.** (D&C 49:24)
Seed of Jacob among people of covenant. **Mormon 3:5** (Mormon 7:10)
Natural branches of Israel grafted in. **1 Nephi 3:4** (1 Nephi 10:14)
Remnant of Israel comes to knowledge of Messiah. **1 Ne. 3:4** (1 Ne. 10:14)
Remnant of House of Israel shall be saved. **Romans 1:43-44** (Romans 9:26-27)

141

REMNANT IN ZION

Remnant returns to Lord, receives revelation. **T&C 129:5** (D&C 113:10)
Jacob not ashamed. Those erred understand. **2 Nephi 11:21** (2 Nephi 27:33-35)
Remnant of seed of Jacob gathered in. **3 Nephi 2:18** (3 Nephi 5:24)
Scattered remnant to have power to bring Zion. **T&C 129:4-5** (D&C 113:7-10)
Seed of Joseph clean through blood of Lamb. **Ether 6:3** (Ether 13:10)
Seed of Joseph dwell within the New Jerusalem. **Ether 6:3** (Ether 13:10)
Remnant of Joseph inherit land, build holy city. **Ether 6:2-3** (Ether 13:6-8)
Israel builds New Jerusalem. Gentiles assist. **3 Nephi 10:1** (3 Nephi 21:21-29)
Gentile chance to repent and assist. **3 Nephi 9:12-10:1** (3 Nephi 21:11-29)
Zion will flourish and rejoice at appointed place. **T&C 26:6** (D&C 42:24-25)
Christ among Jacob in New Jerusalem. **3 Nephi 9:8** (3 Nephi 20:22)

NOTES:

MINISTRY AMONG THE CHRISTIANS

It is anticipated that when turmoil and destruction intensifies in America and throughout the world, that an increasing number of Christians will be willing to receive the Fullness of the Gospel. Much of the division in religion today is the result of doctrinal misinterpretation and centuries of false tradition. And yet because of Jesus Christ, and the power of the Holy Spirit, God will yet lead a broken few into the Truth of All Things. (Moroni 10:1).

GOSPEL OF JESUS CHRIST
Not everyone that says, Lord, Lord, enters Heaven. **Matt 3:47** (Matt 7:21)
Many rejected who say they prophesied in His name **Matt 3:47** (Matt 7:22-23)
Gospel of Jesus Christ. Repent and be baptized. **3Nephi 12:5** (3 Nephi 27: 16)
Speak of the Doctrine of Christ. **2Nephi 13:1** (2 Nephi 31:2)
We talk, preach, prophecy of Christ. **2 Nephi 11:8** (2 Nephi 25:26)
Paul taught the "new doctrine" to the Athenians. **Acts 10:13-15** (Acts 17:22-31)
If any man will do his will, he shall know of the doctrine. **John 6:4** (John 7:17)
He taught doctrine and many things by parables. **Mark 2:11** (Mark 4:2)
You must follow (do) as the Lord or cannot be disciple **Luke 9:8** (Luke 14:26)
You must forsake all to be "my disciple" **Luke 9:9** (Luke 14:33)
He that believeth and is baptized shall be saved. **Mark 8:6** (Mark 16:16)
Baptism is the appointed way to put on Christ. **Galatians 1:12** (Galatians 3:27)
Baptized in my name, Father gives Holy Ghost. **2 Nephi 13:2** (2 Nephi 31:12)
Follow me, and do the things ye have seen me do. **2 Ne. 13:2** (2 Ne. 31:12)
No more doctrine until he comes to you in the flesh. **2 Ne. 14:1** (2 Ne. 32:6)
Straightness and narrowness of the way. **2 Nephi 13:2** (2 Nephi 31:9)
The gospel is to empower endless life, through Jesus the Messiah. **TOJ 1:4**

PRE-MORTAL
All things created spiritually,before naturally on earth. **Gen. 2:11** (Moses 3:4-7)
Generations heavens and earth existed before creation. **Gen. 2:11** (Gen. 2:4-5)
In beginning was the Word. Word was **John 1:1** (John 1:1-5)
Christ was with the Father from the beginning. **2 Nephi 6:6** (2 Nephi 9:15)
Christ foreordained before foundation of world. **1 Peter 1:4** (1 Peter 1:18-20)
Lord God created all the children of men in heaven. **Genesis 211** (Moses 3:4-7)
Before I formed thee in belly I knew thee. **Jeremiah 1:1** (Jeremiah 1:5)
Who did sin (before birth) that he was born blind? John 6:17 (Jn 9:2)
The God of the spirit of all flesh. **Numbers 9:6** (Numbers 16:22)
Brother Jared sees Christ as Spirit before His birth. **Eth. 1:12-13** (Eth. 3:10-16)
Man was also in the beginning with God. **TC 93:10** (D&C 93:29)
Man was created in God's image. **Genesis 2:8** (Genesis 1:26-27)

143

Lord showed Abraham intelligences before the world. **Abr. 6:1** (Abr. 3:22)
The Intelligences organized before the world. **Abraham 6:1** (Abraham 3:22-28)
Foundations of earth…all sons of God shouted for joy? **Job 12:2** (Job 38:4-7)
War in heaven before Eden **Rev. 4:3-5** (Rev. 12:7-12)
Angel before God thrust down in preexistence **TC 69:6** (D&C 76:25-28)
Angel fallen from heaven. **2 Nephi 1:9** (2 Nephi 2:17-18)
Lucifer, son of morning, fallen from heaven. **Is. 6:6** (Isaiah 14:12-15)
Many spirits followed after Lucifer. **Abraham 6:3** (Abraham 3:27-28)
Third part turn away because of agency. **TC 9:11** (D&C 29: 36-38)

PURPOSE OF LIFE
Lord has made these things for his own purpose. **Genesis 1:6** (Moses 1:31)
Spirit of Christ is given to every man. **Moroni 7:3** (Moroni 7:16)
All move upward by gaining light. Advance-learn to be like Christ. **TSJ 1:11**
He gives knowledge to become like Him. **TSJ 1:3**
Adam fell that men might be. **2 Nephi 1:10** (2 Nephi 2:25)
By his fall came death; and we are made partakers. **Moses 4:7** (Moses 6:48)
Without our transgression, never had seed. **Moses 3:4** (Moses 5:11)
Life is time to prepare to meet God. **Alma 16:37** (Alma 34:32)
Their state became a state of probation. **2 Nephi 1:9** (2 Nephi 2:21)
Do not procrastinate day of repentance. **Alma 16:37** (Alma 34:33)
Let not sin therefore reign in your mortal body. **Romans 1:27** (Romans 6:12)
Quicken your mortal body by His Spirit **Romans 1:33** (Romans 8:11)
Same spirit at death, possesses body in eternal world. **Alma 16:37** (Alma 34:34)
Men are free according to the flesh. **2 Nephi 1:10** (2 Nephi 2:27)
All free to choose liberty or death. **2 Nephi 1:10** (2 Nephi 2:26-27)
Neither can natural man abide the presence of God. **T&C 56:3** (D&C 67:12)
This mortal must put on immortality. **Mosiah 8:13** (Mosiah 16:10)
Believe that I am sent by the Most High God, or die burdened with sin. **TJ 6:14**
Dust thou art, and unto dust shalt thou return. **Genesis 2:18** (Moses 4:25).
Fear not, for in this world your joy is not full. **T&C 101:6** (D&C 101:36)
He that has faith on me has endless lives, worlds without end. **TJ 6:18**
Father brings about eternal purpose through Son. **Mormon 2:6** (Mormon 5:14)
All mankind may be saved by obedience. **T&C 146:23** (AoF 1:3)
Be steadfast, Christ may seal you His. **Mosiah 3:3** (Mosiah 5:15)
Raised from this mortality to a state of immortality. **Alma 9:4** (Alma 12:12)
Eternal purposes of the Lord roll on. **Mormon 4:3** (Mormon 8:22)
Lord brings about his eternal purposes. **2 Nephi 1:8** (2 Nephi 2:15)
Lord's purposes fail not. **T&C 69:1** (D&C 76:3)

FAITH

Faith substance of things hoped for. **Hebrews 1:36** (Hebrews 11:1)
Developing the seed of faith. **Alma 16:27-30** (Alma 32:26-43)
All things possible to him that believes. **Mark 5:9** (Mark 9:23)
Faith is not only the principle of action, but of power too. **LoF, First: 13**
Prayer of faith will shall save the sick. **Jacob 1:23** (James 5:14-15)
Faith will move mountains. **Matthew 9:7** (Matthew 17:20)
We walk by faith, not by sight. **2 Corinthians 1:15** (2 Corinthians 5:7)
By grace saved through faith, not yourselves. **Ephesians 1:5** (Ephesians 2:8-9)
Elements required for exercising real faith. **Lecture Third.** (Lecture Third)
Faith is to hope for unseen things that are true. **Alma 16:26** (Alma 32:21)
Greater things for those who exercise faith. **3 Nephi 12:1** (3 Nephi 26:8-10)
Without faith, impossible to please God. **Hebrews 1:38** (Hebrews 11:6)
The just shall live by faith. **Romans 1:3** (Romans 1:17)
Jew and Gentiles must believe or be cut off. **2 Nephi 12:11** (2 Nephi 30:1-2)
If lack wisdom, ask of God and it shall be given you. **Jacob 1:2** (James 1:5-6)
All things denote there is a God. **Alma 16:9** (Alma 30:44)
Receive end of your faith, even salvation of your souls. **1 Peter 1:2** (1 Peter 1:9)
Faith. **T&C Glossary: Faith**

FAITH AND WORKS

By grace are you saved through faith, not self. **Ephesians 1:5** (Ephesians 2:8-9)
Man not justified by works of law, but by faith. **Galatians 1:6** (Galatians 2:16)
Any good thing a man doeth, from Lord. **Ephesians 1:23** (Ephesians 6:8)
The just shall live by faith. **Romans 1:3** (Romans 1:17)
Make the law void through faith? God forbid. **Romans 1:17** (Romans 3:31)
Not everyone says "Lord, Lord," will be saved. **Matthew 3:47** (Matthew 7:21)
Only those who do His will are saved. **Matthew 3:47** (Matthew 7:21)
Teach children all must repent inherit kingdom God. **Genesis 4:9** (Moses 6:57)
If say know Him, but keep not commandments, a liar. **1 John 1:5** (1 John 2:4)
What profit a man to say faith, without works? **Jacob 1:11** (James 2:14-17)
Faith without works is dead. **Jacob 1:11-12** (James 2:17, 20, 26)
Lord redeems men from sin, not in their sins. **Helaman 2:17** (Helaman 5:10)
All mankind may be saved, by obedience to law. **T&C 146:23** (AoF 1:3)
For man's work, receives reward. **1 Corinthians 1:11** (1 Corinthians 3:13-15)
I know thy works and service and patience. **Revelation 1:13** (Revelation 2:19)
Render to every man according to his deeds. **Romans 1:8** (Romans 2:6-11)
Repent and do the first works. Revelation 1:9 (Revelation 2:5)
Doers, not just hearers, are justified before God. Romans 1:9 (Romans 2:13)
Devils recognize and believe on Christ. Not saved. **Jacob 1:12** (James 2:19)
Unclean Spirits recognize, believe on Christ. **Mark 2:6** (Mark 3:11-12)
Whatsoever a man soweth, that shall he reap. **Galatians 1:24** (Galatians 6:7-10)

145

Abound in good works that Christ may seal you His. **Mosiah 3:3** (Mosiah 5:15)
He that follows righteousness, finds life. **Prov. 2:348-349** (Prov. 21:20-21)
To him that overcomes will I give Tree of Life. **Revelation 1:9** (Revelation 2:7)

GRACE AND WORKS
Saved by grace after all we can do. **2 Nephi 11:8** (2 Nephi 25:23)
By grace saved through faith, not of self. **Ephesians 1:5** (Ephesians 2:8-9)
By the law all men are cut off. **2 Nephi 1:6** (2 Nephi 2:5)
Shall we sin under grace? God forbid. **Romans 1:27-28**. (Romans 6:12-19)
If sin willfully after truth, no sacrifice for sins. **Hebrews 1:33** (Hebrews 10:26)
Why call me Lord, and do not what I say? **Luke 5:13** (Luke 6:46-49)
If do works of flesh, shall not enter kingdom. **Gal. 1:21** (Gal. 5:19-21)
Lord redeems men *from* sin, not *in* their sins. **Helaman 2:17** (Helaman 5:10)
By the Spirit you are justified. **Genesis 4:9** (Moses 6:60)
Doers, not just hearers, are justified before God. **Romans 1:9** (Romans 2:13)
Be doers of the word. **Jacob 1:6** (James 1:22-25)
If works good, restored unto that which is good. **Alma 19:9** (Alma 41:1-7)
Overcome to sit with God and Christ on throne. **Revelations 1:16** (Rev. 3:5)
Christ is author of salvation for obedient. **Hebrews 1:12-13** (Hebrews 5:8-9)

WORKS AND JUSTIFICATION
Faith without works is dead. **Jacob 1:12** (James 2:20)
Whatsoever a man soweth, that shall he reap. **Galatians 1:24** (Galatians 6:7-10)
Be doers of the word, not hearers only. **Jacob 1:6** (James 1:22-25)
Doers of the word build house upon a rock. **Matthew 3:48** (Matthew 7:24-27)
If any man do his will, will know of the doctrine. **John 6:4** (John 7:16-17)
Righteous actions accounted through faith in Christ. **Mos. 8:4** (Mos. 14:11)
The just shall live by faith. **Romans 1:1** (Romans 1:7)
Man not justified by works of law, but by faith. **Galatians 1:6** (Galatians 2:16)
By works was man justified and not by works alone. **James 1:12** (James 2:24)
Was not Abraham justified by works? **Jacob 1:12** (James 2:21)
By the spirit you are justified. **Genesis 4:9** (Moses 6:60)
Being now justified by His blood, shall be saved. **Romans 1:22** (Romans 5:9)
Blessed are those who hear word and keep it. **Luke 8:13** (Luke 11:27-28)
There is a reward for the righteous. **Psalms 58** (Psalms 58:11)
If works good, restored unto that which is good. **Alma 19:9** (Alma 41:1-7)
He comes to reward every man according to his work. **Rev. 9:3** (Rev. 22:12-14)
Every man rewarded according to his works. **Matthew 9:3** (Matthew 16:26-27)
God renders unto every man according to deeds. **Romans 1:8** (Romans 2:5-11)
Lord's vengeance on those obey not gospel. **2Thessolians 1:2** (2 Thes. 1:7-10)
Overcome to sit with God and Christ on throne. **Revelations 1:16** (Rev. 3:5)
Keep commandments, endure to end for eternal life. **JSH 15:5** (D&C 14:7)

Endure to the end to be saved. **Matthew 11:3** (Matthew 24;13)
Saved by grace. Judged by works. **2 Nephi 11:8** (2 Nephi 25:23)
Paul looked up to third heaven. **2 Corinthians 1:41** (2 Corinthians 12:1-4)

REPENTANCE
Repent, for the kingdom of God is at hand. **Matthew 3:1** (Matthew 4:17)
Parable of the lost sheep. **Luke 9:11** (Luke 15:3-7)
Life is time for men to prepare to meet God. **Alma 16:37** (Alma 34:32-35)
Days of men prolonged that they might repent. **2 Nephi 1:9** (2 Nephi 2:19-21)
Repent and bring forth fruit of repentance **Mathew 2:2** (Mathew 3:8)
Lord desires all to come unto repentance. **2 Peter 1:12** (2 Peter 3:9)
Christ came to call sinners to repentance. **Matthew 4:8** (Matthew 9:10-13)
Repent, be baptized and receive Holy Ghost. **Moroni 6** (Moroni 6:1-9)
Repent, be baptized and receive Holy Ghost. **Acts 1:12** (Acts 2:37-38)
Come unto Christ, broken heart, contrite spirit. **3 Nephi 4:7** (3 Nephi 9:19-22)
Repentance and baptism for those accountable. **Moroni 8:3** (Moroni 8:10-11)
Repentance and baptism as a witness unto God. **3 Nephi 3:12** (3 Nephi 7:24-25)
Repent, come unto Christ and be in His church. **JSH 10:18-19** (D&C 10:62-67)
Godly sorrow worketh repentance. **2 Corinthians 1:24** (2 Corinthians 7:10)
Repent, Lord suffered so others do not. **T&C 17:5** (D&C 19:15-20)
Justice demands suffering if no repentance. **Alma 19:15-16** (Alma 42:22-25)
Christ sacrifice for those broken heart-contrite spirit. **2 Nephi 1:6** (2 Nephi 2:7)
Having these promises, let us cleanse ourselves. **2 Cor. 1:22** (2 Cor. 7:1)
The Lord remembers sins no more. **T&C 45:9** (D&C 58:42)
Parable of the lost coin. Joy over soul that repents. **Luke 9:12** (Luke 15:8-10)
Except ye repent, ye shall all perish. **Luke 8:30** (Luke 13:1-5)
Devils recognize and believe on Christ. Not saved. **Jacob 1:12** (James 2:19)
Devils recognize and believe on Christ. Not saved. **Mark 2:6** (Mark 3:11-12)
Repent, to avoid the fullness of God's wrath. **Ether 1:7** (Ether 2: 11-12)
Repent or receive testimony of destruction. **T&C 29:6-8** (D&C 43:18-25)
Brought to repentance often means driven out land. **Alma 16:44** (Alma 35:14)
This land choice land, serve God or be swept off. **Ether 1:7** (Ether 2:9-12)
Inhabitants of earth repent or be scourged. **JSH 12:4** (D&C 5:19-20)
If Gentiles repent it will be well with them. **1 Nephi 3:26** (1 Nephi 14:5-7)
The goodness of God leads to repentance. **Romans 1:8** (Romans 2:4)
Worth of souls is great. Joy in those who repent. **JSH 15:31** (D&C 18:10-16)
Most worth to teach repentance. **JSH 15:11** (D&C 16:6)
Whatsoever a man soweth, that shall he reap. **Galatians 1:24** (Galatians 6:7-10)
Through Christ all might be saved by obedience. **T&C 146:23** (D&C 138:4).
Lord redeems men from sin, not in their sins. **Helaman 2:17** (Helaman 5:10)
Repent and endure to end. **2 Nephi 13:2-3** (2 Nephi 31:10-16)
Endure to the end to be saved. **Matthew 11:3** (Matthew 24:13)

147

Repent quickly for the hour is close at hand. **Alma 3:5-6** (Alma 5:27-35)
Hearken unto my voice lest death overtake you. **T&C 31:1-3** (D&C 45: 2-10)
Repentance. **T&C Glossary: Repentance**

BAPTISM AND RE-BAPTISM
Jesus baptized to fulfill all righteousness. **2 Nephi 13:2** (2 Nephi 31:6-12)
Jesus baptized as an example for all. **Matthew 2:4** (Matthew 3:13-17)
He that believeth on me, the works I do he shall do also. **John 9:7** (John 14:12)
Follow me, do the things ye have seen me do. **2 Nephi 13:2** (2 Nephi 31:12)
Gate to enter is repentance-baptism. **2 Nephi 13:3-5** (2 Nephi 31:17-21)
Baptism is the first fruits of repentance. **Moroni 8:5** (Moroni 8:25)
Baptism doth also now save us. **1 Peter 1:14** (1 Peter 3:21)
He that believeth and is baptized shall be saved. **Mark 8:6** (Mark 16:15-16)
Must be born of water and spirit to enter kingdom. **John 2:1-2** (John 3:3-7)
All must be baptized to be saved in kingdom. **2 Nephi 6:7** (2 Nephi 9:23-24)
Must be baptized to ascend into God's presence. **TSJ 2:2**
We have great need of being baptized. **2 Nephi 13:2** (2 Nephi 31:5-7)
Be baptized and forsake sin to ascend into God's presence. **TSJ 2:2**
Baptized in my name, Father gives Holy Ghost. **2 Nephi 13:2** (2 Nephi 31:12)
Commanded to baptize-lay hands for Holy Ghost. **T&C 18:2** (D&C 35:6)
Baptized unto repentance, cleansed unrighteousness. **Alma 5:4** (Alma 7:14-16)
Garments must be washed white, cleansed all stain. **Alma 3:3-5** (Alma 5:21-27)
Old man of sin crucified, body of sin destroyed. **Romans 1:25** (Romans 6:6)
Buried in baptism-death, raised resurrection life. **Romans 1:25** (Romans 6:4)
Buried in baptism, risen in faith from dead. **Colossians 1:7** (Colossians 2:12)
Walk in newness of life. **Romans 1:25** (Romans 6:4)
Those baptized in Christ, have put on Christ. **Galatians 1:12** (Gal 3:27)
Believe and be baptized. **Mark 8:6** (Mark 16-15-16)
Arise and be baptized, and wash away thy sins. **Acts 12:16** (Acts 22:16)
Adam is baptized. **Genesis 4:7** (Moses 6:51-58)
Adam and Eve baptized and born of Spirit. **Genesis 4:10** (Moses 6:65-66)
John baptizes those confessing sin. **Matthew 2:1** (Matthew 3:1-2)
Jesus baptized of John. **Matthew 2:4** (Matthew 3:13-17)
Peter cries repentance and baptizes thousands. **Acts 1:12-13** (Acts 2:37-41)
Paul is baptized. **Acts 11:5** (Acts 19:17-18)
Cornelius vision, Holy Ghost, Gentile baptism **Acts 6:3-8** (Acts 10:1-48)
King Limhi and his people desire baptism. **Mosiah 9:34** (Mosiah 21:33-35)
Alma re-baptizes those coming out apostasy. **Mosiah 9:7-8** (Mosiah 18: 8-17)
Ordained in ministry, baptized unto repentance. **3 Nephi 3:12** (3 Nephi 7:23-26)
Paul re-baptizes disciples. **Acts 11:2** (Acts 19:1-5)
Philip runs to chariot, baptizes eunuch. **Acts 5:7** (Acts 8:35-39)
Samuel protected. Many believe, baptized. **Helaman 5:18** (Helaman 16:3-5)

Twelve desire Holy Ghost, re-baptized, fire. **3 Nephi 9:2** (3 Nephi 19:9-13)
Sign given, people again baptized unto repentance. **3 Nephi 1:6** (3 Nephi 1:23)
All who repented were baptized. **3 Nephi 3:12** (3 Nephi 7:23-26)
Righteous previously baptized survive. **3 Nephi 4:10** (3 Nephi 10:12)
Lord gives Nephi power to baptize, re-baptize. **3 Nephi 5:8** (3 Nephi 11:18-21)
Nephi is re-baptized. **3 Nephi 9:2** (3 Nephi 19:11-12)
Elders, priests, teachers, repent and are rebaptized. **Moroni 6:1** (Moroni 6:1-4)
Alma invites church members to repent, be baptized. **Alma 3:12** (Alma 5:62)
Priesthood of Aaron restored for baptism. **JSH 14:1** (D&C 13:1)
Apostles commissioned to go and baptize. **T&C 55:2** (D&C 68:8-12)
Blessed are those baptized without being stubborn. **Alma 16:25.** (Alma 32:16)
Come all ye Gentiles, repent and be baptized. **3 Nephi 14** (3 Nephi 30:1-2)
Elders, priests, teachers, repent and are rebaptized. **Moroni 6:1** (Moroni 6:1-4)
Go unto the world, preach gospel to every creature. **T&C 55:2** (D&C 68:8-12)

HOLY GHOST
Holy Ghost. **T&C Glossary: Holy Ghost**
Baptizing name of Father, Son, Holy Ghost. **Matthew 13:4** (Matthew 28:19)
Faith, repentance, baptism, and then Holy Ghost. **T&C 35:4** (D&C 49: 11-14)
He shall baptize you with Holy Ghost and fire. **Matthew 2:3** (Matthew 3:11)
Adam baptized with fire and the Holy Ghost. **Genesis 4:10** (Moses 6:66)
Repent, baptized, then remission of sins by fire. **2 Nephi 13:3** (2 Nephi 31:17)
Must be born of water and spirit to enter the kingdom. **John 2:2** (John 3:5)
Christ to go away, that Comforter will come unto us. **John 9:13** (John 16:7)
Another comforter to abide with you forever. **John 9:8** (John 14:16)
When the comforter is come, he will testify of me. **John 9:13** (John 15:26)
I will send Comforter, promise of eternal life. **T&C 86:1** (D&C 88:3-4)
Comforter teaches all things, restores memory of all truth. **TSJ 10:15**
Knowledge by unspeakable gift of Holy Ghost. **T&C 138:21** (D&C 121:26).
Comforter will bring all things to remembrance. **John 9:9** (John 14:26)
Spirit guides you into all truth. **John 9:14** (John 16:13-16)
Truth of all things - by power of Holy Ghost. **Moroni 10:2-4** (Moroni 10:4-19)
Holy Ghost given to those who obey. **Acts 3:7** (Acts 5:32)
Holy Ghost comes upon Gentiles. God no respecter. **Acts 6:6-8** (Acts 10:28-48)
Holy Ghost came, tongues, prophesy. **Acts 11:2** (Acts 19:6)
Meetings are to be led by the Holy Ghost. **Moroni 6:2** (Moroni 6:9)
Fruit of Spirit: love, joy, peace, faith. **Galatians 1:22** (Galatians 5:22-26)
Apostles baptized with Holy Ghost. **Acts 1:7** (Acts 2:1-4)
Paul laid hands-Holy Ghost received. Prophecy. **Acts 11:2** (Acts 19:1-6)
Men ordained by power of Holy Ghost. **Moroni 3** (Moroni 3:4)
Receive the Holy Ghost. **Moroni 2** (Moroni 2:1-3)

GIFTS OF SPIRIT

Desire spiritual gifts to prophecy. **1 Cor. 1:54** (1 Cor. 14:1-3)
Seek ye earnestly the best gifts. **1 Corinthians 1:50** (1 Corinthians 12: 31)
Seek the best gifts to benefit those who love God. **T&C 32:3-4** (D&C 46:8-10)
Covet best gifts, shown a more excellent way. **1 Cor. 1:50** (1 Cor. 12:31)
Concerning spiritual gifts, do not be ignorant. **1 Cor. 1:47-48** (1 Cor. 12:1-11)
Deny not the gifts of God, for they are many. **Moroni 10:3** (Moroni 10:8)
Signs shall follow them that believe. **Mark 8:6 (**Mark 16:17-18)
Many signs and wonders wrought among the people. **Acts 3:4** (Acts 5:12-16)
Gifts of the Spirit listed. **1 Corinthians 1:48 (**1 Corinthians 12: 4-11)
Diversity of gifts come from save Spirit. **1 Corinthians 1:48** (1 Cor. 12:4-11)
Signs, healings, prophecies, tongues, all gifts. **1 Cor. 1:48-51** (1 Cor. 12:4-31)
Gift of the word of wisdom. **1 Corinthians 1:48** (1 Corinthians 12:4-11)
Gift of the word of knowledge. **1 Corinthians 1:48** (1 Corinthians 12:4-11)
Gift of healing and working miracles. **1 Corinthians 1:48** (1 Cor. 12:4-11)
Miracles, healing and casting out devils. **T&C 18:3** (D&C 35:8-9)
Gift of tongues and discerning of spirits. **1 Corinthians 1:48** (1 Cor. 12:4-11)
Zeezrom healed, leaped, baptized, preached. **Alma 10:12, 14** (Alma 15:3,12)
Healing by faith and herbs. Some die in Christ. **T&C 26:11-13** (D&C 42:43-51)
Plants and roots are for diseases and fevers. **Alma 21:16** (Alma 46:40)
Music to heal, cast out evil spirits **1 Samuel 7:19-21** (1 Samuel 16:16-23)
In name of Jesus Christ rise up and walk! **Acts 2:1** (Acts 3:1-8)
Miracles by the power of word of God. **4 Nephi 1:6** (4 Nephi 1:30)
In name of Jesus, trees, mountains, waves obey us. **Jacob 3:2** (Jacob 4:6)
Twelve ordained to heal sickness, cast out devils. **Mark 2:7** (Mark 3:14-15)
Went forth as led by the Spirit of the Lord. **Alma 13:4** (Alma 21:16)
Disciples enact miracles in name of Christ. **4 Nephi 1:2** (4 Nephi 1:5)
Ananias heals Saul from blindness. **Acts 5:9** (Acts 9:17-18)
Paul lays hands on sick and heals **Acts 13:9** (Acts 28:8-9)
Spirit of prophecy, Spirit of revelation, Power of God. **Alma 12:1** (Alma 17:3)

KNOW GOD AND HIS SON

Eternal Life. **T&C Glossary: Eternal Life**

Eternal life is to know God. **John 9:19** (John 17:3)

Seek ye the Lord. **Isaiah 20:2** (Isaiah 55:6)

Worlds, men, and all things were made by Him. **T&C 93:2** (D&C 93:10)

God can roll the earth together as a scroll. **Mormon 2:7** (Mormon 5:23)

At His command, the heavens open. **Ether 1:18** (Ether 4:8-10)

His right hand spans the heavens, stand up together! **1 Ne. 6:3** (1 Ne. 20:13)

Seek ye the Lord. **Isaiah 20:2** (Isaiah 55:6)

Those who seek me early shall find me. **Proverbs 1:36** (Proverbs 8:17)

The sheep follow him for they know his voice. **John 6:24** (John 10:4)

God is love. **1 John 1:19** (1 John 4:8)

God is no respecter of persons. **Acts 6:7** (Acts 10:34)

Glory of God is intelligence, light and truth. **T&C 93:11** (D&C 93:36)

Worlds, men, and all things were made by Him. **T&C 93:2** (D&C 93:10)

To understand and know how and what to worship. **T&C 93:7** (D&C 93:19)

God is not a man that He should lie. **Numbers 10:24** (Numbers 23:19)

The Lord thy God is a merciful God. **Deuteronomy 2:6** (Deuteronomy 4:31)

Thou art a God, ready to pardon. **Nehemiah 2:35-36** (Nehemiah 9:17)

Every man shall know the Lord. **Hebrews 1:23** (Hebrews 8:11)

The sheep follow him for they know his voice. **John 6:24** (John 10:4)

I know the Father, you do not. **John 6:16** (John 8:55)

I ascend unto my Father, and your father. **John 11:2** (John 20:17)

I ascend unto my God, and your God. **John 11:2** (John 20:17)

I will not leave you comfortless, I will come to you. **John 9:8** (John 14:18)

God shall be with them, wipe away tears. **Revelations 8:8** (Revelation 21:3-4)

The Father and Son will come and make their abode. **John 9:8** (John 14:23)

See my face and know that I am. **T&C 93:1** (D&C 93:1)

Every man shall know the Lord. **Hebrews 1:23** (Hebrews 8:11)

Sheep follow him for they know his voice. **John 6:24** (John 10:4)

Spans the heavens, stand up together! **1 Nephi 6:3** (1 Nephi 20:13)

God can roll earth together as a scroll. **Mormon 2:7** (Mormon 5:23)

His command, the heavens open. **Ether 1:18** (Ether 4:9)

Be still and know that I am God. **Psalms 46:3**. (Psalms 46:10)

NATURE OF GOD (TRINITY)
God already perfect. Jesus is made perfect. **Hebrews 1:13** (Hebrews 5:9)
The head of Christ is God. **1 Corinthians 1:44** (1 Corinthians 11:3)
Christ is the image of His Father. **Hebrews 1:1** (Hebrews 1:1-3)
God anointed Jesus with power and is with Him **Acts 6:7** (Acts 10:38)
Father, Son, Holy Ghost at baptism of Jesus. **Matthew 2:4** (Matthew 3:15-17)
Father speaks to the Son from heaven. **John 8:3** (John 12:28-29)
Father announces He is pleased with His Son **3 Nephi 5:2** (3 Nephi 11:3-7)
Jesus places promise of His Father upon the twelve. **Luke 14:7** (Luke 24:49)
As my Father hath sent me, even so send I you. **John 11:3** (John 20:21)
My Father worketh, and I work. **John 5:3-4** (John 5:17-23)
Word against Holy Ghost not forgiven. **Matthew 6:13** (Matthew 12:31-32)
I and my Father are one. **John 6:29** (John 10:30)
One God, one mediator, the man Christ Jesus **1 Timothy 1:6** (1 Timothy 2:5).
Testimony of two. Jesus of self. God of Jesus. **John 6:12** (John 8:17-18)
Stephen sees both the Father and Son. **Acts 4:10** (Acts 7:55-56)
Jesus raised up by God-exalted on His right hand. **Acts 1:11** (Acts 2:32-33)
No man has seen the Father without hearing Him testify of Christ. **TJ 1:4**
I know the Father, you do not. **John 6:16** (John 8:55)
I ascend unto my Father, and your father. **John 11:2** (John 20:17)
I ascend unto my God, and your God. **John 11:2** (John 20:17)
Touch me not, not yet ascended to my Father. **John 11:2** (John 20:17)
Baptize in name Father, Son, Holy Ghost. **Matthew 13:4** (Matthew 28:16-20)
Joseph Smith sees both the Father and Son. **JSH 2:4** (J.S. History 17)

APOSTASY AFTER JESUS CHRIST
Jews thought they understood the scriptures. **John 5:7** (John 5:39)
Jews looking past the mark. **Jacob 3:5** (Jacob 4:14)
Ye do err not knowing the scripture. **Matthew 10:22** (Matthew 22:29)
Pattern of idolatry and apostasy. **Judges 1:6.** (Judges 2:17-23)
Idols set up in heart. Separated from Lord. **Ezekiel 5:8** (Ezekiel 14:2-7)
Grievous wolves to enter in among the flock. **Acts 12:4** (Acts 20:29-31)
Traditions of Fathers limit receiving light and truth. **T&C 93:11.** (D&C 93: 39)
Two churches only. Church of Lamb, Church devil **1 Nephi 3:25** (1 Nephi 14:1)
Spiritual wickedness high places. **Ephesians 1:25** (Ephesians 6:12)
Prophets prophecy falsely and people love it. **Jeremiah 3:7** (Jeremiah 5:30-31)
False prophets deceive many. **Matthew 11:25-11:3** (Matthew 24:11-12, 23-24)
Beware of false prophets in sheep's clothing. **Matthew 3:46** (Matthew 7:15)
False prophets do not profit people **Jeremiah 8:19** (Jeremiah 23:32)
Lord against them that prophecy false dreams **Jeremiah 8:19**. (Jeremiah 23:32)
False prophets follow own spirit. **Ezekiel 5:3** (Ezekiel 13:1-3)
Those preach from their own understanding only gratify their pride. (TSJ 6:5)

If message unpopular, say he is false prophet. **Hel. 5:7** (Hel. 13:26-27)
If message popular, say he is a prophet. **Helaman 5:7** (Helaman 13:26-27)
Rebellious desire smooth language, deceits. **Isa. 9:7, 3-5:5** (Isa. 30:1, 8-11)
Exchanging pleasantries. **Isaiah 9:7, 3-5:5** (Isaiah 30:1, 8-11)
Teachings are tables full of vomit. **Isaiah 8;2-3** (Isaiah 28:8-9)
People not be able to endure sound doctrine. **2 Timothy 1:10** (2 Timothy 4: 3-4)
Famine in the land of hearing the Word of God. **Amos 1:25-31** (Amos 8-11)
Earth is defiled, changed ordinance, broken covenant. **Isaiah 7:1** (Isaiah 24:1-6)
Satan soweth tares, they drive church into wilderness **T&C 84:1** (D&C 86:3)
After Apostles fall asleep, tares choke the wheat. **T&C 84:1** (D&C 86:2-3)
Shepherds feed themselves-not the flock. **Ezekiel 17:5** (Ezekiel 34:2-3)
Lost shepherd's and wandering sheep. **Ezekiel 17:5-7** (Ezekiel 34:6-13)
Do not feed flock for filthy lucre. **1 Peter 1:19** (1 Peter 5:2)
Priestcraft: get gain and praise of world. **3 Nephi 11:17** (2 Nephi 26:29)
Priestcraft led to the crucifixion of Jesus. **2 Nephi 7:1** (2 Nephi 10:5)
The true shepherd does not profit from the sheep. **TSJ 7:11**
Leaders cause people to err and be destroyed. **Isaiah 4:3** (Isaiah 9:16)
Land shall be utterly emptied, utterly spoiled. **Isaiah 7:1** (Isaiah 24:3)
Darkness shall cover the earth, gross darkness people. **Isaiah 22** (Isaiah 60:2)
Falling away before great day of the Lord. **2 Thessalonians 1:4** (2 Thess. 2:3-4)

BIBLE ERRORS AND OMISSIONS

Many other signs Jesus did not written in this book. **John 11:5** (John 20:30)
World could not contain books should be written. **John 11:13** (John 21:25)
Many other signs Jesus did not written in this book. **John 11:5** (John 20:30)
Book of Remembrance kept by Adam. **Genesis 3:14** (Moses 6:5-6)
Book of Covenant mentioned, not in Bible. **Exodus 13:25** (Exodus 24:7)
Book of Gad missing-mentioned in Bible **1 Chron. 12:19** (1 Chron. 29:29)
Bible mentions the book of the prophet Esaias. **Luke 4:2** (Luke 4:17)
Prophecy of Ahijah mentioned, not in Bible. **2 Chron. 3:14** (2 Chron. 9:29)
Book of Shemaiah. **2 Chronicles 4:18** (2 Chronicles 12:15)
Book of Jehu. **2 Chronicles 7:34** (2 Chronicles 20:34)
Book of Jasher not in Bible. **Joshua 2:19** (Joshua 10:13)
Book of the Wars of the Lord. **Numbers 10:8** (Numbers 21:14)
Book of Samuel the Seer. **1 Chronicles 12:19** (1 Chronicles 29:29)
Book of Gad the Seer. **1 Chronicles 12:19** (1 Chronicles 29:29)
Book of Nathan the Prophet. **2 Chronicles 6:9** (2 Chronicles 9:29)
Sayings of the Seers. **2 Chronicles 17:6** (2 Chronicles 33:19)
The Manner of Kingdom, written by Samuel. **1 Samuel 4:22** (1 Samuel 10:25)
The Acts of Uzziah, written by Isaiah. **2 Chronicles 13:9** (2 Chronicles 26:22)
Christ should be a Nazarene. **Matthew 1:12** (Matthew 2:23)
Elias must restore all things before Christ. **Matthew 9:5** (Matthew 17:10)

Epistle of Paul to Corinthians-predates current 1st Cor. **1 Cor. 3:8** (1 Cor. 5:9)
An earlier Epistle to the Ephesians. **Ephesians 1:8** (Ephesians 3:3)
An Epistle to the Church at Laodicea. **Colossians 1:18** (Colossians 4:16)
Prophecies of Enoch. **Judas !:3** (Jude 1:14)
Precious parts of Gospel purged from Bible. **1 Nephi 3:22** (1 Nephi 13:33)
Lost revelations-scriptures to be revealed. **2 Nephi 12:10** (2 Nephi 29:11-14)
Latter day scripture witeness for the Bible **1 Nephi 3:24** (1 Nephi 13:38-40)
Lost truth restored in Book of Mormon. **1 Nephi 3:23** (1 Nephi 13:34-35)
One like Moses will give world lost writings. **Genesis 1:7** (Moses 1:40-41)
Lord will judge world out of books written. **2 Nephi 12:10** (2 Nephi 29:11-14)

RAPTURE
They deliver you up to be afflicted-killed. **Matthew 11:3,7** (Matthew 24:9-14)
Church not endure sound doctrine. Deceived. **2 Tim. 1:10** (2 Tim. 4: 3-4)
If they persecute me, they will persecute you. **John 9:12** (John 15:20)
Tribulation of elect will be greatest in history. **Matthew 11:5** (Matthew 24:22)
For the sake of the elect, days shortened. **Matthew 11:5** (Matthew 24:22)
No rapture, washed white in Lamb's blood. **Rev. 2:16** (Rev. 7:14)
We are accounted as sheep for the slaughter. **Romans 1:37** (Romans 8:36)
They shall persecute you in last days. **Luke 12:15** (Luke 21:12)
Judgement must begin at the house of God. **1 Peter 1:18** (1 Peter 4:17-18)
The righteous suffered through great tribulation. **Revelation 2:15-16** (7: 11-17)

APOSTASY OF MODERN DAY CHURCHES
Holy Church of God polluted. **Mormon 4:5** (Mormon 8:38)
Spiritual wickedness high places. **Ephesians 1:25** (Ephesians 6:12)
Last days will be perilous times. **2 Timothy 1:8** (2 Timothy 3:1-7)
Many will not endure sound doctrine. **2 Timothy 1:10** (2 Timothy 4:3-4)
Famine in the land of hearing word of Lord. **Amos 1:27** (Amos 8:11)
Some have wrested scriptures-gone far astray. **Alma 19:9** (Alma 41:1)
Teachings are tables full of vomit. **Isaiah 8:2-3** (Isaiah 28:8-9)
Falling away before coming of Lord. **2 Thessalonians 1:4** (2 Thess. 2:1-3)
Grievous wolves come in among the flock. **Acts 12:4** (Acts 20:29-31)
Beware of false prophets in sheep's clothing. **Matthew 3:46** (Matthew 7:15)
Leaders cause people to err and be destroyed. **Isaiah 4:3** (Isaiah 9:16)
Lost shepherds and wandering sheep. **Ezekiel 17:5-7** (Ezekiel 34:6-13)
Shepherds feed themselves-not the flock. **Ezekiel 17:5.** (Ezekiel 34:2-3)
Do not feed flock for filthy lucre. **1 Peter 1:19** (1 Peter 5:2)
Priestcraft: to get gain and praise of world. **2 Nephi 11:17** (2 Nephi 26:29)
Priestcraft led to the crucifixion of Jesus. **2 Nephi 7:1** (2 Nephi 10:5)
Churches for gain-popularity consumed as stubble. **1 Nephi 7:5** (1 Nephi 22:23)
Church pride grinds on the poor. **2 Nephi 11:15** (2 Nephi 26:20)

Those labor for money and not Zion shall perish. **2 Ne. 11:17** (2 Ne. 26:31)
Broken covenant, changed ordinances **Isaiah 7:1.** (Isaiah 24:5)
Broken covenant, cites despised, highways wasted. **Isaiah 11:4** (Isaiah 33:8)
False prophets do not profit people **Jeremiah 8:19** (Jeremiah 23:32)
False prophets follow their own spirit. **Ezekiel 5:3** (Ezekiel 13:1-3)
Message unpopular, people say false prophet. **Hel. 5:7** (Hel. 13:26-27)
Message popular, people say a prophet. **Heleman 5:7** (Helaman 13:26-27)
Leaders prophecy falsely and people love it. **Jeremiah 3:7** (Jeremiah 5:30-31)
Rebellious desire smooth language, deceits. **Isa. 12:1 4:5-5:3** (Isa. 30:1, 8-11)
Church: exchanging pleasantries. **Isaiah 12:1 4:5-5:3** (Isaiah 30:1,8-11)
Church: breaking up because of pride. **3 Nephi 3:2** (3 Nephi 6:10-14)
Priests cast poor out of synagogue. Some teachable. **Alma 16:23** (Alma 32:5)
Traditions of father's limit receiving light and truth. **T&C 93:11** (D&C 93: 39)
Pattern of idolatry and apostasy. **Judges 1:6** (Judges 2:17-23)
Idols in heart. Stumble and separated from Lord. **Ezekiel 5:8** (Ezekiel 14:2-7)
Trust in Lord, cursed is he that trusts in man. **Jeremiah 6:12**(Jeremiah 17:5-7)
Looking past the mark of Christ. **Jacob 3:5** (Jacob 4:14)
Christ is the only keeper of the gate. **2 Nephi 6:11** (2 Nephi 9:41)

JOSEPH SMITH AND THE BOOK OF MORMON
God is unchanging. **Hebrews 1:59-63** (Hebrews. 13:8-20)
Lord will do nothing save reveals His secret to prophets. **Amos 1:9** (Amos 3:7)
Can know a true or false prophet by fruits. **Matthew 3:46** (Matthew 7:15-16)
Fruit of Spirit: love, joy, peace, faith. **Galatians 1:22** (Galatians 5:22-26)
Spirit guides you into all truth. **John 9:14** (John 16:13-16)
Gain knowledge by the gift of Holy Ghost. **T&C 138:21** (D&C 121:26).
Words spoken by the Holy Spirit are scripture. **D&C 55:1** (D&C 68:3-4)
Man not live bread alone, but every word of God. **Matthew 2:5** (Matthew 4:4)
Only part of what Jesus said and did recorded in Bible. **John 11:3** (John 21:25)
Jesus teaches there are other sheep not of this fold. **John 6:26** (John 10:16)
Gospel will be given to another nation. **Matthew 10:13** (Matthew 21 :43)
Know ye not there are more nations then one? **2 Ne. 12:9-10** (2 Ne. 29: 7-12)
Stick of Judah, Stick of Joseph. Together. **Ezekiel 19:4** (Ezekiel 37:15-19)
Book of Mormon contains the fullness of the gospel. **JSH 16:3** (D&C 20:9)
Everlasting gospel comes with the angels **D&C 86:24** (D&C 88:103)
John sees angel preaching gospel in last days. **Revelation 5:2** (Revelation 14:6)
Several called to preach and testify of Christ. **3 Nephi 3:4** (3 Nephi 6:20)
Prophecy occurring after the death of Jesus. **Acts 11:2** (Acts 19:6)
Gentiles say, have a Bible-need no other Bible. **2 Ne. 12:8-9** (2 Ne. 29: 3-5)
Other scriptures wrested to their own destruction. **2 Peter 1:14** (2 Peter 3:16)
Choose things true, pure, of good report. **Philippians1:15** (Philippians 4:8)
Ask God, He will manifest the truth to you. **Moroni 10:2** (Moroni 10:4)

155

PRESERVING THE RESTORATION

Christ is only keeper of the gate. **2 Nephi 6:11** (2 Nephi 9:41)
The course of the Lord is one eternal round. **1 Nephi 3:5** (1 Nephi 10:19)
The Lord gives pattern in all things. **T&C 39:4** (D&C 52:14)
Truth is things as they really are, really will be. **Jacob 3:4** (Jacob 4:13)
Truth: things as they are, were, and are to come. **T&C 93:8** (D&C 93:24)
Men are free to choose. **2 Nephi 1:10** (2 Nephi 2:27)
Lords church can be overthrown by transgression. **Mos. 11:26** (Mos. 27:13)
Satan lulls church away into carnal security, **2 Nephi 12:4** (2 Nephi 28:21)
Masses say "All is well in Zion" **2 Nephi 12:4** (2 Nephi 28:21)
Joseph identifies church as a Gentile Church. **T&C 123:18** (D&C 109:60)
Christ prophesies Gentile church loses fulness. **3 Nephi 7:5** (3 Nephi 16:10-11)
Gentiles receive not the fulness, but reject it. **T&C 31:7** (D&C 45:28-30)
Wo unto the Gentiles…they will deny me **2 Nephi 12:7** (2 Nephi 28:32)
House of God needs set in order. **T&C 83:4** (D&C 85:7)
Lord sets hand second time to restore people. **2 Nephi 11:6** (2 Nephi 25:17)
Lord offers hand second time to nourish and prune. **Jacob 4:1** (Jacob 6:2)
Joseph's marvelous work has yet to occur. **JS History 11:2** (D&C 4:1)
The Lord brings forth His strange act. **T&C 101:20** (D&C 101:95)
Strange act to prune vineyard last time. **T&C 94:1** (D&C 95:4)
Dispensation. **T&C Glossary**
Dispensation of the Fullness of Times. **T&C Glossary**
Fullness of the Gospel. **T&C Glossary**
Entering Lord's real church through repentance. **JS History 10:19** (D&C 10:67)
Few only that do not lift themselves in pride. **Mormon 4:5** (Mormon 8:36)
Few humble followers Christ. **2 Nephi 12:2** (2 Nephi 28:14)
Humble overcome false precepts of men. **2 Nephi 12:2** (2 Nephi 28:14)
Scriptures wrested to their own destruction. **2 Peter 1:14** (2 Peter 3:16)
Scriptures given for salvation of elect. **T&C 18:6** (D&C 35:20–21)
Remnant of Israel receives revelation. **T&C 129:5** (D&C 113:9-10)
Lord sends his angels then and now. **Alma 19:3** (Alma 39:19)
Everlasting Gospel comes with the angels. **T&C 86:24** (D&C 88:103)
Several called to preach and testify of Christ. **3 Nephi 3:4** (3 Nephi 6:20)
Blessings or cursing Israel? Repent-obey covenant. **Lev. 13:8-16** (Lev. 26:1-46)
Righteous Gentiles offered covenant in last days **3 Nephi 10:1** (3 Nephi 21:22)
Gentiles offered covenant, Christ in midst. **3 Nephi 10:1** (3 Nephi 21:22-25)
Incline ear to everlasting covenant, mercies David. **Isaiah 20:1** (Isaiah 55:3)
New name of David given unto Denver Snuffer. **T&C 162:1**
God has given David for a witness unto the people. **Isaiah 20:1** (Isaiah 55:3-4)
Covenant of Peace through servant David. **Eze. 17:10-11** (Eze. 34:22-27)
The Pass through Denver Snuffer. **T&C 163:1-4**
Gethsemane through Denver Snuffer. **T&C 161:1-31**

A Sign through Denver Snuffer. **T&C 160:1-5**
An End of Authority through Denver Snuffer. **T&C 166:1-4**
Seven Women through Denver Snuffer. **T&C 167:1**
The Resurrection through Denver Snuffer. **T&C 169:1-4**
His Return through Denver Snuffer. **T&C 164:1**
The Train through Denver Snuffer. **T&C 172:1-5**
Prayer for Covenant through Denver Snuffer. **T&C 156:1-8**
Answer and Covenant through Denver Snuffer **T&C 157:1-66**
Servant marred-but spared in God's hand. **3 Nephi 9:12** (3 Nephi 21:9-10)
Watchmen see eye to eye when Lord brings Zion. **3 Nephi 7:6** (Isaiah 52:8)
Old things are done away, all things new. **3 Nephi 5:31** (3 Nephi 12: 47)
All invited heaven, to sit down Holy Fathers. **Helaman 2:7** (Helaman 3:27-30)
Seeking for the blessings of the Fathers. **Abraham 1:1** (Abraham 1:2-3)
Elijah keys to seal hearts of fathers to children. **TC Ref.** (D&C 27:9-12)
Elijah hearts of fathers to children, children to fathers. **Mal. 1:12** (Mal. 4:4-6)
Fathers and children must be welded together. **T&C 151:14** (D&C 128:18)
Promises made to fathers, in the hearts of children. **JS History 3:4** (D&C 2:1-3)
Dispensation fullness. Glory-keys since Adam. **T&C 151:14** (D&C 128:18)
Priesthood from the Fathers. **Abraham 1:1** (Abraham 1:4)
Those called to bring Zion with priesthood. **T&C 129:4** (D&C 113:7-8)
God will gather in one all things. Fullness of times. **TC Ref.** (D&C 27:13)
Fullness of the Gospel. **T&C Glossary**
Brought to repentance often = driven out of the land. **Alma 16:44** (Alma 35:14)
Upon my house it shall begin. **T&C 124:6** (D&C 112:25)
Gentiles. **T&C Glossary**
Parable that Gentiles would be destroyed. **Matt 10:16** (JST Matt 21:56)
Do not gather in haste, brings confusion-pestilence. **T&C 50:6** (D&C 63:24)
God's message to those who seek Zion at the last day **Isaiah 18:7** (Isaiah 52)
Lord takes one of a city and two of a family to Zion. **Jeremiah 2:3** (Jer. 3:14)
Believing Gentiles numbered among Lamanites. **3 Nephi 10:1** (3 Nephi 21: 22)
The first shall be last and the last first **Jacob 3:25** (Jacob 5:63)
Restitution of all things. **Acts 2:3** (Acts 3:21)
New Heaven. **T&C Glossary**
New Earth. **T&C Glossary**
New Heaven/New Earth. New Jerusalem. **Ether 6:3** (Ether 13:1-12)

NEW COVENANT-ANCIENT

Lord's course is one eternal round. **1 Nephi 3:5** (1 Nephi 10:19)
Everlasting covenant existed in beginning. **T&C 35:3** (D&C 49:9)
Everlasting covenant sent as standard to prepare people. **T&C 31:3** (D&C 45:9)
Oath and Covenant. **T&C Glossary: Oath and Covenant**
The Lord gives pattern in all things. **T&C 39:4** (D&C 52:14)
God covenants with Adam and Eve. **Genesis 4:10** (Moses 6:64-66)
All things confirmed unto Adam by holy ordinance. **Genesis 3:13** (Moses 5:59)
Adam-Eve covenant through sacrifice, baptism. **Genesis 4:10** (Moses 6:64-66)
God covenants with Noah and his seed. **Genesis 5:22** (Genesis 9:8-17)
Abraham seeks for the blessings of the fathers. **Abraham 1:1** (Abraham 1:2)
Abrahamic covenant. **Genesis 7:29** (Genesis 17:2-7)
Abraham received priesthood through the fathers. **T&C 82:10** (D&C 84:14-16)
Abraham promised his posterity to be numerous. **Genesis 7:29** (Genesis 17:2-6)
Seed of Abraham blessed Gospel, salvation. **Abraham 3:1** (Abraham 2:11)
Blessings of Abraham passed Isaac to Jacob. **Genesis 9:20** (Genesis 28:10-16)
God covenants Jacob/Israel. Given land-seed. **Gen. 9:55-56** (Gen. 35:10-15)
Covenant: Abram given land for seed forever. **Genesis 7:11** (Genesis 13:14-16)
Covenant: Abraham's posterity as sands of sea. **Genesis 8:7** (Genesis 22:17-18)
All invited enter gate, sit with Holy Fathers. **Helaman 2:7** (Helaman 3:27-30)
Israel invited keep covenant-be peculiar treasure. **Exodus 12:1** (Exodus 19:1-5)
Elijah keys seal hearts fathers to children. **JS History 3:4** (JS History 1:38-39)
Hearts fathers to children, children to fathers. **Malachi 1:11-12** (Malachi 4:4-6)
Fathers and children must be welded together. **T&C 151:14** (D&C 128:18)
Promises made to the fathers-in hearts of children. **JS History 3:4** (D&C 2:1-3)
Becoming heirs to Christ. (Abrahamic covenant) **Galatians 1:12** (Gal. 3:26-29)
Israel invited keep covenant-kingdom of priests. **Exodus 12:1** (Exodus 19:1-6)
Ordinances changed, broken everlasting covenant. **Isaiah 7:1** (Isaiah 24:5-6)
Blessings-cursings declared for Israel. **Leviticus 13:8-16** (Leviticus 26:1-46)
Gather together those make covenant by sacrifice. **Psalms 50:1** (Psalms 50:5)
Christ is the messenger of the covenant. **Malachi 1:6** (Malachi 3:1)
Christ is mediator of the new covenant. **Hebrews 1:22-23** (Hebrews 8:6-13)
Those hear Christ, children of the covenant. **3 Nephi 9:8**. (3 Nephi 20:21-26)
Lord sends his angels then and now. **Alma 19:3** (Alma 39:19)
Men are free to choose. **2 Nephi 1:10** (2 Nephi 2:27)
Come, Lord will make an everlasting covenant. **Isaiah 20:1** (Isaiah 55:3)
Cry out, Abba Father! Receive adoption. **Romans 1:34** (Romans 8:15-17)
Covenant. **T&C Glossary**

NEW COVENANT-MODERN

Great and marvelous work begins words Christ. **3 Nephi 9:12** (3 Nephi 21:9-10)
That mine everlasting covenant might be established. **T&C 54:4** (D&C 1:22)
New - Everlasting covenant from the beginning. **JS History 18:8** (D&C 22:1)
Oath and Covenant. **T&C Glossary: Oath and Covenant**
Old covenants done away, no entry law Moses. **JS History 18:8** (D&C 22:1-2)
Old things are done away, all becomes new. **3 Nephi 5:31** (3 Nephi 12: 47)
Without Christ, strangers from covenants. **Ephesians 1:6** (Ephesians 2:12)
Stand by my servant Joseph Smith faithfully. **JS History 13:9** (D&C 6:18)
Oath and covenant of the priesthood. **T&C 82:17** (D&C 84:33-40)
Church under condemnation, vanity-unbelief. **T&C 82:20** (D&C 84:54-55)
Satan lulls church away into carnal security, **2 Nephi 12:4** (2 Nephi 28:21)
Masses say "All is well in Zion" **2 Nephi 12:4** (2 Nephi 28:21)
Joseph identifies church as a Gentile Church. **T&C 123:18** (D&C 109:60)
Christ prophesies Gentile church loses fulness. **3 Nephi 7:5** (3 Nephi 16:10-11)
Gentiles receive not the fulness but reject it. **T&C 31:6**-7 (D&C 45:28-30)
Wo unto the Gentiles…they will deny me **2 Nephi 12:7** (2 Nephi 28:32)
Ordinances changed, broken everlasting covenant. **Isaiah 7:1** (Isaiah 24:5-6)
House of God needs to be set in order. **T&C 83:4** (D&C 85:7)
Lord sets hand second time to restore people. **2 Nephi 11:6** (2 Nephi 25:17)
Lord offers hand second time to nourish and prune. **Jacob 4:1** (Jacob 6:2)
Covenant with His laws in their heart and mind. **Heb. 1:31** (Heb. 10:16)
Marvelous work has yet to occur. **JS History 11:2** (D&C 4:1)
The Lord brings forth His strange act. **T&C 101:20** (D&C 101:95)
Strange act to prune vineyard last time. **T&C 94:1** (D&C 95:4)
Several called to preach and testify of Christ. **3 Nephi 3:4** (3 Nephi 6:20)
When men covenant they are salt of the earth. **T&C 101:7** (D&C 101:39-40)
Gentiles who repent are covenant people. **2 Nephi 12:11** (2 Nephi 30:1-2)
Whosoever repents, comes unto me, my church. **JS History 10:19** (D&C 10:67)
Willing to enter covenant, be called name of Christ. **Mosiah 3:1** (Mosiah 5:5)
Baptism and re-baptism covenant. **Mosiah 9:7-8** (Mosiah 18:8-13)
If Gentiles repent, covenant established. **3 Nephi 10:1** (3 Nephi 21:22)
Few only that do not lift themselves in pride. **Mormon 4:5** (Mormon 8:36)
Few humble followers of Christ. **2 Nephi 12:2** (2 Nephi 28:14)
Humble overcome false precepts of men. **2 Nephi 12:2** (2 Nephi 28:14)
Scriptures wrested to their own destruction. **2 Peter 1:14** (2 Peter 3:16)
Scriptures given for salvation of elect. **T&C 18:6** (D&C 35:20–21)
Remnant of Israel receives revelation. **T&C 129:5** (D&C 113:9-10)
God makes new covenant with House of Israel. **Jer. 12:9** (Jer. 31:31-34)
Lord sends his angels then and now. **Alma 19:3** (Alma 39:19)
Angels prepare men for covenant work. **Moroni 7:6-7** (Moroni 7:31-38)
Lord has sent his angel to the people to cry repentance. **Alma 7:6** (Alma 9:25)
Everlasting Gospel comes from the angels. **T&C 86:24** (D&C 88:103)

Righteous Gentiles offered covenant in last days **3 Nephi 10:1** (3 Nephi 21:22-23)
Time Gentiles offered covenant, Christ in midst. **3 Nephi 10:1** (3 Nephi 21:25)
Lord is the messenger of the covenant. **Malachi 1:6** (Malachi 3:1)
Everlasting covenant given unto the people. **Isaiah 20:1** (Isaiah 55:3-4)
God has given David for a witness unto the people. **Isaiah 20:1** (Isaiah 55:3)
The new name of David given to Denver Snuffer. **T&C 162**
Prayer for Covenant through Denver Snuffer. **T&C 156**
Answer and Covenant through Denver Snuffer. **T&C 157**
Covenant of peace offered by servant David. **Ezek. 17:9-11** (Ezek. 34:22-27)
Blessings or cursing Israel? Repent-obey covenant. **Lev. 13:8-16** (Lev. 26:1-46)
Come-hear everlasting covenant, sure mercies David. **Isaiah 20:1** (Isaiah 55:3)
Incline your ear, Lord will make covenant with you. **Isaiah 20:1** (Isaiah 55:3)
One mighty and strong to set the House of God in order. **T&C 83:4** (D&C 85:7)
Those who will not believe what man declares. **3 Nephi 9:12** (3 Nephi 21:9)
Don't condemn things God, because of man. **Mor. 8:3-4** (Mor. 8:12-17)
Servant marred, but life of servant in God's hand. **3 Nephi 9:12** (3 Nephi 21:10)
Covenant of His peace not removed. **3 Nephi 10:2** (3 Nephi 22:10)
Need plates to preserve language of fathers. **1 Nephi 1:12** (1 Nephi 3:19)
Old things are done away, all things new. **3 Nephi 5:31** (3 Nephi 12: 47)
All invited heaven, to sit down Holy Fathers. **Helaman 2:7** (Helaman 3:27-30)
Seeking for the blessings of the Fathers. **Abraham 1:1** (Abraham 1:2-3)
Hearts fathers to children, children to fathers. **Malachi 1:11-12** (Malachi 4:4-6)
Elijah keys seal hearts fathers to children. **JS History 3:4** (JS History 1:38-39)
Fathers and children must be welded together. **T&C 151:14** (D&C 128:18)
Promises to fathers, in the hearts of children. **JS History 3:4** (D&C 2:1-3)
Covenants must be sealed by HSP. **Glossary Holy Spirit Promise** (D&C 132:7)
Watchmen cry let us go up to Zion. **Jeremiah 12:5-6** (Jeremiah 31:6-14)
Watchmen finally see eye to eye. **Isaiah 18:8** (Isaiah 52:8)
They will ask way to Zion-to make perpetual covenant. **Jer. 18:2** (Jer. 50:5)
Come let us join ourselves to Lord in perpetual covenant. **Jer. 18:2** (Jer. 50:5)
Because of covenant made, become children of Christ. **Mosiah 3:2** (Mosiah 5:7)
Gather together those make covenant by sacrifice. **Psalms 50:1** (Psalms 50:5)
Those willing to observe covenants are accepted. **T&C 96:3** (D&C 97:8)
Disbelieving cut off from covenant people. **3 Nephi 9:12** (3 Nephi 21:11)
Covenant people blessed-safe in wilderness. **Ezekiel 17:9-11** (Ezekiel 34:22-31)
Dispensation of the fullness of times. **T&C 151:14 (**D&C 128:18)
Restitution of all things. **Acts 2:3** (Acts 3:21)
Redeemer will keep His word and come to Zion. **Isaiah 21:2** (Isaiah 59:20-21)
Dispensation fullness times. Glory-keys since Adam. **T&C 151:14** (D&C 128:18)
New Heaven/New Earth established for the pure. **Ether 6:1-3** (Ether 13:1-12)

ZION IN AMERICA

Seek to establish the cause of Zion. **JSH 1:3-5.** (D&C 6:6)
Flee Babylon and declare work of the Lord in Zion. **Jer.18:10-11.** (Jer. 51:6-10)
Go ye out from Babylon. Be clean. **T&C 58:1-2** (D&C 133:5-7)
Zion is the pure in heart. **T&C 96:7** (D&C 97:21)
ZION: one heart, one mind. No poor among them **Genesis 4:14** (Moses 7:18)
City of Enoch taken before flood. **Gen. 4:14-15, 22** (Moses 7:18-23, 62-64)
Enoch and his people walked with God **Moses 4:23** (Moses 7:69)
Enoch walked with God; and God took him. **Moses 4:23** (Genesis 5:24)
The Lord has taken them of Zion unto Himself. **T&C 22:1** (D&C 38:4)
Enoch's Zion is FLED. **Genesis 4:23** (Moses 7:69)
ZION as a city of holiness taken to heaven. **Genesis 4:14-15** (Moses 7:18-23)
The Lord shall bring Zion back again. **Isaiah 52:8** (Isaiah 52:8)
New Jerusalem will come back out heaven. **Rev. 1:18** (Rev. 3:11)
Posterity looks upward, Zion looks downward. **Gen. 5:22.** (JST Gen. 9:21-23)
Kingdom of Zion is kingdom of our God. **T&C 107:7** (D&C 105:32)
Land of Zion and Jerusalem turned to own place. **T&C 58:3.** (D&C 133:23-24)
Two places. From Zion law, Jerusalem the word. **Isaiah 1:5** (Isaiah 2:2-3)
Two places.Lord speaks from Zion, Jerusalem. **D&C 58:3** (D&C 133:21-22)
Two places. Those left in Zion, those remain Jerusalem. **Isa. 1:12** (Isa. 4:2-4)
Two places. Zion is wilderness. Jerusalem desolation. **Isa. 24:5** (Isa. 64:10)
Jerusalem called city of Zion-captured by David.**1 Chron. 6:19.** (1 Chron. 11:5)
New Jerusalem built upon land of America. **Ether 6:2** (Ether 13:5-6)
New Jerusalem will be in this land. **3 Nephi 9:8** (3 Nephi 20:22)
New Jerusalem built on this land unto seed Joseph. **Ether 6:1-3** (Ether 13:1-12)
Remnant of Joseph build a Holy City on this land. **Ether 6:3** (Ether 13:8-10)
Lost ten tribes return from North. **Jeremiah 2:3** (Jeremiah 3:18)
Out of Zion shall go forth the law. **Isaiah 1:5** (Isaiah 2:3)
When city prepared, gather in one to be His people **T&C 26:2** (D&C 42:9)
Zion invitation to mountains. To walk in light Lord. **Isaiah 1:5-6** (Isaiah 2:2-5)
Lord performs His work upon Mount Zion. **2 Nephi 9:17** (2 Nephi 20:12)
Zion flourish in hills, rejoice at place in mountains. **T&C 26:6** (D&C 42:24-25)
Lord's house established in tops mountains. **Isaiah 1:5** (Isaiah 2:2)
Lord will come to His temple, bring judgement. **T&C 58:1** (D&C 133:2-3)
How blessed they seek Zion. Beautiful on mount. **1 Nephi 3:23** (1 Nephi13: 37)
Land of inheritance for your children. Jesus King. **T&C 22:6** (D&C 38:20)
New Jerusalem: a land to flee for peace-safety. **T&C 31:13-15** (D&C 45:62-71)
Ye are come mount Sion, city living God. **Hebrews 1:56** (Hebrews 12:22-24)
Stand Mount Zion! Sing Songs of Joy. **T&C 58:6** (D&C 133:55-56)
Lamb stand upon mount Sion, with 144,000. **Revelation 5:1** (Revelation 14:1)
Lamb will stand on Mount Zion with 144,000. **T&C 58:3** (D&C 133:18-23)
Praise! For the Lord has brought again Zion. **T&C 82:27-28** (D&C 84:98-102)

Lord shall appear in glory and build up Zion. **Psalms 102:2** (Psalms 102:16)
Cry and shout inhabitant Zion: great Holy One of Israel. **Isa. 5:6**. (Isa. 12:6)
God Reigns in Zion. **Mosiah 7:17** (Mosiah 12:21)
New Heaven and New Earth. The New Jerusalem. **Ether 6:1-3** (Ether 13:1-12)

RESTORATION OF ALL THINGS
I will bring forth a marvelous work and a wonder. **Isaiah 9:5** (Isaiah 29:13-14)
A marvelous work and a wonder is about to come forth. **JSH 11:2** (D&C 4:1-2)
Gospel of the kingdom preached all the world. **Matthew 11:7** (Matthew 24:14)
Prophecy occurring after the death of Jesus. **Acts 11:2** (Acts 19:6)
According to proportion of faith, let us prophecy. **Romans 1:60** (Romans 12:6)
Prophecy helps those that will believe. **1 Cor. 1:57** (1 Cor. 14:22)
The times of the restitution of all things. **Acts 2:3** (Acts 3:19-24)
Everlasting gospel preached unto those on earth. **Revelation 5:2** (Rev. 14:6-7)
Lord will reestablish Ephraim in last days. **Jeremiah 12:5-10** (Jeremiah 31)
Lord create new covenant with Judah. **Jeremiah 5-10** (Jeremiah 31)
I will make an everlasting covenant with you. **Isaiah 20:1** (Isaiah 55:3-5)
I will make an everlasting covenant in the last days. **Isaiah 23** (Isaiah 61:8)

ETERNAL PROGRESSION
There are many Gods, many Lords. **1 Corinthians 1:32** (1 Corinthians 8:5-6)
In my Father's house are many mansions. **John 9:6** (John 14:2)
Today thou shalt be with me in paradise. **Luke 13:22** (Luke 23:43)
Christ preached to the spirits in prison. **1 Peter 1:14** (1 Peter 3:18-20)
Ye are god's; and all are children Most High. **Psalms 82:2** (Psalms 82:6)
Is it not written in you law, I said ye are gods? **John 6:30** (John 10:34-36)
The kingdom of God is within you. **Luke 10:2** (Luke 17:20-21)
Cry out, Abba Father! Receive spirit adoption. **Romans 1:34** (Romans 8:15-17)
We are children God - joint heirs with Christ. **Romans 1:34** (Romans 8:14-18)
Jesus Christ: not robbery to be equal God. **Philippians 1:7** (Philippians 2:5-6)
God's work and glory is eternal life of man. **Genesis 1:7** (Moses 1:39)
Be ye therefore perfect as your father in Heaven. **Matthew 3:26** (Matthew 5:48)
Man is become as one of us, to know good - evil. **Genesis 2:19** (Genesis 3:22)
As many obtain authority gain right to ascend **TSJ 1:4**
If you want to ascend to Heavenly Council, you must heed messengers. **TSJ 2:3**
Whoever drinks from living water…shall live from eternity to eternity. **TSJ 4:3**
Anyone who helps me with harvesting souls will save their own. **TSJ 4:8**
Son of Man comes to save the lost. **Luke 10:7** (Luke 18:10)
We are engraved upon His Hands. **1 Nephi 6:8** (1 Nephi 21:16)
Those blinded by falseness, can see or remain blind. **TSJ 7:8**
Those who believe and follow His Son will escape limitations of sin. **TSJ 2:4**
Disciple not above Master, those perfect are as Master. **Luke 5:5** (Luke 6:40)

162

Advance to be like Him. **TSJ 1:12**
Knowledge to become like Him. **TSJ 1:3**
Teaching every man to be perfect in Christ. **1 Col. 1:5** (1 Col. 1:28)
He that overcomes shall inherit all things. **Revelation 8:6** (Revelations 20:7-8)
Followers will also finish the path…at the place my Father dwells. **TSJ 10:10**
Be steadfast, Christ may seal you His. **Mosiah 3:3** (Mosiah 5:15)
Eternal purposes of the Lord roll on. **Mormon 4:3** (Mormon 8:22)
Lord brings about his eternal purposes. **2 Nephi 1:8** (2 Nephi 2:15)
Lord's purposes fail not. **T&C 69:1** (D&C 76:3)
For ever. **T&C Glossary: For Ever, Eternity, Eternal Life.**
Exaltation. **T&C Glossary: Exaltation, Eternity, Eternal Life.**

NOTES:

MINISTRY AMONG THE JEWS

The terms "Jew" and "Gentile" have diverse applications and multiple levels of meaning. Complexities include numerous historical, cultural, and genealogical factors that influence interpretation. Scripture in this section may apply to Orthodox Jews, "Messianic Jews," Lamanites, the lost ten tribes, and/or the entire House of Israel.

LAW OF GOD
God hath given a law to all things. **T&C 86:6** (D&C 88:42–43)
Light of Christ is the law all things are governed. **T&C 86:1** (D&C 88:7–13)
All laws are spiritual. **T&C 9:9** (D&C 29:34)
Law is schoolmaster to bring us unto Christ. **Gal. 1:10-11** (Gal. 3:19–24)
The law of the Lord is perfect, converting the soul. **Psalms 19:2** (Psalms 19:7)
God gave commandments to Adam. **Genesis 2:9,13** (Genesis 1:28, 2:16–17)
God gave laws to Noah. **Genesis 5:21** (Genesis 9:1)
Mary's purification fulfilled according to law of Moses. **Luke 2:4** (Luke 2:22)
Law of the Lord says every male holy to the Lord. **Luke 2:4** (Luke 2:23)
Where there is no law, there is no punishment. **2 Nephi 6:7** (2 Nephi 9:25)
There is a law given. **Alma 19:15** (Alma 42:17–22)
Men will be judged according to law. **Alma 19:15** (Alma 42:23)
Children of Israel given strict law performances. **Mosiah 8:1** (Mosiah 13:29-30)
Disobedience = law carnal commandments. **T&C 82:14** (D&C 84:23–27)
We keep law of Moses-look forward to Christ. **2 Nephi 11:8-9** (2 Ne. 25:24–30)
Salvation not by law of Moses alone. **Mosiah 7:17-8:2** (Mosiah 12:27–13:32)
In me is the law of Moses fulfilled. **3 Nephi 4:1-2** (3 Ne. 9:17)
Law given unto Moses hath an end in me. **3 Nephi 7:1** (3 Ne. 15:1–10)
The Lord is our lawgiver. **Isaiah 11:5** (Isaiah 33:22)
There is one lawgiver. **Jacob 1:17** (James 4:12)
Jesus Christ is the law. **3 Nephi 7:3** (3 Nephi 15:9)

PROPHECY

Temple to be destroyed. Not one stone upon another. **Matt 11:1** (Matt. 24:1-2)

Jews will crucify their God. **2 Nephi 7:1** (2 Nephi 10:3)

Seek diligently to turn hearts Jews unto prophets. **T&C 98:3** (D&C 98:16-17)

Lord will keep covenant to House of Israel. **3 Nephi 13:7-8** (3 Nephi 29:1-9)

Gentiles reject truth, gospel to House of Israel. **3 Nephi 7:5** (3 Nephi 16:10)

Moroni's Plea: O Jerusalem, Awake and Arise. **Mor. 10:6** (Mor. 10: 31-32)

Lord set his hand second time. No other Savior. **2 Ne. 11:6** (2 Ne. 25:17-18)

Turn hearts Jews unto prophets, prophets unto Jews. **T&C 98:3** (D&C 98:17)

Jews begin to believe Jesus Christ is Messiah. **2 Nephi 12:12** (2 Nephi 30:7)

Tribe of Judah shall be sanctified. **T&C 58:3** (D&C 133:34-35)

Jews restored through the Book of Mormon. **Mormon 2:6** (Mormon 5:13-14)

Books convince Jew and Gentile of truth. **1 Nephi 3:24** (1 Nephi 13:38-39)

Jews and Gentiles granted repentance unto life. **Acts 6:9** (Acts 11:18)

Jews restored in the latter days. **1 Nephi 4:3-4** (1 Nephi 15:18-20)

Prayer children of Judah may return to their lands. **T&C 123:18** (D&C 109:64)

When believe in Christ, restored lands inheritance. **2 Nephi 7:2** (2 Nephi 10:7)

Remnant scattered and gathered. **1 Nephi 7:2-3** (1 Nephi 22:4-12)

He that scattered Israel will gather them. **Jeremiah 12:5-6** (Jeremiah 31:7-12)

Day comes Jews believe and are gathered. **2 Nephi 7:2** (2 Nephi 10:7-8)

Seed of Jacob gathered four quarters of earth. **3 Nephi 2:18** (3 Nephi 5:21-26)

Those scattered, gathered to fulfill covenant. **Ether 6:3** (Ether 13:11)

Scattered remnant power to bring Zion. **T&C 129:4-5** (D&C 113: 7-10)

Remnant of Jacob shall return to God. **2 Nephi 9:18** (2 Nephi 20:20-22)

Prophets prophecy in Jerusalem. **Revelation 3:15-18** (Rev. 11:3-14)

Prophets killed, 3 1/2 days ascend into heaven. **Rev. 3:15-17** (Rev. 11:7-12)

Jews surviving in Jerusalem shall be called holy. **Isaiah 1:2** (Isaiah 4:3)

Jews alive Second Coming will know Christ. **Zech. 1:34-35** (Zech. 12:8-11)

Jews shall ask, what are these wounds? **Zechariah 1:36** (Zechariah 13:6)

Jews weep because they persecuted their king. **T&C 31:11** (D&C 45:51-53)

Inhabitants of Jerusalem washed in the blood of Lamb. **Ether 6:3** (Ether 13:11)

Israel comforted in Jerusalem. **Isaiah 25:2** (Isaiah 66:13)

Remnant called unto Sion. **Romans 1:43-45** (Romans 9:26-33)

Old Jerusalem, New Jerusalem, seed of Joseph. **Ether 6:1-3** (Ether 13:1-12)

Land of Zion and Jerusalem turned to own place. **T&C 58:3** (D&C 133:23-24)

OLD JERUSALEM
Jesus is born as King of the Jews. **Matthew 1:6** (Matthew 2:2)
Lord hot against Israel for transgressing covenant. **Judges 1:6** (Judges 2:20)
Without Christ we are strangers from covenants. **Eph. 1:6** (Eph. 2:12)
No other nation would crucify their God. **2 Nephi 7:1** (2 Nephi 10:3-6)
Jews hated for despising Holy One of Israel. **1 Nephi 5:37** (1 Nephi 19:13-14).
Jerusalem trodden, until time of Gentiles fulfilled. **Luke 12:16** (Luke 21:22-24).
Lord's vineyard becomes scattered and desolate. **Isaiah 1:13** (Isaiah 5:1-7)
Lord's vineyard, Israel scattered and desolate. **Isaiah 1:13** (Isaiah 5:1-7)
Blindness to Israel, until fullness Gentiles comes. **Rom. 1:56** (Rom. 11:25)
Remnant scattered among nations, but gathered. **T&C 31:4-:4** (D&C 45:17-25)
Lord's vineyard, House of Israel is dried up waste. **Isa. 1:13-15** (Isa. 5:1-13)
Jerusalem judgements, then remnant comes. **Ezekiel 5:11** (Ezekiel 14:21-23)
Jews who will not repent will be cut off. **2 Nephi 12:11** (2 Nephi 30:2)
Remnant of House of Israel shall be saved. **Romans 1:43-44** (Romans 9:26-27)
Jerusalem to be redeemed. **Jeremiah 13:7** (Jeremiah 33:10-11)
Prayer children of Judah may return their lands. **D&C 123:18** (D&C 109:64)
Jews restored in the latter days. **1 Nephi 4:3-4** (1 Nephi 15:18-20)
Time of the gathering. **Luke 12:16** (Luke 21:24)
When believe Christ, restored lands inheritance. **2 Nephi 7:2** (2 Nephi 10:7-8)
Lord will cause Jews in captivity to return. **Jeremiah 13:5** (32:36-44)
Scattered Jews to return to Jerusalem. **2 Nephi 11:4** (2 Nephi 25:9-10)
Dispersed of Judah gathered. **Isaiah 5:5** (Isaiah 11:12)
Judah shall inherit portion in Holy Land. **Zechariah 1:7** (Zechariah 2:12)
Ten tribes gathered. **3 Nephi 10:1** (3 Nephi 21:24-29)
Remnant scattered and gathered. **1 Nephi 7:2-3** (1 Nephi 22:4-12)
Seed of Jacob gathered four quarters of earth. **3 Nephi 2:18** (3 Nephi 5:21-26)
Remnant returns to Lord, receives revelation. **T&C 129:5** (D&C 113:10)
Remnant called unto Sion. **Romans 1:43-45** (Romans 9: 26-33)
Those scattered, gathered to fulfill covenant. **Ether 6:3** (Ether 13:11)
Scattered, gather to fulfill covenant made Abraham. **Ether 6:3** (Ether 13:11)
Jerusalem built up again unto the Lord. **Ether 6:2** (Ether 13:5)
Scattered remnant power to bring Zion. **D&C 129:4-5** (D&C 113: 7-10)
Remnant of Jacob shall return to God. **2 Nephi 9:18** (2 Nephi 20:20-22)
All nations gather against Jerusalem to battle. **Zech. 1:38-39** (Zech. 14:1-9)
When Jerusalem compassed armies, desolation is nigh. **Luke 8:22** (Luke 21:20)
Prophets prophecy in Jerusalem. **Revelation 3:15-18** (Revelations 11:3-14)
Prophets killed, 3 1/2 days ascend into heaven. **Rev. 3:15-17** (Rev. 11:7-12)
Jews surviving in Jerusalem shall be called holy. **Isaiah 1:12** (Isaiah 4:3)
Jacob not ashamed. Those erred understand. **2 Nephi 11:21** (2 Nephi 27:33-35)
When Son of man comes, redemption is nigh. **Luke 12:17** (Luke 21:27-28)
Inhabitants of Jerusalem washed in the blood of Lamb. **Ether 6:3** (Ether 13:11)

Jews alive Second Coming will know Christ. **Zech. 1:34-35** (Zech. 12:8-11)
Jews shall ask, what are these wounds? **Zechariah 1:36** (Zechariah 13:6)
Jews weep because they persecuted their king. **D&C 31:11** (D&C 45:51-53)
Israel comforted in Jerusalem. **Isaiah 25:2** (Isaiah 66:13)
Break forth in joy, Lord hath redeemed Jerusalem. **Isaiah 18:8** (Isaiah 52:9-10)
Sing and rejoice! O daughter of Jerusalem. **Zeph. 1:12** (Zeph. 3:14-20)

NEW JERUSALEM
Seek to establish the cause of **JSH 13:6**(D&C 6:6)
Flee Babylon, declare work of Lord in Zion. **Jer. 18:10-11** (Jeremiah 51:6-10)
Go ye out from Babylon. Be clean. **T&C 58:1-2** (D&C 133:5-7)
Enoch and his people walked with God. **Genesis 4:23** (Moses 7:69)
ZION as a city of holiness taken up to heaven. **Gen. 4:14-15** (Moses 7:18-23)
Enoch's Zion is FLED. **Genesis 4:23** (Moses 7:69)
New Jerusalem will come back out heaven. **Rev. 1:18** (Rev. 3:12)
Posterity looks upward, Zion looks downward. **Gen. 5:22** (JST Gen. 9:21-23)
Kingdom of Zion is kingdom of our God. **T&C 107:7** (D&C 105:32)
New Jerusalem built upon land of America. **Ether 6:2** (Ether 13:5-6)
New Jerusalem will be in this land. **3 Nephi 9:8** (3 Nephi 20:22)
New Jerusalem built on this land unto seed Joseph. **Ether 6:2-3** (Ether 13:1-12)
Remnant of Joseph build a Holy City on this land. **Ether 6:3** (Ether 13:8-10)
Lost ten tribes return from North. **Jeremiah 2:3** (Jeremiah 3:18)
Zion and Jerusalem turned back own place. **T&C 58:3** (D&C 133:23-24)
Two places. From Zion law, Jerusalem the word. **Isaiah 1:5** (Isaiah 2:2-3)
Two places. Lords voice from Zion, Jerusalem. **T&C 58:3** (D&C 133:21-22)
Two places. Those in Zion, those remain Jerusalem. **Isaiah 1:12** (Isaiah 4:2-4)
Two places. Zion is wilderness. Jerusalem desolation. **Isa. 24:5** (Isa. 64:10)
Zion invitation to mountains. To walk in light Lord. **Isaiah 1:5-6** (Isaiah 2:2-5)
Purchase land for Zion. **T&C 50:7** (D&C 63:25-27)
Zion in the Lords hand. Better to purchase land. **T&C 50:7** (D&C 63:25-30)
No curse upon the land when Lord comes. **T&C 22:6** (D&C 38:18)
Prepare all things and do not gather in haste. **T&C 101:15** (D&C 101:68-69)
Do not gather in haste, brings confusion-pestilence. **T&C 50:6** (D&C 63:24)
When city prepared, gather in one to be His people. **T&C 26:2** (D&C 42:9)
Lord performs His work upon Mount Zion. **2 Nephi 9:17** (2 Nephi 20:12)
Powers of heaven in midst this people. Zion. **3 Nephi 9:8** (3 Nephi 20: 22)
Zion flourish in hills, rejoice at place in mountains. **T&C 35:8** (D&C 49:25)
Zion gather in Holy places, kings crowned. **T&C 101:3** (D&C 101:11-22)
Lord's house established in tops mountains. **Isaiah 1:5** (Isaiah 2:2)
Lord will come to His temple, bring judgement. **T&C 58:1** (D&C 133:2-3)
How blessed they seek Zion. Beautiful on mount. **1 Nephi 3:23** (1 Nephi13: 37)
New Jerusalem: land to flee for peace-safety. **T&C 31:13-15** (D&C 45:62-71)

Stand Mount Zion! Sing Songs of Joy. **T&C 58:6** (D&C 133:55-56)
Zion is with me. **Genesis 4:19** (Moses 7:47)
Lamb will stand on Mount Zion with 144,000. **T&C 58:3** (D&C 133:18-23)
Praise! For the Lord has brought again Zion. **T&C 82:27** (D&C 84:98-102)
Lord shall appear in glory and build up Zion. **Psalms 102:2** (Psalms 102:16)
God Reigns in Zion. **Mosiah 7:17** (Mosiah 12:21)
New Heaven and New Earth. The New Jerusalem. **Ether 6:1-3** (Ether 13:1-12)

THE STICK OF JOSEPH IN THE HAND OF EPHRAIM

TWO STICKS

The word of the Lord came again unto me, saying, Moreover, you son of man, take one stick and write upon it: For Judah, and for the children of Israel his companions. Then take another stick and write upon it: For Joseph, the stick of Ephraim, and for all the house of Israel his companions. And join them one to another, into one stick, and they shall become one in your hand. And when the children of your people shall speak unto you, saying, Will you not show us what you mean by these? Say unto them, Thus says the Lord God: Behold, I will take the stick of Joseph which is in the hand of Ephraim, and the tribes of Israel his fellows, and will put them with him, even with the stick of Judah, and make them one stick; and they shall be one in my hand. And the sticks on which you write shall be in your hand before their eyes. (RE Ezekiel 19:4)

The Stick of Joseph in the Hand of Ephraim is dedicated to *Mashiach*, the house of Israel, and the Y'hudim-or Jewish people.

In response to this sacred text, (written 2500 years ago to both *Jew and Gentile)*, all within the covenant are invited to assist the Y'hudim and grow in our preparation to receive the ancient gospel.

References in the RE Book of Mormon and The Stick of Joseph in the Hand of Ephraim share the same numbering. They can be accessed in either book. This current summary is introductory and not exhaustive.

FULFILLING PROPHECY

The "two sticks" prophecy. **Ezekiel 19:4**
The two writings to come together. **2 Nephi 2:4**
Joseph's branches to climb over a wall. **Gen. 49:22**
Joseph's branches stretch to the sea. **Ps. 80:2, 12**
A branch of Joseph broken off. **2 Nephi 2:2**
Israel's words to speak from the dust. **Isaiah 29:3-4**
A sealed book prophesied. **Isaiah 29:11-12**
The destroyed to speak out of the ground in a sealed book. **2 Nephi 11:13-14**
Truth to come out of the earth. **Ps. 85:11**
A prince of Zedekiah to be transplanted. **Ezek. 17:12-14, 22-24**
The seed of Zedekiah slain, except Muloch. **Hel. 3:9**
The scattered branches to be grafted in again. **1 Nephi 3:4**
Other tribes to honor Joseph. **Gen. 37:5-9**

THE GATHERING OF ISRAEL

Scattered Israel to be gathered. **3 Nephi 9:7-8**
Scattered Israel to be gathered. **3 Nephi 10:1**
Scattered Israel to be gathered. **Deut. 30:3-5**
Scattered Israel to be gathered. **Isa. 11:12**
Scattered Israel to be gathered. **Jer. 23:3-8**
Scattered Israel to be gathered. **Ezek. 37:21-23**
Scattered Israel to be gathered. **Zech. 2:6-12**
The sign the gathering has begun. **3 Nephi 9:11**

NEW COVENANT TO COME

Repentant gentiles to receive the covenant. **2 Nephi 12:11**
Repentant gentiles to receive the covenant. **3 Nephi 10:1**
God to offer Israel a new covenant. **Jer. 31:31-34**
God will deliver his covenant people. **2 Nephi 5:5**
God will remember his covenants. **3 Nephi 7:5**

THE REMNANT OF THE JEWS

"The covenant requires some work to be done among the remnant of the Jews and some work to be done among the Native Americans. That is something that is being attended to but not everything that is going on is necessarily something that ought to be broadcast publicly for everyone and everywhere. We all have our obligations and we all have our responsibilities. Some people have very specific responsibilities that they've accepted and that they're discharging to take care of things involved in the covenant...(Denver Snuffer, The Restoration's Shattered Promises and Great Hope, Q&A Pg. 20)

A PRECIOUS FEW

"Christ's ministry was relatively modest in it's accomplishment in terms of the people He influenced directly...the fact is that precious few people have allowed the message of the Book of Mormon, that was intended to redeem not only latter-day gentiles but to redeem a remnant of the natives that were on this continent, and to ultimately redeem some of the Jews that remain as a remnant and to bring them together in a cause that will make the earth herself rejoice because wickedness has ceased from off her face." (Denver Snuffer, Remembering the New Covenant, pg. 13)

NOTES:

MINISTRY AMONG LATTER DAY SAINTS

"If the gentiles will repent and return unto me,
saith the Father, behold, they shall be numbered
among my people, O house of Israel."
3 Nephi 7:5

God and His Word confirm that *The Church of Jesus Christ of Latter Day Saints* is currently in a state of apostasy. Observing how the LDS institution is violating scripture, while simultaneously fulfilling prophecy, is useful only if it results in personal repentance. The following summary is provided to encourage all who trust in the Lord to choose truth over tradition.

It is written, *"...If they will repent and hearken unto my words, and harden not their hearts, I will establish my church among them, and they shall come in unto the covenant and be numbered among this the remnant of Jacob, unto whom I have given this land for their inheritance; And they shall assist my people, the remnant of Jacob, and also as many of the house of Israel as shall come, that they may build a city, which shall be called the New Jerusalem."* (3 Nephi 10:1).

Today only a few *"humble followers of Christ"* (2 Nephi 12:2) seek a repentance sufficient to "assist" the Remnant in establishing Zion. (3 Nephi 9:11).

Despite the "awful situation" we find ourselves in, (Ether 3:18), there is hope for those willing to cast off religious vanity and unbelief. Denver Snuffer explains, *"Ephraim the envious, drunkard, headstrong, idolater, and rebellious will finally repent in the last days and allow the Lord to rule over him. It will be as if Ephraim were never cast off. Ephraim will then provide those returning "crowns of glory," or in other words the intelligence, which is light and truth, or the knowledge of God. At that point no one will tell another, "Know ye the Lord," because all will know Him, from the least to the greatest. Some few Gentiles will be included."* [6]

The following summary encourages Latter Day Saints to trust in the Lord and receive greater light. Prioritizing eternal truth over institutional tradition is the pattern that allows a broken valiant few to contribute to the establishment of Zion.

RESTORATION

This brief summary relates to a few of the restoration elements in scripture. Much of the historical process and teaching is documented within church history records.

1805: Joseph Smith is born. **JSH 1:2** (JS History 1:3)
1820: First vision with Father and Son. **JSH 2:4** (JS History 1:16-17)
1820: Joseph told religious creeds abomination. **JSH 2:5** (JSH 1:18-19)
1823: Joseph visited by angel and instructed. **JSH 3:1-12** (JSH 1:29-47)
1827: Joseph obtains the plates. **JSH 6:1** (JS History 1:59)
1828: Book of Lehi and 116 pages are lost. **JSH 9, 10** (D&C 3:5-15)
1829: Aaronic priesthood given to Joseph-Oliver. **JSH 14:1** (D&C 13:1)
1829: 3 and 8 Witnesses shown gold plates. **JSH 15:16-22** (D&C Intro)
1829: Oliver Cowdery scribe for Joseph. **JSH 13:24-25** (D&C 9:1, 4)
1830: Book of Mormon printed. **BOM Intro** (BOM Intro)
1830: Church of Christ is established. **T&C 54:5** (D&C 1:30)
1831: Joseph to translate New Testament. **T&C 31:13** (D&C 45:60-61)
1831: Book of Commandments coming. **T&C 54:1-2** (D&C 1, Preface)
1833: Commanded build house for translation. **T&C 97:3** (D&C 94:10)
1834: Print the fullness of scriptures. **T&C 105:13** (D&C 104:58)
1835: Translation of Book of Abraham. **T&C 145** (Book of Abraham)
1835: Lecture first of Lectures on Faith. **T&C 110** (Lecture First)
1835: Doctrine and Covenants published. **T&C 54** (D&C 1, Preface)
1842: Facsimiles Book of Abraham published. **T&C 145:1-7** (Abr. 1-5)
1842: Wentworth letter, articles of faith. **T&C 146:21-33** (AoF: 1-13)
1844: Joseph and Hyrum martyred for Christ. **Heb. 1:42** (Heb. 11:13)

APOSTASY AFTER JOSEPH SMITH

God cannot look upon sin any degree of allowance. **T&C 54:5** (D&C 1:31)
Joseph Smith identifies LDS as Gentile Church. **T&C 123:18** (D&C 109:60)
Christ prophesies Gentiles will lose fullness. **3 Nephi 7:5** (3 Nephi 16:10-11)
Christ confirms church lost fullness of priesthood. **T&C 141:10** (D&C 124:28)
Gentiles perceive not the light, reject it. **T&C 31:6-7** (D&C 45:28-30)
Wo unto the Gentiles…they will deny me **2 Nephi 12:7** (2 Nephi 28:32)
Why have ye transfigured Word of God? **Mormon 4:5** (Mormon 8:33)
Church comes under condemnation. **T&C 82:20** (D&C 84:54-56)
Condemnation is to receive not the light. **T&C 93:10** (D&C 93: 32)
Gentiles rejecting the fullness as remnant gathered **T&C 31:6** (D&C 45:26-29)
Moroni sees our day and mourns. **Mormon 4:5** (Mormon 8:35-41)
Temple defiled by changing ordinances. **Isaiah 7:1** (Isaiah 24:5)
Unrighteous dominion = Amen to priesthood. **T&C 139:5** (D&C 121:36-37)
Priesthood keys and authority. **T&C Glossary Keys**

Tares persecute wheat-drive church into wilderness. **T&C 84:1-2** (D&C 86:1-7)
Lord's church overthrown by transgression. **Mosiah 11:20** (Mosiah 27:13)
Church of God polluted. **Mormon 4:5** (Mormon 8:38)
Tares persecute wheat-drive church into wilderness. **T&C 84:1-2** (D&C 86:1-7)
House of God still needs to be set in order. **T&C 83:4** (D&C 85:7)
Upon Lord's house shall troubles begin. **D&C 124:6** (D&C 112:25)
Gentile stewards of Gospel to be destroyed. **Matt. 10:16** (JST Matt. 21:56)
Destroyed unknowingly. **T&C Glossary: Destroy**

RELIGIOUS LEADERS

Jesus Christ is the only keeper of the gate. **2 Nephi 6:11** (2 Nephi 9:41)
Trust in Jesus Christ, not the arm of flesh. **2 Nephi 3:8** (2 Nephi 4:34)
Trust in Lord; cursed is he that trusts in man. **Jer. 6:12** (Jer. 17:5-7)
Looking past the mark of Christ. **Jacob 3:5** (Jacob 4:14)
Know a true or false prophet by his fruits. **Matt. 3:46** (Matt. 7:15-16)
Fruit of Spirit: love, joy, peace, faith. **Galatians 1:22** (Galatians 5:22-26)
Samuel Lamanite warns of popular prophets. **Hel. 5:7** (Hel. 13:26-27)
Prophets can lie. **Ezekiel 5:3-4** (Ezekiel 13:7-8)
Do not trust a prophet more than God. **1 Kings 3:11-20** (1 Kings 13:1-32)
A Prophet can be deceived. **Ezekiel 5:9** (Ezekiel 14:9)
Shepherds feed themselves-not the flock. **Ezekiel 17:5** (Ezekiel 34:2-3)
Lost shepherds and wandering sheep. **Ezekiel 17:5-7** (Ezekiel 34:6-13)
Do not feed flock for filthy lucre. **1 Peter 1:19** (1 Peter 5:2)
Priestcraft: get gain and praise of world. **3 Nephi 11:17** (2 Nephi 26:29)
Priestcraft led to the crucifixion of Jesus. **2 Nephi 7:1** (2 Nephi 10:5)
The true shepherd does not profit from sheep. **TSJ 7:11**
Enforced priestcraft leads to destruction. **Alma 1:2** (Alma 1:12)
Spiritual wickedness high places. **Ephesians 1:25** (Ephesians 6:12)
Prophets prophecy falsely and people love it. **Jer. 3:7** (Jer. 5:30-31)
Cursed for hearkening to precepts of men. **2 Nephi 12:6** (2 Nephi 28:31
Traditions of fathers limit light-truth received. **T&C 93:11** (D&C 93:39)
Why have ye transfigured the holy word of God? **Mor. 4:5** (Mor. 8:33)
False prophets deceive many. **Matt. 11:3,6** (Matt. 24:11-12, 23-24)
Beware of false prophets in sheep's clothing. **Matt. 3:46** (Matt. 7:15)
Apostles fall asleep, tares choke the wheat. **T&C 84:1** (D&C 86:2-3)
Satan sows tares, drive church into wilderness. **T&C 84:1** (D&C 86:3)
Leaders cause people to err and be destroyed. **Isaiah 4:3** (Isaiah 9:16)
Because you claim, "We see", therefore your sins remain. **TSJ 7:8**
False prophets do not profit people. **Jeremiah 8:19** (Jeremiah 23:32)
Lord against them that prophecy false dreams. **Jer. 8:19** (Jer. 23:32)
False prophets follow own spirit. **Ezekiel 5:3** (Ezekiel 13:1-3)
Those preach from own understanding, gratify their pride. **TSJ 6:5**

If message unpopular, say false prophet. **Hel. 5:7** (Hel. 13:26-27)
If message popular, say a prophet. **Hel. 5:7** (Hel. 13:26-27)
Rebellious desire smooth language-deceit. **Isa. 9:7, 9** (Isa. 30:1, 8-11)
Famine in the land of hearing word of Lord. **Amos 1:27** (Amos 8:11)
False prophecy and the people love it. **Jeremiah 3:7** (Jeremiah 5:30-31)
Prophets have erred. **Isaiah 8:2** (Isaiah 28:7-8)
Teachings are tables full of vomit. **Isaiah 8:2-3** (Isaiah 28:8-9)
Unrighteous dominion of leaders. **T&C 139:5-7** (D&C 121: 34-44)
Priests cast poor out of synagogue. **Alma 16:23** (Alma 32:5)
Lord cannot look upon sin with any allowance. **T&C 54:5** (D&C 1:31)
Those who labor for money shall perish. **2 Nephi 11:17** (2 Nephi 26:31)
Gentiles who worship men destroyed. **Matt. 10:15-16** (JST Matt. 21:56)
Idolizing deceived prophets = destroyed. **Ezek. 5:9** (Ezek. 14:9-10)
Grievous wolves come in among the flock. **Acts 12:4** (Acts 20:29-31)

RELIGIOUS CULTURE
Two Churches Only. Church Lamb, Church devil. **1 Ne. 3:27** (1 Ne. 14:10)
Traditions of Fathers limit receiving light and truth. **T&C 93:11** (D&C 93:39)
Pattern of idolatry and apostasy. **Judges 1:6** (Judges 2:17-23)
Idols in the heart. Separated from Lord. **Ezekiel 5:8** (Ezekiel 14:2-7)
Cursed for hearkening to precepts of men. **2 Nephi 12:6** (2 Nephi 28:31)
Samuel Principle. People rejecting God. **1 Samuel 4:2** (1 Samuel 8:7-9)
All must follow God over a prophet. **1 Kings 3:11-20** (1 Kings 13:1-34)
Laman incorrectly knows Jerusalem righteous. **1 Ne. 5:17** (1 Ne. 17:21-22)
All is well in Zion. **2 Nephi 12:4** (2 Nephi 28:21)
Signs of religious apostasy. **1 Nephi 7:4** (1 Nephi 22:23)
People wrest scriptures and do not understand them. **JSH 10:18** (D&C 10:63)
Moroni sees our doing and mourns. **Mormon 4:5** (Mormon 8:35-41)
BOM to come forth in due time by way of the Gentile. **BOM Title Page**
LDS identified with the Gentiles. **T&C 123:18** (D&C 109:60)
Warning to Church. **T&C 50:14-15** (D&C 63:60-64)
Church pride. Grind on poor. **2 Nephi 11:15** (2 Nephi 26:20)
Repent or condemned church will be cut off. **T&C 50:14-15** (D&C 63:61-64)
Proud and drunkards of Ephraim. **Isaiah 8:1-4** (Isaiah 28:1-18)
Church can be overthrown if people transgress. **Mosiah 11:20** (Mosiah 27:13)
Temple defiled, ordinances changed. **Isaiah 7:1** (Isaiah 24:5)
Losing fullness of priesthood, temple needed. **T&C 141:10** (D&C 124:28)
Glory of God is intelligence. **T&C 93:11** (D&C 93:36)
Grow line upon line. **2 Nephi 12:6** (2 Nephi 28:30)
To know not mysteries, is to be in chains of hell. **Alma 9:3** (Alma 12:11)
Find mysteries-bring many to knowledge of truth. **JSH 13:8** (D&C 6:11)
Find out mysteries-to convince many of error. **JSH 13:8** (D&C 6:11)

Wo unto him that sayeth he has enough. **2 Nephi 12:6** (2 Nephi 28:27-29)
Receive the light or lose it. **T&C 29:3** (D&C 43:9-10)
The lesser and greater portion of the word. **Alma 9:3** (Alma 12:10)
Some have wrested scriptures-gone far astray. **Alma 19:9** (Alma 41:1)
Church teaching the preparatory gospel. **T&C 82:14** (D&C 84: 26-27)
Gentiles rejecting the fullness. **T&C 31:6-7** (D&C 45:26-29)
Contention, jarrings, envy, strife, pollute inheritances.**T&C 101:2** (D&C 101:6)
Church Pride, Grind on Poor. **2 Nephi 11:15** (2 Nephi 26:20)
Tithing is for the Poor. **Genesis 7:21 (**JST Genesis 14:39)
All is well in Zion, need no more. **2 Nephi 12:5** (2 Nephi 28:24)
False prophets cause people to err. **Jeremiah 8:19** (Jeremiah 23:15-32)
Rebellious desire smooth language and deceits. **Isaiah 9:7, 9** (Isaiah 30:1, 8-11)
Unbelief. **T&C Glossary: Unbelief**
Dwindle in Unbelief. **T&C Glossary: Dwindle in Unbelief.**
Tares persecute wheat-drive church into wilderness. **T&C 84:1** (D&C 86:1-7)
The real Church of Christ **JSH 10:19** (D&C 10:67)
Those who follow the Lord know how to worship. **TSJ 4:5 (John 4:22-24)**
Fullness of the Priesthood Lost. **T&C 141:10** (D&C 124:28)
Need Nauvoo temple done to restore lost fullness. **T&C 141:10** (D&C 124:28)
Church Breaking Up because of pride. **3 Nephi 3:2** (3 Nephi 6:7-14)
Gentiles shall be destroyed. **Matthew 10:16** (JST Matthew 21:56)

PROPHETIC WARNINGS TO LATTER DAY SAINTS
Moroni sees our day and mourns. **Mormon 4:5** (Mormon 8:35-41)
God cannot look upon sin any degree of allowance. **T&C 54:5** (D&C 1:31)
Church comes under condemnation. **T&C 82:20** (D&C 84:54-56)
Condemnation is to receive not the light. **T&C 93:10** (D&C 93:32)
LDS identified with the Gentiles. **T&C 123:18** (D&C 109:60)
Gentiles rejecting the fullness. **T&C 31:6-7** (D&C 45:26-29)
Two Churches Only. Church Lamb, Church devil. **1 Ne. 3:27** (1 Ne. 14:10)
Priestcraft. **T&C Glossary: Priestcraft**
Unbelief. **T&C Glossary: Unbelief, Dwindle in Unbelief**
Fullness of the Priesthood lost. **T&C 141:10** (D&C 124:28)
Warning to church. **T&C 50:14-15** (D&C 63:60-64)
Repent or be condemned - church cut off. **T&C 50:14-15** (D&C 63:61-64)
Church can be overthrown by transgression. **Mosiah 11:26** (Mosiah 27:13)
Last days will be perilous times. **2 Timothy 1:8** (2 Timothy 3:1-7)
Many will not endure sound doctrine. **2 Timothy 1:10** (2 Timothy 4:3-4)
Having a form of Godliness but denying power. **2 Timothy 1:8** (2 Timothy 3:5)
Ever learning, never come knowledge of truth. **2 Timothy 1:8** (2 Timothy 3:7)
Many blinded, know not where to find the truth. **T&C 139:15** (D&C 123:12)
Satan lulls church away into carnal security. **2 Nephi 12:4** (2 Nephi 28:21)

Masses erroneously say "All is well in Zion." **2 Nephi 12:4** (2 Nephi 28:21)
Why have ye transfigured Word of God? **Mormon 4:5** (Mormon 8:33)
Fullness of the Priesthood lost. **T&C 141:10** (D&C 124:28)
Temple defiled by changing ordinances. **Isaiah 7:1** (Isaiah 24:5)
Unrighteous dominion = Amen to priesthood. **T&C 139:5** (D&C 121:36-37)
Priesthood keys and authority. **T&C Glossary Keys**
Tares persecute wheat-drive church into wilderness. **T&C 84:1-2** (D&C 86:1-7)
Lord's church overthrown by transgression. **Mosiah 11:20** (Mosiah 27:13) Holy
Church of God polluted. **Mormon 4:5** (Mormon 8:38)
Proud and drunkards of Ephraim. **Isaiah 8:1-4** (Isaiah 28:1-18)
Church breaking up because of pride. **3 Nephi 3:2** (3 Nephi 6:10-14)
Churches built for gain/popularity, consumed. **1 Nephi 7:5** (1 Nephi 22:23)
Members chose money over Zion. **T&C 107:2** (D&C 105:8)
Famine in the land of hearing word of Lord. **Amos 1:27** (Amos 8:11)
Satan soweth tares, church driven into wilderness. **T&C 84:1** (D&C 86:3)
Falling away before the coming of the Lord. **2 Thess. 1:4** (2 Thess. 2:1-3)
An End of Authority through Denver Snuffer. **T&C 166**
Upon my house it shall begin. **T&C 124:6** (D&C 112:25-26)
Gentiles shall be destroyed. **Matthew 10:15** (JST Mathew 21:56)
Zion can only be built on laws Celestial Kingdom. **T&C 107:1** (D&C 105:6)
Few only that do not lift themselves in pride. **Mormon 4:5** (Mormon 8:36)
Humble overcome false precepts of men. **2 Nephi 12:2** (2 Nephi 28:14)
Few humble followers of Christ in latter-days. **2 Nephi 12:2** (2 Nephi 28:14)

TIMES OF THE GENTILES
Times of the Gentiles. **T&C Glossary**: Times of the Gentiles
Fullness of the Gospel will go to the Gentiles. **3 Nephi 7:4** (3 Nephi 16:7)
Book of Mormon to come forth by way of Gentile. **BOM Title Page**
LDS are identified with Gentiles. **T&C 123:18** (D&C 109:60)
Gentiles invited into House of Israel. **3 Nephi 14:1** (3 Nephi 30:1-2)
Much of my Gospel brought to Gentiles. **1 Nephi 3:23** (1 Nephi 13:34)
Gentiles reject fullness, precepts of men. **T&C 31:6-7** (D&C 45: 26-31)
Lord will set his hand second time. **Jacob 4:1** (Jacob 6:2)
Several called to preach and testify of Christ. **3 Nephi 3:4** (3 Nephi 6:20)
John sees angel preaching gospel in last days. **Rev. 5:2** (Rev. 14:6)
If Gentiles repent-enter covenant, part of Jacob. **3 Ne. 10:1** (3 Ne. 21:22)
Bible-other books convince Gentiles of truth. **1 Ne. 3:24** (1 Ne. 13:38-39)
Repentant Gentiles assist New Jerusalem. **3 Ne. 9:12-10:1** (3 Ne. 21:11-29)
Gentiles are to restore Jews/Lamanites. Mormon 2:6-7 (Mormon 5:13-24)
Repentant Gentiles numbered House of Israel. **3 Ne. 7:5** (3 Ne. 16:13)
A few humble followers of Christ. **2 Nephi 12:2** (2 Nephi 28:14)
Come unto Christ, receive greater things. **Ether 1:18-19** (Ether 4:12-13-15)

New Heaven/New Earth. New Jerusalem. **Ether 6:1-3** (Ether 13:1-12)
Remnant scattered until times Gentiles fulfilled. **T&C 31:5-6** (D&C 45:22-25)
Gentiles reject fullness. Gospel to House Israel. **3 Nephi 7:5** (3 Nephi 16:10-12)
Gospel given to remnant of Lehi's seed. **1 Nephi 4:3** (1 Nephi 15:13-14)
House of Israel. T&C Glossary: House of Israel
Remnant. **T&C Glossary: Remnant**

PRESERVING THE RESTORATION

Christ is only keeper of the gate. **2 Nephi 6:11** (2 Nephi 9:41)
The course of the Lord is one eternal round. **1 Nephi 3:5** (1 Nephi 10:19)
The Lord gives pattern in all things. **T&C 39:4** (D&C 52:14)
Truth is things as they really are, really will be. **Jacob 3:4** (Jacob 4:13)
Truth: things as they are, were, and are to come. **T&C 93:8** (D&C 93:24)
Men are free to choose. **2 Nephi 1:10** (2 Nephi 2:27)
Lords church can be overthrown by transgression. **Mos. 11:26** (Mos. 27:13)
Satan lulls church away into carnal security, **2 Nephi 12:4** (2 Nephi 28:21)
Masses say "All is well in Zion" **2 Nephi 12:4** (2 Nephi 28:21)
Joseph identifies church as a Gentile Church. **T&C 123:18** (D&C 109:60)
Christ prophesies Gentile church loses fulness. **3 Nephi 7:5** (3 Nephi 16:10-11)
Gentiles receive not the fulness, but reject it. **T&C 31:7** (D&C 45:28-30)
Wo unto the Gentiles…they will deny me **2 Nephi 12:7** (2 Nephi 28:32)
House of God needs set in order. **T&C 83:4** (D&C 85:7)
Lord sets hand second time to restore people. **2 Nephi 11:6** (2 Nephi 25:17)
Lord offers hand second time to nourish and prune. **Jacob 4:1** (Jacob 6:2)
Joseph's marvelous work has yet to occur. **JS History 11:2** (D&C 4:1)
The Lord brings forth His strange act. **T&C 101:20** (D&C 101:95)
Strange act to prune vineyard last time. **T&C 94:1** (D&C 95:4)
Dispensation. **T&C Glossary**
Dispensation of the Fullness of Times. **T&C Glossary**
Fullness of the Gospel. **T&C Glossary**
Entering Lord's real church through repentance. **JS History 10:19** (D&C 10:67)
Few only that do not lift themselves in pride. **Mormon 4:5** (Mormon 8:36)
Few humble followers Christ. **2 Nephi 12:2** (2 Nephi 28:14)
Humble overcome false precepts of men. **2 Nephi 12:2** (2 Nephi 28:14)
Scriptures wrested to their own destruction. **2 Peter 1:14** (2 Peter 3:16)
Scriptures given for salvation of elect. **T&C 18:6** (D&C 35:20–21)
Remnant of Israel receives revelation. **T&C 129:5** (D&C 113:9-10)
Lord sends his angels then and now. **Alma 19:3** (Alma 39:19)
Everlasting Gospel comes with the angels. **T&C 86:24** (D&C 88:103)
Several called to preach and testify of Christ. **3 Nephi 3:4** (3 Nephi 6:20)
Blessings or cursing Israel? Repent-obey covenant. **Lev. 13:8-16** (Lev. 26:1-46)
Righteous Gentiles offered covenant in last days **3 Nephi 10:1** (3 Nephi 21:22)

Gentiles offered covenant, Christ in midst. **3 Nephi 10:1** (3 Nephi 21:22-25)
Incline ear to everlasting covenant, mercies David. **Isaiah 20:1** (Isaiah 55:3)
New name of David given unto Denver Snuffer. **T&C 162:1**
God has given David for a witness unto the people. **Isaiah 20:1** (Isaiah 55:3-4)
Covenant of Peace through servant David. **Eze. 17:10-11** (Eze. 34:22-27)
The Pass through Denver Snuffer. **T&C 163:1-4**
Gethsemane through Denver Snuffer. **T&C 161:1-31**
A Sign through Denver Snuffer. **T&C 160:1-5**
An End of Authority through Denver Snuffer. **T&C 166:1-4**
Seven Women through Denver Snuffer. **T&C 167:1**
The Resurrection through Denver Snuffer. **T&C 169:1-4**
His Return through Denver Snuffer. **T&C 164:1**
The Train through Denver Snuffer. **T&C 172:1-5**
Prayer for Covenant through Denver Snuffer. **T&C 156:1-8**
Answer and Covenant through Denver Snuffer **T&C 157:1-66**
Servant marred-but spared in God's hand. **3 Nephi 9:12** (3 Nephi 21:9-10)
Need plates to preserve language of fathers. **1 Nephi 1:12** (1 Nephi 3:19)
Watchmen see eye to eye when Lord brings Zion. **3 Nephi 7:6** (Isaiah 52:8)
Old things are done away, all things new. **3 Nephi 5:31** (3 Nephi 12: 47)
All invited heaven, to sit down Holy Fathers. **Helaman 2:7** (Helaman 3:27-30)
Seeking for the blessings of the Fathers. **Abraham 1:1** (Abraham 1:2-3)
Elijah keys to seal hearts of fathers to children. **TC Ref.** (D&C 27:9-12)
Elijah hearts of fathers to children, children to fathers. **Mal. 1:12** (Mal. 4:4-6)
Fathers and children must be welded together. **T&C 151:14** (D&C 128:18)
Promises made to fathers, in the hearts of children. **JS History 3:4** (D&C 2:1-3)
Dispensation fullness. Glory-keys since Adam. **T&C 151:14** (D&C 128:18)
Priesthood from the Fathers. **Abraham 1:1** (Abraham 1:4)
Those called to bring Zion with priesthood. **T&C 129:4** (D&C 113:7-8)
God will gather in one all things. Fullness of times. **TC Ref.** (D&C 27:13)
Fullness of the Gospel. **T&C Glossary**
Brought to repentance often = driven out of the land. **Alma 16:44** (Alma 35:14)
Upon my house it shall begin. **T&C 124:6** (D&C 112:25)
Gentiles. **T&C Glossary**
Parable that Gentiles would be destroyed. **Matt 10:16** (JST Matt 21:56)
Do not gather in haste, brings confusion-pestilence. **T&C 50:6** (D&C 63:24)
God's message to those who seek Zion at the last day **Isaiah 18:7** (Isaiah 52)
Lord takes one of a city and two of a family to Zion. **Jeremiah 2:3** (Jer. 3:14)
Believing Gentiles numbered among Lamanites. **3 Nephi 10:1** (3 Nephi 21: 22)
The first shall be last and the last first **Jacob 3:25** (Jacob 5:63)
Restitution of all things. **Acts 2:3** (Acts 3:21)
New Heaven. **T&C Glossary**
New Earth. **T&C Glossary**
New Heaven/New Earth. New Jerusalem. **Ether 6:3** (Ether 13:1-12)

Consider that the new covenant does not include the Church of Jesus Christ of Latter Day Saints as the final form of Christ's church. What if the new covenant containing the fullness is the marvelous work and wonder that is still in the future and has not yet happened. (1 Ne 3:26; 1 Ne 14:1-7). As prophesied Joseph Smith accomplished a great work in bringing forth essential revelation, scripture, and prophecy. But the fullness initially offered to the Gentiles was conditional upon their obedience. (D&C 33:7; D&C 93:20). Because the church was placed under condemnation for treating lightly the covenant contained in the Book of Mormon the fullness was withdrawn. (D&C 27:12; D&C 84:57). The saints were also reprimanded for not publishing the Joseph Smith Translation of the Bible (D&C 88:12-14; D&C 104:58-60). The Lord promised to restore "*that which was lost to you*" (which included the fullness of the priesthood) if they would build the Nauvoo Temple. The temple was never fully completed and eventually destroyed. (D&C 49:9; D&C 124:43-49). There is no record that the fullness was ever restored. Joseph and his appointed heir, Hyrum, were martyred before the fullness could be restored. The pattern involving covenant, apostasy, and restoration is how the Lord works with every generation. (D&C 61:1; D&C 35:1). Today, as part of His strange act He once again offers the new covenant. (Jacob 1-2, D&C 101:95).

Gentile Fulfillment

"And in that day shall be heard of wars and rumors of wars, and the whole earth shall be in commotion, and men's hearts shall fail them, and they shall say that Christ delayeth his coming until the end of the earth. And the love of men shall wax cold, and iniquity shall abound. And when the times of the Gentiles is come in, a light shall break forth among them that sit in darkness, and it shall be the fulness of my gospel; But they receive it not; for they perceive not the light, and they turn their hearts from me because of the precepts of men. And in that generation shall the times of the Gentiles be fulfilled."
T&C 31:6

NOTES:

CORRELATION TABLES
OLD TESTAMENT

RE	KJV/NIV/RSV
GEN 1	–
GEN 2	GEN 1–3
GEN 3	GEN 4–5
GEN 4	–
GEN 5	GEN 6–9
GEN 6	GEN 10–11
GEN 7	GEN 12–20
GEN 8	GEN 21–25:18
GEN 9	GEN 25:19–35
GEN 10	GEN 36
GEN 11	GEN 37–46:7
GEN 12	GEN 46:8–50
EXO 1	EXO 1–2
EXO 2	EXO 3–4
EXO 3	EXO 5
EXO 4	EXO 6–7
EXO 5	EXO 8
EXO 6	EXO 9
EXO 7	EXO 10
EXO 8	EXO 11–13
EXO 9	EXO 14–15:21
EXO 10	EXO 15:22–17
EXO 11	EXO 18
EXO 12	EXO 19–20
EXO 13	EXO 21–24
EXO 14	EXO 25–27
EXO 15	EXO 28–29:37
EXO 16	EXO 29:38–31
EXO 17	EXO 32–33:6

EXO 18	EXO 33:7–34:28
EXO 19	EXO 34:29–39
EXO 20	EXO 40
LEV 1	LEV 1–6:8
LEV 2	LEV 6:9–10
LEV 3	LEV 11
LEV 4	LEV 12–14
LEV 5	LEV 15
LEV 6	LEV 16
LEV 7	LEV 17–18:5
LEV 8	LEV 18:6–30
LEV 9	LEV 19–20
LEV 10	LEV 21–22
LEV 11	LEV 23–24:9
LEV 12	LEV 24:10–23
LEV 13	LEV 25–26
LEV 14	LEV 27
NUM 1	NUM 1–3:4
NUM 2	NUM 3:5–4
NUM 3	NUM 5
NUM 4	NUM 6
NUM 5	NUM 7:1–88
NUM 6	NUM 7:89–8
NUM 7	NUM 9–12
NUM 8	NUM 13–15
NUM 9	NUM 16–19
NUM 10	NUM 20–24
NUM 11	NUM 25–27:11
NUM 12	NUM 27:12–30
NUM 13	NUM 31–36
DEUT 1	DEUT 1–3
DEUT 2	DEUT 2–6:9
DEUT 3	DEUT 6:10–11:17
DEUT 4	DEUT 11:18–13

DEUT 5	DEUT 14–17:13
DEUT 6	DEUT 17:14–20
DEUT 7	DEUT 21–26
DEUT 8	DEUT 27–29:1
DEUT 9	DEUT 29:2–34
JOSH 1	JOSH 1–5
JOSH 2	JOSH 6–12
JOSH 3	JOSH 13–21
JOSH 4	JOSH 22
JOSH 5	JOSH 23–24
JUDG 1	JUDG 1–3:6
JUDG 2	JUDG 3:7–5
JUDG 3	JUDG 6–8:32
JUDG 4	JUDG 8:33–10:5
JUDG 5	JUDG 10:6–12
JUDG 6	JUDG 13–16
JUDG 7	JUDG 17–18
JUDG 8	JUDG 19–21
RUTH 1	RUTH 1
RUTH 2	RUTH 2
RUTH 3	RUTH 3–4
1 SAM 1	1 SAM 1–2:11
1 SAM 2	1 SAM 2:12–4:1
1 SAM 3	1 SAM 4:1–7
1 SAM 4	1 SAM 8–10
1 SAM 5	1 SAM 11–12
1 SAM 6	1 SAM 13–14
1 SAM 7	1 SAM 15–16
1 SAM 8	1 SAM 17–19:7
1 SAM 9	1 SAM 19:8–24
1 SAM 10	1 SAM 25–27:7
1 SAM 11	1 SAM 27:8–28
1 SAM 12	1 SAM 29–31
2 SAM 1	2 SAM 1–5:5

2 SAM 2	2 SAM 5:5–8
2 SAM 3	2 SAM 9–10
2 SAM 4	2 SAM 11–12:25
2 SAM 5	2 SAM 12:25–15:6
2 SAM 6	2 SAM 15:7–16:14
2 SAM 7	2 SAM 16:15–18:18
2 SAM 8	2 SAM 18:19–20
2 SAM 9	2 SAM 21
2 SAM 10	2 SAM 22
2 SAM 11	2 SAM 23
2 SAM 12	2 SAM 24
1 KGS 1	1 KGS 1
1 KGS 2	1 KGS 2–11
1 KGS 3	1 KGS 12–16
1 KGS 4	1 KGS 17–22
2 KGS 1	2 KGS 1–2
2 KGS 2	2 KGS 3–9
2 KGS 3	2 KGS 10
2 KGS 4	2 KGS 11–13
2 KGS 5	2 KGS 14–17
2 KGS 6	2 KGS 18–20
2 KGS 7	2 KGS 21–23
2 KGS 8	2 KGS 24–25
1 CHR 1	1 CHR 1–2:1
1 CHR 2	1 CHR 2:2–4:23
1 CHR 3	1 CHR 4:24–5
1 CHR 4	1 CHR 6
1 CHR 5	1 CHR 7
1 CHR 6	1 CHR 8–10
1 CHR 7	1 CHR 11–12
1 CHR 8	1 CHR 13–16
1 CHR 9	1 CHR 17–20
1 CHR 10	1 CHR 21–22
1 CHR 11	1 CHR 23–27

1 CHR 12	1 CHR 28–29
2 CHR 1	2 CHR 1–5:1
2 CHR 2	2 CHR 5:2–7
2 CHR 3	2 CHR 8–9
2 CHR 4	2 CHR 10–12
2 CHR 5	2 CHR 13–14:1
2 CHR 6	2 CHR 14:2–16
2 CHR 7	2 CHR 17–20
2 CHR 8	2 CHR 21–22:1
2 CHR 9	2 CHR 22:1–5
2 CHR 10	2 CHR 23
2 CHR 11	2 CHR 24
2 CHR 12	2 CHR 25
2 CHR 13	2 CHR 26
2 CHR 14	2 CHR 27
2 CHR 15	2 CHR 28
2 CHR 16	2 CHR 29–32
2 CHR 17	2 CHR 33
2 CHR 18	2 CHR 34–35
2 CHR 19	2 CHR 36
EZRA 1	EZRA 1–6
EZRA 2	EZRA 7–10
NEH 1	NEH 1–2:8
NEH 2	NEH 2:9–13
ESTR	ESTR 1–10
JOB 1	JOB 1
JOB 2	JOB 2–3
JOB 3	JOB 4–7
JOB 4	JOB 8–10
JOB 5	JOB 11–14
JOB 6	JOB 15–17
JOB 7	JOB 18–19
JOB 8	JOB 20–21
JOB 9	JOB 22–24

JOB 10	JOB 25–31
JOB 11	JOB 32–37
JOB 12	JOB 38–42:6
JOB 13	JOB 42:7–17
PSALMS	PSALMS
PROV 1	PROV 1–9
PROV 2	PROV 10–22:16
PROV 3	PROV 22:17–24
PROV 4	PROV 25–29
PROV 5	PROV 30
PROV 6	PROV 31
ECCL	ECCL 1–12
ISA 1	ISA 1–5
ISA 2	ISA 6
ISA 3	ISA 7–8
ISA 4	ISA 9–10:19
ISA 5	ISA 10:20–12
ISA 6	ISA 13–23
ISA 7	ISA 24–27
ISA 8	ISA 28–29:10
ISA 9	ISA 29:11–30:26
ISA 10	ISA 30:26–31
ISA 11	ISA 32–33
ISA 12	ISA 34–35
ISA 13	36–40:2
ISA 14	ISA 40:3–31
ISA 15	ISA 41–46
ISA 16	ISA 47
ISA 17	ISA 48–50:3
ISA 18	ISA 50:4–52:12
ISA 19	ISA 52:13–54
ISA 20	ISA 55–58
ISA 21	ISA 59
ISA 22	ISA 60

ISA 23	ISA 61
ISA 24	ISA 62–65
ISA 25	ISA 66
JER 1	JER 1–3:5
JER 2	JER 3:6–4:18
JER 3	JER 4:19–6
JER 4	JER 7–10
JER 5	JER 11–13
JER 6	JER 14–17:11
JER 7	JER 17:12–27
JER 8	JER 18–24
JER 9	JER 25
JER 10	JER 26–28
JER 11	JER 29
JER 12	JER 30–31
JER 13	JER 32–33
JER 14	JER 34–35
JER 15	JER 36–39:14
JER 16	JER 39:15–44
JER 17	JER 45–49
JER 18	JER 50–51
JER 19	JER 52
LAM	LAM 1–5
EZEK 1	EZEK 1–5
EZEK 2	EZEK 6–7
EZEK 3	EZEK 8–11
EZEK 4	EZEK 12:1–20
EZEK 5	EZEK 12:21–14
EZEK 6	EZEK 15–16
EZEK 7	EZEK 17
EZEK 8	EZEK 18–19
EZEK 9	EZEK 20
EZEK 10	EZEK 21–22
EZEK 11	EZEK 23

EZEK 12	EZEK 24
EZEK 13	EZEK 25
EZEK 14	EZEK 26–28
EZEK 15	EZEK 29–32
EZEK 16	EZEK 33:1–20
EZEK 17	EZEK 33:21–34
EZEK 18	EZEK 35–36
EZEK 19	EZEK 37
EZEK 20	EZEK 38–39
EZEK 21	EZEK 40–48
DAN 1	DAN 1
DAN 2	DAN 2
DAN 3	DAN 3
DAN 4	DAN 4
DAN 5	DAN 5
DAN 6	DAN 6
DAN 7	DAN 7
DAN 8	DAN 8
DAN 9	DAN 9
DAN 10	DAN 10-12
HOSEA 1	HOSEA 1–3
HOSEA 2	HOSEA 4–14
JOEL	JOEL 1–3
AMOS	AMOS 1–9
OBADIAH	OBADIAH
JONAH	JONAH 1–4
MICAH	MICAH 1–7
NAHUM	NAHUM 1–3
HAB 1	HAB
HAB 2	HAB
ZEPH	ZEPH 1–3
HAG	HAG 1–2
ZECH	ZECH 1–14
MAL	MAL 1–4

OLD
TESTAMENT

KJV/NIV/RSV	RE
–	GEN 1
GEN 1	GEN 2:1–8
GEN 2	GEN 2:8–14
GEN 3	GEN 2:15–20
GEN 4	GEN 3:1–14
GEN 5	GEN 3:15–23
–	GEN 4
GEN 6	GEN 5:1–12
GEN 7	GEN 5:13–16
GEN 8	GEN 5:17–21
GEN 9	GEN 5:21–24
GEN 10	GEN 6:1–5
GEN 11	GEN 6:6–8
GEN 12	GEN 7:1–5
GEN 13	GEN 7:6–13
GEN 14	GEN 7:12–22
GEN 15	GEN 7:23–25
GEN 16	GEN 7:26–28
GEN 17	GEN 7:29–35
GEN 18	GEN 7:36–40
GEN 19	GEN 7:41–46
GEN 20	GEN 7:47–48
GEN 21	GEN 8:1–4
GEN 22	GEN 8:5–8
GEN 23	GEN 8:9–10
GEN 24	GEN 8:11–18
GEN 25	GEN 8:19–9:3
GEN 26	GEN 9:4–11
GEN 27	GEN 9:12–17

NUM 13	NUM 8:1–5
NUM 14	NUM 8:6–13
NUM 15	NUM 8:14–18
NUM 16	NUM 9:1–10
NUM 17	NUM 9:11–12
NUM 18	NUM 9:13–16
NUM 19	NUM 9:17–20
NUM 20	NUM 10:1–5
NUM 21	NUM 10:6–13
NUM 22	NUM 10:14–20
NUM 23	NUM 10:20–25
NUM 24	NUM 10:26–34
NUM 25	NUM 11:1–3
NUM 26	NUM 11:4–17
NUM 27	NUM 11:18–12:3
NUM 28	NUM 12:4–7
NUM 29	NUM 12:8–18
NUM 30	NUM 12:19–23
NUM 31	NUM 13:1–8
NUM 32	NUM 13:9–14
NUM 33	NUM 13:15–20
NUM 34	NUM 13:21–25
NUM 35	NUM 13:26–33
NUM 36	NUM 13:34–36
DEUT 1	DEUT 1:1–4
DEUT 2	DEUT 1:5–9
DEUT 3	DEUT 1:10–14
DEUT 4	DEUT 2:1–8
DEUT 5	DEUT 2:9–12
DEUT 6	DEUT 2:13–3:3
DEUT 7	DEUT 3:4–7
DEUT 8	DEUT 3:8–9
DEUT 9	DEUT 3:10–15
DEUT 10	DEUT 3:16–19

DEUT 11	DEUT 3:20–4:2
DEUT 12	DEUT 4:3–1
DEUT 13	DEUT 4:11–13
DEUT 14	DEUT 5:1–5
DEUT 15	DEUT 5:6–8
DEUT 16	DEUT 5:9–13
DEUT 17	DEUT 5:14–6:1
DEUT 18	DEUT 6:2–4
DEUT 19	DEUT 6:5–10
DEUT 20	DEUT 6:11–14
DEUT 21	DEUT 7:1–5
DEUT 22	DEUT 7:6–9
DEUT 23	DEUT 7:10–12
DEUT 24	DEUT 7:13–22
DEUT 25	DEUT 7:23–28
DEUT 26	DEUT 7:29–31
DEUT 27	DEUT 8:1–3
DEUT 28	DEUT 8:4–13
DEUT 29	DEUT 8:14–9:3
DEUT 30	DEUT 9:4–7
DEUT 31	DEUT 9:8–14
DEUT 32	DEUT 9:14–21
DEUT 33	DEUT 9:22–33
DEUT 34	DEUT 9:34–35
JOSH 1	JOSH 1:1–3
JOSH 2	JOSH 1:4–7
JOSH 3	JOSH 1:8–10
JOSH 4	JOSH 1:11–13
JOSH 5	JOSH 1:14–17
JOSH 6	JOSH 2:1–5
JOSH 7	JOSH 2:6–10
JOSH 8	JOSH 2:11–14
JOSH 9	JOSH 2:15–16
JOSH 10	JOSH 2:17–23

JUDG 21	JUDG 8:8–11
RUTH 1	RUTH 1
RUTH 2	RUTH 2
RUTH 3	RUTH 3:1–3
RUTH 4	RUTH 3:4–6
1 SAM 1	1 SAM 1:1–7
1 SAM 2	1 SAM 1:7–2:7
1 SAM 3	1 SAM 2:8–13
1 SAM 4	1 SAM 2:13–3:7
1 SAM 5	1 SAM 3:8–11
1 SAM 6	1 SAM 3:11–19
1 SAM 7	1 SAM 3:19–24
1 SAM 8	1 SAM 4:1–4
1 SAM 9	1 SAM 4:5–13
1 SAM 10	1 SAM 4:1–22
1 SAM 11	1 SAM 5:1–5
1 SAM 12	1 SAM 5:6–12
1 SAM 13	1 SAM 6:1–6
1 SAM 14	1 SAM 6:7–7:2
1 SAM 15	1 SAM 7:2–13
1 SAM 16	1 SAM 7:14–21
1 SAM 17	1 SAM 8:1–18
1 SAM 18	1 SAM 8:19–28
1 SAM 19	1 SAM 8:29–9:5
1 SAM 20	1 SAM 9:6–15
1 SAM 21	1 SAM 9:16–19
1 SAM 22	1 SAM 9:20–27
1 SAM 23	1 SAM 9:28–35
1 SAM 24	1 SAM 9:36–42
1 SAM 25	1 SAM 10:1–15
1 SAM 26	1 SAM 10:16–23
1 SAM 27	1 SAM 10:24–11:2
1 SAM 28	1 SAM 11:3–11
1 SAM 29	1 SAM 12:1–4

1 SAM 30	1 SAM 12:5–14
1 SAM 31	1 SAM 12:15–19
2 SAM 1	2 SAM 1:1–7
2 SAM 2	2 SAM 1:8–15
2 SAM 3	2 SAM 1:16–26
2 SAM 4	2 SAM 1:27–31
2 SAM 5	2 SAM 1:32–2:6
2 SAM 6	2 SAM 2:7–13
2 SAM 7	2 SAM 2:14–21
2 SAM 8	2 SAM 2:22–27
2 SAM 9	2 SAM 3:1–4
2 SAM 10	2 SAM 3:5–11
2 SAM 11	2 SAM 4:1–11
2 SAM 12	2 SAM 4:11–5:2
2 SAM 13	2 SAM 5:3–17
2 SAM 14	2 SAM 5:18–27
2 SAM 15	2 SAM 5:28–6:8
2 SAM 16	2 SAM 6:9–7:2
2 SAM 17	2 SAM 7:3–11
2 SAM 18	2 SAM 7:12–8:4
2 SAM 19	2 SAM 8:5–16
2 SAM 20	2 SAM 8:17–26
2 SAM 21	2 SAM 9
2 SAM 22	2 SAM 10
2 SAM 23	2 SAM 11
2 SAM 24	2 SAM 12
1 KGS 1	1 KGS 1
1 KGS 2	1 KGS 2:1–14
1 KGS 3	1 KGS 2:15–21
1 KGS 4	1 KGS 2:22–26
1 KGS 5	1 KGS 2:27–30
1 KGS 6	1 KGS 2:31–39
1 KGS 7	1 KGS 2:40–50
1 KGS 8	1 KGS 2:51–69

2 CHR 1	2 CHR 1:1-4
2 CHR 2	2 CHR 1:5-12
2 CHR 3	2 CHR 1:13-18
2 CHR 4	2 CHR 1:19-24
2 CHR 5	2 CHR 1:25-2:4
2 CHR 6	2 CHR 2:5-19
2 CHR 7	2 CHR 2:20-27
2 CHR 8	2 CHR 3:1-6
2 CHR 9	2 CHR 3:7-14
2 CHR 10	2 CHR 4:1-6
2 CHR 11	2 CHR 4:7-11
2 CHR 12	2 CHR 4:12-18
2 CHR 13	2 CHR 5:1-6
2 CHR 14	2 CHR 5:7-6:5
2 CHR 15	2 CHR 6:6-10
2 CHR 16	2 CHR 6:11-14
2 CHR 17	2 CHR 7:1-5
2 CHR 18	2 CHR 7:6-18
2 CHR 19	2 CHR 7:19-22
2 CHR 20	2 CHR 7:23-35
2 CHR 21	2 CHR 8:1-8
2 CHR 22	2 CHR 8:8-9:5
2 CHR 23	2 CHR 10
2 CHR 24	2 CHR 11
2 CHR 25	2 CHR 12
2 CHR 26	2 CHR 13
2 CHR 27	2 CHR 14
2 CHR 28	2 CHR 15
2 CHR 29	2 CHR 16:1-12
2 CHR 30	2 CHR 16:13-19
2 CHR 31	2 CHR 16:20-28
2 CHR 32	2 CHR 16:29-40
2 CHR 33	2 CHR 17
2 CHR 34	2 CHR 18:1-14

PROV 25	PROV 4:1–23
PROV 26	PROV 4:24–47
PROV 27	PROV 4:48–69
PROV 28	PROV 4:70–97
PROV 29	PROV 4:98–124
PROV 30	PROV 5
PROV 31	PROV 6
ECCL 1	ECCL 1:1-3
ECCL 2	ECCL 1:4-9
ECCL 3	ECCL 1:10-14
ECCL 4	ECCL 1:15-18
ECCL 5	ECCL 1:19-23
ECCL 6	ECCL 1:24-26
ECCL 7	ECCL 1:27-32
ECCL 8	ECCL 1:32-36
ECCL 9	ECCL 1:37-41
ECCL 10	ECCL 1:42-52
ECCL 11	ECCL 1:53-57
ECCL 12	ECCL 1:58-60
SONG-SOLOMON	–
ISA 1	ISA 1:1–4
ISA 2	ISA 1:5–8
ISA 3	ISA 1:9–10
ISA 4	ISA 1:11–12
ISA 5	ISA 1:13–20
ISA 6	ISA 2
ISA 7	ISA 3:1–3
ISA 8	ISA 3:4–7
ISA 9	ISA 4:1–4
ISA 10	ISA 4:5–5:3
ISA 11	ISA 5:4–5
ISA 12	ISA 5:6
ISA 13	ISA 6:1–3
ISA 14	ISA 6:4–8

ISA 49	ISA 17:5–8
ISA 50	ISA 17:9–18:1
ISA 51	ISA 18:2–6
ISA 52	ISA 18:7–19:1
ISA 53	ISA 19:2–3
ISA 54	ISA 19:4–5
ISA 55	ISA 20:1–2
ISA 56	ISA 20:3–4
ISA 57	ISA 20:5–6
ISA 58	ISA 20:7
ISA 59	ISA 21
ISA 60	ISA 22
ISA 61	ISA 23
ISA 62	ISA 24:1
ISA 63	ISA 24:2–4
ISA 64	ISA 24:5
ISA 65	ISA 24:6–9
ISA 66	ISA 25
JER 1	JER 1:1–3
JER 2	JER 1:4–9
JER 3	JER 1:10–2:4
JER 4	JER 2:5–3:2
JER 5	JER 3:3–7
JER 6	JER 3:8–10
JER 7	JER 4:1–4
JER 8	JER 4:5–9
JER 9	JER 4:10–13
JER 10	JER 4:14–18
JER 11	JER 5:1–3
JER 12	JER 5:4–7
JER 13	JER 5:8–10
JER 14	JER 6:1–4
JER 15	JER 6:5–8
JER 16	JER 6:9–10

HOSEA 2	HOSEA 1:5–10
HOSEA 3	HOSEA 1:11
HOSEA 4	HOSEA 2:1–3
HOSEA 5	HOSEA 2:4–6
HOSEA 6	HOSEA 2:7–9
HOSEA 7	HOSEA 2:10–12
HOSEA 8	HOSEA 2:13–16
HOSEA 9	HOSEA 2:17–22
HOSEA 10	HOSEA 2:23–27
HOSEA 11	HOSEA 2:28–30
HOSEA 12	HOSEA 2:30–34
HOSEA 13	HOSEA 2:34–38
HOSEA 14	HOSEA 2:39–40
JOEL 1	JOEL 1:1–5
JOEL 2	JOEL 1:6–12
JOEL 3	JOEL 1:13–16
AMOS 1	AMOS 1:1–5
AMOS 2	AMOS 1:6–8
AMOS 3	AMOS 1:9–10
AMOS 4	AMOS 1:11–12
AMOS 5	AMOS 1:13–16
AMOS 6	AMOS 1:17–19
AMOS 7	AMOS 1:20–24
AMOS 8	AMOS 1:25–27
AMOS 9	AMOS 1:28–31
OBADIAH	OBADIAH
JONAH 1	JONAH 1:1–5
JONAH 2	JONAH 1:5
JONAH 3	JONAH 1:6–8
JONAH 4	JONAH 1:9–11
MICAH 1	MICAH 1:1–2
MICAH 2	MICAH 1:3–6
MICAH 3	MICAH 1:7–8
MICAH 4	MICAH 1:9–10

MICAH 5	MICAH 1:11–13
MICAH 6	MICAH 1:14–15
MICAH 7	MICAH 1:16–18
NAHUM 1	NAHUM 1:1–3
NAHUM 2	NAHUM 1:–4
NAHUM 3	NAHUM 1:5–9
HAB 1	HAB 1:1–3
HAB 2	HAB 1:4–10
HAB 3	HAB 2
ZEPH 1	ZEPH 1:1–5
ZEPH 2	ZEPH 1:6–9
ZEPH 3	ZEPH 1:10–12
HAG 1	HAG 1:1–3
HAG 2	HAG 1:4–6
ZECH 1	ZECH 1:1–4
ZECH 2	ZECH 1:5–7
ZECH 3	ZECH 1:8
ZECH 4	ZECH 1:9–11
ZECH 5	ZECH 1:12–13
ZECH 6	ZECH 1:14–15
ZECH 7	ZECH 1:16–18
ZECH 8	ZECH 1:19–24
ZECH 9	ZECH 1:25–26
ZECH 10	ZECH 1:27–29
ZECH 11	ZECH 1:30–32
ZECH 12	ZECH 1:33–35
ZECH 13	ZECH 1:36–37
ZECH 14	ZECH 1:38–42
MAL 1	MAL 1:1–2
MAL 2	MAL 1:3–5
MAL 3	MAL 1:6–9
MAL 4	MAL 1:10–12

NEW TESTAMENT CORRELATIONS

RE	KJV/NIV/RSV
MATT 1	MATT 1–2
MATT 2	MATT 3 & 4:1-12
MATT 3	MATT 4:12 to 7
MATT 4	MATT 8 to 9:37
MATT 5	MATT 9:38 to 10
MATT 6	MATT 11–12
MATT 7	MATT 13
MATT 8	MATT 14 to 16:12
MATT 9	MATT 16:13 to 20:16
MATT 10	MATT 20:17 to 23
MATT 11	MATT 24 to 26:5
MATT 12	MATT 26:6 to 27
MATT 13	MATT 28
MARK 1	MARK 1 to 2:12
MARK 2	MARK 2:13 to 5:20
MARK 3	MARK 5:21 to 6:29
MARK 4	MARK 6:30 to 8:26
MARK 5	MARK 8:27 to 12
MARK 6	MARK 13
MARK 7	MARK 14 & 15
MARK 8	MARK 16
LUKE 1	LUKE 1
LUKE 2	LUKE 2:1–40
LUKE 3	LUKE 2:41 to 4:13
LUKE 4	LUKE 4:14 to 6:11
LUKE 5	LUKE 6:12 to 7
LUKE 6	LUKE 8
LUKE 7	LUKE 9:1–49
LUKE 8	LUKE 9:50 to 13:21
LUKE 9	LUKE 13:22 to 17:10
LUKE 10	LUKE 17:11 to 18:30

LUKE 11	LUKE 18:31 to 19:27
LUKE 12	LUKE 19:28 to 21
LUKE 13	LUKE 22 & 23
LUKE 14	LUKE 24
JOHN 1	JOHN 1 & 2
JOHN 2	JOHN 3:1–21
JOHN 3	JOHN 3:22 to 4:4
JOHN 4	JOHN 4:5 to 5:1
JOHN 5	JOHN 5:2 to 6
JOHN 6	JOHN 7 to 10
JOHN 7	JOHN 11 to 12:11
JOHN 8	JOHN 12:12–50
JOHN 9	JOHN 13 to 17
JOHN 10	JOHN 18 & 19
JOHN 11	JOHN 20 & 21
ACTS 1	ACTS 1 & 2
ACTS 2	ACTS 3 to 4:31
ACTS 3	ACTS 4:32 to 5
ACTS 4	ACTS 6 to 8:1
ACTS 5	ACTS 8:1 to 9:31
ACTS 6	ACTS 9:32 to 11:18
ACTS 7	ACTS 11:19 to 12
ACTS 8	ACTS 13
ACTS 9	ACTS 14 to 15:35
ACTS 10	ACTS 15:36 to 18:23
ACTS 11	ACTS 18:24 to 20:6
ACTS 12	ACTS 20:7–26
ACTS 13	ACTS 27 & 28
ROMANS	ROMANS 1

1 COR.	1 CORINTHIANS
2 COR.	2 CORINTIANS
GALATIANS	GALATIANS
EPHESIANS	EPHESIANS
PHILLIPIANS	PHILLIPIANS
COLOSSIANS	COLOSSIANS
1 THESS	1 THESS
2 THESS	2 THESS
1 TIMOTHY	1 TIMOTHY
2 TIMOTHY	2 TIMOTHY
TITUS	TITUS
PHILEMON	PHILEMON
HEBREWS	HEBREWS
JACOB	JAMES
1 PETER	1 PETER
2 PETER	2 PETER
1 JOHN	1 JOHN
2 JOHN	2 JOHN
3 JOHN	3 JOHN
JUDAS	JUDE
REV. 1	REV. 1 & 2
REV. 2	REV. 3 to 8:1
REV. 3	REV. 8:2 to 11
REV. 4	REV. 12 & 13
REV. 5	REV. 14
REV. 6	REV. 15 to 17
REV. 7	REV. 18 to 19:10
REV. 8	REV. 19:11 to 22

NEW
TESTAMENT

KJV/NIV/RV	RE
MATT 1	MATT 1:1–5
MATT 2	MATT 1:6–14
MATT 3	MATT 2:1–4
MATT 4	MATT 2:5–8 & 3:1–4
MATT 5	MATT 3:4–26
MATT 6	MATT 3:27–39
MATT 7	MATT 3:40–49
MATT 8	MATT 4:1–6
MATT 9	MATT 4:7–4:15
MATT 10	MATT 4:15 & 5:1–8
MATT 11	MATT 6:1–8
MATT 12	MATT 6:9–18
MATT 13	MATT 7
MATT 14	MATT 8:1–7
MATT 15	MATT 8:8–14
MATT 16	MATT 8:15–16 & 9:1–3
MATT 17	MATT 9:4–9
MATT 18	MATT 9:10–17
MATT 19	MATT 9:18–24
MATT 20	MATT 9:25–26 & 10:1–4
MATT 21	MATT 10:5–16
MATT 22	MATT 10:17–24
MATT 23	MATT 10:25–37
MATT 24	MATT 11:1–14
MATT 25	MATT 11:15–25
MATT 26	MATT 11:26–27, 12:1 16
MATT 27	MATT 12:17–33
MATT 28	MATT 13
MARK 1	MARK 1:1–9
MARK 2	MARK 1:10–11 & 2:1–4

ACTS 10	ACTS 6:3–8
ACTS 11	ACTS 6:9 & 7:1–2
ACTS 12	ACTS 7:3–8
ACTS 13	ACTS 8
ACTS 14	ACTS 9:1–5
ACTS 15	ACTS 9:6–10 & 10:1
ACTS 16	ACTS 10:2–9
ACTS 17	ACTS 10:10–15
ACTS 18	ACTS 10:16–19 & 11:1
ACTS 19	ACTS 11:2–10
ACTS 20	ACTS 11:11 & 12:1–5
ACTS 21	ACTS 12:6–14
ACTS 22	ACTS 12:14–20
ACTS 23	ACTS 12:20–27
ACTS 24	ACTS 12:28–33
ACTS 25	ACTS 12:34–38
ACTS 26	ACTS 12:38–45
ACTS 27	ACTS 13:1–7
ACTS 28	ACTS 13:8–13
ROM 1	ROM 1:1–6
ROM 2	ROM 1:7–11
ROM 3	ROM 1:12–17
ROM 4	ROM 1:18–21
ROM 5	ROM 1:21–24
ROM 6	ROM 1:25–28
ROM 7	ROM 1:29–32
ROM 8	ROM 1:33–37
ROM 9	ROM 1:38–45
ROM 10	ROM 1:46–50
ROM 11	ROM 1:51–58
ROM 12	ROM 1:59–62
ROM 13	ROM 1:63–66
ROM 14	ROM 1:67–72
ROM 15	ROM 1:73–78

GAL 5	GAL 1:17–22
GAL 6	GAL 1:23–26
EPH 1	EPH 1:1–3
EPH 2	EPH 1:4–7
EPH 3	EPH 1:8–11
EPH 4	EPH 1:12–16
EPH 5	EPH 1:16–21
EPH 6	EPH 1:22–26
PHIL 1	PHIL 1:1–5
PHIL 2	PHIL 1:6–10
PHIL 3	PHIL 1:11–13
PHIL 4	PHIL 1:14–18
COL 1	COL 1:1–5
COL 2	COL 1:6–10
COL 3	COL 1:11–15
COL 4	COL 1:15–19
1 THESS 1	1 THESS 1:1–2
1 THESS 2	1 THESS 1:3–6
1 THESS 3	1 THESS 1:7–9
1 THESS 4	1 THESS 1:10–12
1 THESS 5	1 THESS 1:13–15
2 THESS 1	2 THESS 1:1–3
2 THESS 2	2 THESS 1:4–6
2 THESS 3	2 THESS 1:7–10
1 TIM 1	1 TIM 1:1–5
1 TIM 2	1 TIM 1:6–7
1 TIM 3	1 TIM 1:8–9
1 TIM 4	1 TIM 1:10–12
1 TIM 5	1 TIM 1:13–15
1 TIM 6	1 TIM 1:16–19
2 TIM 1	2 TIM 1:1–4
2 TIM 2	2 TIM 1:5–7
2 TIM 3	2 TIM 1:8–9
2 TIM 4	2 TIM 1:10–12

TITUS 1	TITUS 1:1–2
TITUS 2	TITUS 1:3
TITUS 3	TITUS 1:3–5
PHILEMON	PHILEMON
HEB 1	HEB 1:1–2
HEB 2	HEB 1:3–5
HEB 3	HEB 1:6–8
HEB 4	HEB 1:9–11
HEB 5	HEB 1:12–14
HEB 6	HEB 1:14–16
HEB 7	HEB 1:17–21
HEB 8	HEB 1:22–23
HEB 9	HEB 1:24–28
HEB 10	HEB 1:29–35
HEB 11	HEB 1:36–50
HEB 12	HEB 1:51–57
HEB 13	HEB 1:58–64
JAMES 1	JACOB 1:1–7
JAMES 2	JACOB 1:8–12
JAMES 3	JACOB 1:13–14
JAMES 4	JACOB 1:15–18
JAMES 5	JACOB 1:19–25
1 PET 1	1 PET 1:1–5
1 PET 2	1 PET 1:6–9
1 PET 3	1 PET 1:10–14
1 PET 4	1 PET 1:15–18
1 PET 5	1 PET 1:19–21
2 PET 1	2 PET 1:1–5
2 PET 2	2 PET 1:6–10
2 PET 3	2 PET 1:11–15
1 JOHN 1	1 JOHN 1:1–3
1 JOHN 2	1 JOHN 1:4–12
1 JOHN 3	1 JOHN 1:13–17
1 JOHN 4	1 JOHN 1:18–20

1 JOHN 5	1 JOHN 1:21–26
2 JOHN	2 JOHN
3 JOHN	3 JOHN
JUDE	JUDAS
REV 1	REV 1:1–7
REV 2	REV 1:8–15
REV 3	REV 1:16–20
REV 4	REV 2:1–3
REV 5	REV 2:4–6
REV 6	REV 2:7–12
REV 7	REV 2:13–16
REV 8	REV 2:17 & REV 3:1–5
REV 9	REV 3:6–10
REV 10	REV3:11–13
REV 11	REV 3:14–20
REV 12	REV 4:1–5
REV 13	REV 4:6–10
REV 14	REV 5
REV 15	REV 6:1–2
REV 16	REV 6:2–9
REV 17	REV 6:10–13
REV 18	REV 7:1–7
REV 19	REV 7:8–10 & 8:1–3
REV 20	REV 8:4–7
REV 21	REV 8:8–12
REV 22	REV 8:13–15 & REV 9

BOOK OF MORMON

RE	LDS
1 NEPHI 1	1 NEPHI 1–5
1 NEPHI 2	1 NEPHI 6–9
1 NEPHI 3	1 NEPHI 10–14
1 NEPHI 4	1 NEPHI 15
1 NEPHI 5	1 NEPHI 16–19:21
1 NEPHI 6	1 NEPHI 19:22–21
1 NEPHI 7	1 NEPHI 22
2 NEPHI 1	2 NEPHI 1–2
2 NEPHI 2	2 NEPHI 3
2 NEPHI 3	2 NEPHI 4
2 NEPHI 4	2 NEPHI 5
2 NEPHI 5	2 NEPHI 6–8
2 NEPHI 6	2 NEPHI 9
2 NEPHI 7	2 NEPHI 10
2 NEPHI 8	2 NEPHI 11–15
2 NEPHI 9	2 NEPHI 16–22
2 NEPHI 10	2 NEPHI 23–24
2 NEPHI 11	2 NEPHI 25–27
2 NEPHI 12	2 NEPHI 28–30
2 NEPHI 13	2 NEPHI 31
2 NEPHI 14	2 NEPHI 32
2 NEPHI 15	2 NEPHI 33
JACOB 1	JACOB 1
JACOB 2	JACOB 2
JACOB 3	JACOB 3
JACOB 4	JACOB 4
JACOB 5	JACOB 5
ENOS	ENOS
JAROM	JAROM
OMNI	OMNI
MORMON	MORMON

MOSIAH 1	MOSIAH 1–3
MOSIAH 2	MOSIAH 4
MOSIAH 3	MOSIAH 5
MOSIAH 4	MOSIAH 6
MOSIAH 5	MOSIAH 7–8
MOSIAH 6	MOSIAH 9–10
MOSIAH 7	MOSIAH 11–13:24
MOSIAH 8	MOSIAH 13:25–16
MOSIAH 9	MOSIAH 17–21
MOSIAH10	MOSIAH 22
MOSIAH11	MOSIAH 23–27
MOSIAH12	MOSIAH 28:1-19
MOSIAH13	MOSIAH 28:20–29
ALMA 1	ALMA 1–3
ALMA 2	ALMA 4
ALMA 3	ALMA 5
ALMA 4	ALMA 6
ALMA 5	ALMA 7
ALMA 6	ALMA 8
ALMA 7	ALMA 9
ALMA 8	ALMA 10–11
ALMA 9	ALMA 12–13:9
ALMA 10	ALMA 13:10–15
ALMA 11	ALMA 16
ALMA 12	ALMA 17–20
ALMA 13	ALMA 21–22
ALMA 14	ALMA 23–26
ALMA 15	ALMA 27–29
ALMA 16	ALMA 30–35
ALMA 17	ALMA 36–37
ALMA 18	ALMA 38
ALMA 19	ALMA 39–42
ALMA 20	ALMA 43–44
ALMA 21	ALMA 45–49

ALMA 22	ALMA 50
ALMA 23	ALMA 51
ALMA 24	ALMA 52–53
ALMA 25	ALMA 54–55
ALMA 26	ALMA 56–58
ALMA 27	ALMA 59–60
ALMA 28	ALMA 61
ALMA 29	ALMA 62
ALMA 30	ALMA 63
HELAMAN1	HELAMAN 1–2
HELAMAN2	HELAMAN 3–6
HELAMAN3	HELAMAN 7–10
HELAMAN4	HELAMAN 11–12
HELAMAN5	HELAMAN 13–16
3 NEPHI 1	3 NEPHI 1–2
3 NEPHI 2	3 NEPHI 3–5
3 NEPHI 3	3 NEPHI 6–7
3 NEPHI 4	3 NEPHI 8–10
3 NEPHI 5	3 NEPHI 11–13:24
3 NEPHI 6	3 NEPHI 13:25–14
3 NEPHI 7	3 NEPHI 15–16
3 NEPHI 8	3 NEPHI 17–18
3 NEPHI 9	3 NEPHI 19–21:21
3 NEPHI 10	3 NEPHI 21:22–23:13
3 NEPHI 11	3 NEPHI 23:14–26:5
3 NEPHI 12	3 NEPHI 26:6–27:22
3 NEPHI 13	3 NEPHI 27:23–29
3 NEPHI 14	3 NEPHI 30
4 NEPHI	4 NEPHI
MORMON 1	MORMON 1–3
MORMON 2	MORMON 4–5
MORMON 3	MORMON 6–7
MORMON 4	MORMON 8–9

ETHER 1	ETHER 1–4
ETHER 2	ETHER 5
ETHER 3	ETHER 6–8
ETHER 4	ETHER 9–11
ETHER 5	ETHER 12
ETHER 6	ETHER 13–15
MORONI 1	MORONI 1
MORONI 2	MORONI 2
MORONI 3	MORONI 3
MORONI 4	MORONI 4
MORONI 5	MORONI 5
MORONI 6	MORONI 6
MORONI 7	MORONI 7
MORONI 8	MORONI 8
MORONI 9	MORONI 9
MORONI 10	MORONI 10

LDS	RE
1 NE 1	1 NE 1:1–5
1 NE 2	1 NE 1:6–9
1 NE 3	1 NE 1:10–14
1 NE 4	1 NE 1:15–20
1 NE 5	1 NE 1:21–23
1 NE 6	1 NE 2:1
1 NE 7	1 NE 2:2–5
1 NE 8	1 NE 2:6–13
1 NE 9	1 NE 2:13–14
1 NE 10	1 NE 3:1–5
1 NE 11	1 NE 3:6–14
1 NE 12	1 NE 3:15–18
1 NE 13	1 NE 3:19–24
1 NE 14	1 NE 3:25–31
1 NE 15	1 NE 4
1 NE 16	1 NE 5:1–10
1 NE 17	1 NE 5:11–23
1 NE 18	1 NE 5:24–33
1 NE 19	1 NE 5:34–38 & 6:1-2
1 NE 20	1 NE 6:2–5
1 NE 21	1 NE 6:6–10
1 NE 22	1 NE 7
2 NE 1	2 NE 1:1–5
2 NE 2	2 NE 1:6–11
2 NE 3	2 NE 2
2 NE 4	2 NE 3
2 NE 5	2 NE 4
2 NE 6	2 NE 5:1–5
2 NE 7	2 NE 5:6–7
2 NE 8	2 NE 5:8–12
2 NE 9	2 NE 6
2 NE 10	2 NE 7
2 NE 11	2 NE 8:1–3

2 NE 12	2 NE 8:4–6
2 NE 13	2 NE 8:7–8
2 NE 14	2 NE 8:9–10
2 NE 15	2 NE 8:11–18
2 NE 16	2 NE 9:1–2
2 NE 17	2 NE 9:3–5
2 NE 18	2 NE 9:6–9
2 NE 19	2 NE 9:10–13
2 NE 20	2 NE 9:14–19
2 NE 21	2 NE 9:20–21
2 NE 22	2 NE 9:22
2 NE 23	2 NE 10:1–2
2 NE 24	2 NE 10:3–7
2 NE 25	2 NE 11:1–9
2 NE 26	2 NE 11:10–17
2 NE 27	2 NE 11:18–21
2 NE 28	2 NE 12:1–7
2 NE 29	2 NE 12:8–10
2 NE 30	2 NE 12:11–13
2 NE 31	2 NE 13
2 NE 32	2 NE 14
2 NE 33	2 NE 15
JACOB 1	JACOB 1
JACOB 2	JACOB 2:1–9
JACOB 3	JACOB 2:10–13
JACOB 4	JACOB 3:1–6
JACOB 5	JACOB 3:7–28
JACOB 6	JACOB 4
JACOB 7	JACOB 5
ENOS	ENOS
JAROM	JAROM
OMNI	OMNI
MORMON	MORMON
MSH 1	MSH 1:1–4

MSH 2	MSH 1:5–12
MSH 3	MSH 1:13–18
MSH 4	MSH 2
MSH 5	MSH 3
MSH 6	MSH 4
MSH 7	MSH 5:1–10
MSH 8	MSH 5:11–14
MSH 9	MSH 6:1–5
MSH 10	MSH 6:6–14
MSH 11	MSH 7:1–9
MSH 12	MSH 7:10–18
MSH 13	MSH 7:19–21 & 8:1-2
MSH 14	MSH 8:3–4
MSH 15	MSH 8:5–11
MSH 16	MSH 8:12–14
MSH 17	MSH 9:1–5
MSH 18	MSH 9:6–13
MSH 19	MSH 9:14–20
MSH 20	MSH 9:21–26
MSH 21	MSH 9:27–34
MSH 22	MSH 10
MSH 23	MSH 11:1–6
MSH 24	MSH 11:7–12
MSH 25	MSH 11:13–17
MSH 26	MSH 11:18–23
MSH 27	MSH 11:23–29
MSH 28	MSH 12:1–4,13:1
MSH 29	MSH 13:2–11
ALMA 1	ALMA 1:1–7
ALMA 2	ALMA 1:8–16
ALMA 3	ALMA 1:17–21
ALMA 4	ALMA 2
ALMA 5	ALMA 3
ALMA 6	ALMA 4

ALMA 7	ALMA 5
ALMA 8	ALMA 6
ALMA 9	ALMA 7
ALMA 10	ALMA 8:1–7
ALMA 11	ALMA 8:8–18
ALMA 12	ALMA 9:1–10
ALMA 13	ALMA 10:1–4
ALMA 14	ALMA 10:5–11
ALMA 15	ALMA 10:12–16
ALMA 16	ALMA 11
ALMA 17	ALMA 12:1–10
ALMA 18	ALMA 12:11–17
ALMA 19	ALMA 12:18–26
ALMA 20	ALMA 12:27–32
ALMA 21	ALMA 13:1–6
ALMA 22	ALMA 13:6–14
ALMA 23	ALMA 14:1–4
ALMA 24	ALMA 14:5–12
ALMA 25	ALMA 14:13–15
ALMA 26	ALMA 14:16–21
ALMA 27	ALMA 15:1–9
ALMA 28	ALMA 15:10–11
ALMA 29	ALMA 15:12–14
ALMA 30	ALMA 16:1–15
ALMA 31	ALMA 16:16–21
ALMA 32	ALMA 16:22–30
ALMA 33	ALMA 16:31–32
ALMA 34	ALMA 16:33–38
ALMA 35	ALMA 16:39–45
ALMA 36	ALMA 17:1–6
ALMA 37	ALMA 17:7–17
ALMA 38	ALMA 18
ALMA 39	ALMA 19:1–3

MORONI 6	MORONI 6
MORONI 7	MORONI 7
MORONI 8	MORONI 8
MORONI 9	MORONI 9
MORONI10	MORONI 10

TEACHINGS AND COMMANDMENTS
CORRELATIONS

RE	LDS	CoC
JSH 3:4	2	–
JSH 10:1–6; See also 2	3	2
JSH 10:8–21	10	3
JSH 11:2–3	4	4
JSH 12:2–7	5	5
JSH 13:3–5	6	6
JSH 13:18–19	7	7
JSH 13:21–23; See also 3	8	8
JSH 13:24–28	9	9
JSH 14:1	13	–
JSH 14:7–16	11	10
JSH 14:18–21	12	11
JSH 15:3–7	14	12
JSH 15:8–9	15	13
JSH 15:10–11	16	14
JSH 15:14–15	17	15
JSH 15:27–38	18	16
JSH 16:2–28	20	17
JSH 17; See also 4	19	18
JSH 18:3–5	21	19
JSH 18:8	22	20
JSH 18:10–14	23	21
2	3	2
3	8	8
4	19	18
5	25	24
6	26	25

7	24	23
8	27:1–5	26
9	29	28
10	28	27
11	30:1–4	29
12	30:5–8	–
13	30:9–11	–
14	31	30
15	32	31
16	33	32
17	34	33
18	35	34
19	36	35
20	37	37
21	74	74
22	38	38
23	39	39
24	40	40
25	41	41
26	42:1–72	42
27	–	–
28	42:74–77	–
29	43	43
30	44	44
31	45	45
32	46	46
33	47	47
34	48	48
35	49	49
36	50	50
37	–	–
38	51	51
39	52	52
40	53	53

41	54	54
42	55	55
43	56	56
44	57	57
45	58	58
46	59	59
47	60	60
48	61	61
49	62	62
50	63	63
51	64	64
52	66	66
53	65	65
54	1	1
55	68	68
56	67	67
57	–	–
58	133	–
59	–	–
60	69	69
61	70	70
62	71	71
63	72:1–8	72
64	72:9–23	72
65	72:24–26	72
66	73	73
–	74	74
67	75:1–22	75
68	75:23–36	75
69	76	76
70	78	77
71	80	79
72	79	78
73	81	80

74	77	–
75	–	–
76	–	–
77	–	–
78	82	81
79	83:1–5	82
80	–	–
81	99	96
82	84	83
83:3–5	85	–
84	86	84
85	87	–
86	88:1–126	85
87	88:127–137	85
88	–	–
89	89	86
90	90	87
91	91	88
92	92	89
93	93	90
94	95	92
95	96	93
96	97	94
97	94	91
98	98	95
99	–	–
100	100	97
	(Orig 101)	111
101	101	98
102	–	–
103	102	99
104	103	100
105	104	101
106	–	–

107	105	102
108	106	103
109	–	–
110 (LoF)	–	–
111	–	–
112	–	–
113	–	–
114	–	–
115	–	–
116	–	–
117	–	–
118	–	–
119	–	–
120	–	–
–	107	104
121	108	–
122:4–6	137	–
123	109	–
	111	–
124	112	105
125	–	–
126	–	–
127	–	–
128	–	–
129	113	–
130	114	–
131	115	–
132	116	–
133	117	–
134	118	–
135	119	106
136	120	–
137	–	–
138:4–6,11–22	121:1–33	–

139:5–9	121:34 -122	–
139:13–16	123	
140	–	–
141	124	107-Appendix
142	–	–
–	–	108A
143	125	–
144	–	–
145 (BoA)	PGP	–
146	–	–
147	–	–
148	–	–
149	–	–
–	126	–
150	127	109 Appendix
151	128	110-Appendix
152	–	–
153	–	–
154:9–20	107:40–57	–
–	129	–
–	130	–
–	131	–
–	132	–
–	133	108
155	–	–
156	–	–
157:26–32	110	–
158	–	–
159	–	–
160	–	–
161	–	–

162	–	–
163	–	–
164	–	–
165	–	–
166	–	–
167	–	–
168	–	–
169	–	–
170	–	–
171	–	–
172	–	–
173	–	–
174	–	–
175	–	–
176	–	–
–	134	112
–	135	113
–	136	–
–	137	–
–	138	–
–	OD 1	–
–	OD 2	–
Genesis 1	Moses 1	22
Genesis 7	Moses 7	36
–	–	114-(165)

Notes:

Notes:

APPENDIX

Doctrine of Christ

Baptism Covenant

Baptism Ordinance

Sacrament Prayers

Covenant Offering

Covenant Promise

Doctrine of Christ

Behold, verily, verily, I say unto you, I will declare unto you my doctrine. And this is my doctrine, and it is the doctrine which the Father hath given unto me; and I bear record of the Father, and the Father beareth record of me, and the Holy Ghost beareth record of the Father and me; and I bear record that the Father commandeth all men, everywhere, to repent and believe in me. And whoso believeth in me, and is baptized, the same shall be saved; and they are they who shall inherit the kingdom of God. And whoso believeth not in me, and is not baptized, shall be damned. Verily, verily, I say unto you, that this is my doctrine, and I bear record of it from the Father; and whoso believeth in me believeth in the Father also; and unto him will the Father bear record of me, for he will visit him with fire and with the Holy Ghost. And thus will the Father bear record of me, and the Holy Ghost will bear record unto him of the Father and me; for the Father, and I, and the Holy Ghost are one. And again I say unto you, ye must repent, and become as a little child, and be baptized in my name, or ye can in nowise receive these things. And again I say unto you, ye must repent, and be baptized in my name, and become as a little child, or ye can in nowise inherit the kingdom of God. Verily, verily, I say unto you, that this is my doctrine, and whoso buildeth upon this buildeth upon my rock, and the gates of hell shall not prevail against them. And whoso shall declare more or less than this, and establish it for my doctrine, the same cometh of evil, and is not built upon my rock; but he buildeth upon a sandy foundation, and the gates of hell stand open to receive such when the floods come and the winds beat upon them. Therefore, go forth unto this people, and declare the words which I have spoken, unto the ends of the earth. (3 Nephi 5:9).

Baptism Covenant

And it came to pass that he said unto them, Behold, here are the waters of Mormon — for thus were they called. And now as ye are desirous to come into the fold of God and to be called his people and are willing to bear one another's burdens, that they may be light, yea, and are willing to mourn with those that mourn, yea, and comfort those that stand in need of comfort, and to stand as witnesses of God at all times and in all things and in all places that ye may be in, even until death, that ye may be redeemed of God and be numbered with those of the first resurrection, that ye may have Eternal life. Now I say unto you, If this be the desire of your hearts, what have you against being baptized in the name of the Lord, as a witness before him that ye have entered into a covenant with him, that ye will serve him and keep his commandments, that he may pour out his Spirit more abundantly upon you? And now when the people had heard these words, they clapped their hands for joy and exclaimed, This is the desire of our hearts. (Mosiah 9:7)

Baptism Ordinance

Verily I say unto you, that whoso repenteth of his sins through your words, and desireth to be baptized in my name, on this wise shall ye baptize them — Behold, ye shall go down and stand in the water, and in my name shall ye baptize them. And now behold, these are the words which ye shall say, calling them by name, saying: **Having authority given me of Jesus Christ, I baptize you in the name of the Father, and of the Son, and of the Holy Ghost. Amen.** *And then shall ye immerse them in the water, and come forth again out of the water. And after this manner shall ye baptize in my name; for behold, verily I say unto you, that the Father, and the Son, and the Holy Ghost are one; and I am in the Father, and the Father in me, and the Father and I are one.* (3 Nephi 5:8)

Common Practice

*"Having authority given me of Jesus Christ,
I baptize you in the name of the Father,
and of the Son, and of the Holy Ghost.
Amen."* [7]

Sacrament Prayer for Bread

O God, the Eternal Father, we ask thee in the name of thy Son, Jesus Christ, to bless and sanctify this bread to the souls of all those who partake of it; that they may eat in remembrance of the body of thy Son, and witness unto thee, O God, the Eternal Father, that they are willing to take upon them the name of thy Son, and always remember him, and keep his commandments which he hath given them, that they may always have his Spirit to be with them. Amen. (Moroni 4:1)

Sacrament Prayer for Wine

O God, the Eternal Father, we ask thee, in the name of thy Son, Jesus Christ, to bless and sanctify this wine to the souls of all those who drink of it, that they may do it in remembrance of the blood of thy Son, which was shed for them; that they may witness unto thee, O God, the Eternal Father, that they do always remember him, that they may have his Spirit to be with them. Amen. (Moroni 5:1).

SACRAMENT
STICK OF JOSEPH

*The manner of their elders and kohanim administering the flesh
and blood6 of Mashiach unto the assembly. And they administered
it according to the mitzvot of Mashiach; wherefore, we know that
the manner to be true. And the elder or kohen did minister it; and
they did kneel down with the assembly and pray to the Father in
the name of Mashiach, saying,*

BLESSING OF THE BREAD

*O Elohim the Eternal Father, we ask you in the name of your Son
Yeshua HaMashiach to bless and sanctify this bread to the souls of
all those who partake of it, that they may eat in remembrance of the
body of your Son, and witness unto you, O Elohim the Eternal
Father, that they are willing to take upon them the name of your
Son, and always remember him, and keep his mitzvot which he has
given them, that they may always have his ruach to be with them.
Amen.* (Moroni 4:1)

ADMINISTERING OF THE WINE

*The manner of administering the wine. Behold, they took the cup
and said, O Elohim the Eternal Father, we ask you in the name of
your Son Yeshua HaMashiach to bless and sanctify this wine to
the souls of all those who drink of it, that they may do it in
remembrance of the blood of your Son, which was shed for them,
that they may witness unto you, O Elohim the Eternal Father, that
they do always remember him, that they may have his ruach to be
with them. Amen.* (Moroni 5:1)

Covenant

Covenant invitation revealed by God and delivered through Denver Snuffer on September 23, 2017 at the Boise Idaho General Conference.

There are four questions I will read. Please remain seated until the four questions have all been read. If after you hear all four questions you can answer, Yes to all four, then you will be asked to stand and say, Yes to accept:

First: Do you believe all the words of the Lord which have been read to you this day, and know them to be true and from the Lord Jesus Christ who has condescended to provide them to you, and do you covenant with Him to cease to do evil and to seek to continually do good?

Second: Do you have faith in these things and receive the scriptures approved by the Lord as a standard to govern you in your daily walk in life, to accept the obligations established by the Book of Mormon as a covenant and to use the scriptures to correct yourselves and to guide your words, thoughts and deeds?

Third: Do you agree to assist all others who covenant to likewise accept this standard to govern their lives to keep the Lord's will, to succor those who stand in need, to lighten the burdens of your brothers and sisters whenever you are able, and to help care for the poor among you?

Fourth: And do you covenant to seek to become of one heart with those who seek the Lord to establish His righteousness?

If you agree, please stand wherever you are located, either here or in a remote location, to be recognized and numbered by God and His angels. All those standing please confirm you are willing to accept this covenant by saying, Yes.[8]

Covenant Promise
(Answer and Covenant, T&C 158:9-20)

Now, hear the words of the Lord to those who receive this covenant this day:

All you who have turned from your wicked ways and repented of your evil doings, of lying and deceiving, and of all whoredoms, and of secret abominations, idolatries, murders, priestcrafts, envying, and strife, and from all wickedness and abominations, and have come unto me, and been baptized in my name, and have received a remission of your sins, and received the Holy Ghost, are now numbered with my people who are of the house of Israel. I say to you: Teach your children to honor me. Seek to recover the lost sheep remnant of this land and of Israel and no longer forsake them. Bring them unto me and teach them of my ways to walk in them. And I, the Lord your God, will be with you and will never forsake you and I will lead you in the path which will bring peace to you in the troubling season now fast approaching.

I will raise you up and protect you, abide with you, and gather you in due time, and this shall be a land of promise to you as your inheritance from me. The Earth will yield her increase, and you will flourish upon the mountains and upon the hills, and the wicked will not come against you because the fear of the Lord will be with you. I will visit my house, which the remnant of my people shall build, and I will dwell therein, to be among you, and no one will need to say, *Know ye the Lord*, for you all shall know me, from the least to the greatest. I will teach you things that have been hidden from the foundation of the world and your understanding will reach unto Heaven.

And you shall be called the children of the Most High God, and I will preserve you against the harvest. And the angels sent to harvest the world will gather the wicked into bundles to be burned, but will pass over you as my peculiar treasure. But if you do not honor me, nor seek to recover my people Israel, nor teach your children to honor me, nor care for the poor among you, nor help lighten one another's burdens, then you have no promise from me and I will raise up other people who will honor and serve me and give unto them this land, and if they repent I will abide with them.

The time is now far spent, therefore labor with me and do not forsake my covenant to perform it; study my words and let them be the standard for your faith and I will add thereto many treasures. Love one another and you will be mine, and I will preserve you, and raise you up, and abide with you for ever.

AMEN. [9]

STATEMENT OF PRINCIPLES

A Statement of Principles, *adopted by the covenant people, 30 September, 2018, in answer to the commandment given by the Lord in the* Answer to Prayer for Covenant.

1 We, as a covenant people, were commanded by God to develop a statement of principles to be used as a guide and standard. The following statement is the result of the contributions of many. As a people, we agreed to the following methodology in its creation: we confined ourselves to the words of the Lord as found in our canonized scriptures and given to his servants Joseph Smith Jr. and Denver Snuffer Jr.

2 We, as a people, therefore stand as witnesses to the work of Jesus Christ in our day and declare as truth and with soberness that God has set his hand yet again to call his people to labor in preparing the way for Jesus Christ's return. We invite all who receive this witness to come and learn of his ways. Therefore, as commanded by the Lord, we as a covenant people offer the following statement of principles to help guide you in this process.

A GUIDE AND STANDARD

3 The Lord commanded us, *I require a statement of principles to be adopted by the mutual agreement of my people, for if you cannot do so, you will be unable to accomplish other works that I will require at your hands. When you have an agreed statement of principles, I require it to also be added as a guide and standard for my people to follow. Remember there are others who know nothing, as yet, of my work now underway, and therefore the guide and standard is to bless, benefit and inform them.*[1]

JESUS CHRIST

4 The Lord admonished us, *I descended below it all, and now the sorrows of you all, and have borne the grief of it all and I say to you, Forgive one another. Be tender with one another, pursue judgment, bless the oppressed, care for the orphan, and uplift the widow in her need for I have redeemed you from being orphaned and taken you that you are no longer a widowed people. Rejoice in me, and rejoice with your brethren and sisters who are mine also. Be one.[2] For you to unite I must admonish and instruct you, for my will is to have you love one another.[3] It is not enough to say you love God; you must also love your fellow man.[4] I have given to you my doctrine, and have also revealed teachings, commandments, precepts, and principles to guide you and it is not meet that I command you in all things — reason together and apply what I have given you, and it will be enough.[5] Each of you must equally walk truly in my path, not only to profess, but to do as you profess.[6] Love one another and you will be mine, and I will preserve you, and raise you up, and abide with you for ever.[7]*

The Doctrine of Jesus Christ

5 The Lord proclaimed, *I will declare unto you my doctrine. And this is my doctrine, and it is the doctrine which the Father hath given unto me — and I bear record of the Father, and the Father beareth record of me, and the holy ghost beareth record of the Father and me — and I bear record that the Father commandeth all men everywhere to repent and believe in me. And whoso believeth in me, and is baptized, the same shall be saved, and they are they who shall inherit the kingdom of God. And whoso believeth not in me and is not baptized shall be damned. Verily, verily I say unto you that this is my doctrine and I bear record of it from the Father. And whoso believeth in me believeth in the Father also, and unto him will the Father bear record of me for he will visit him with fire and with the holy ghost. And thus will the Father bear record of me and the holy ghost will bear*

255

record unto him of the Father and me, for the Father and I and the
holy ghost are one. And again I say unto you, ye must repent and
become as a little child and be baptized in my name or ye can in
nowise receive these things. And again I say unto you, ye must
repent, and be baptized in my name, and become as a little child, or
ye can in nowise inherit the kingdom of God. Verily, verily I say
unto you that this is my doctrine. And whoso buildeth upon this
buildeth upon my rock, and the gates of hell shall not prevail
against them. And whoso shall declare more or less than this, and
establisheth it for my doctrine, the same cometh of evil and is not
built upon my rock, but he buildeth upon a sandy foundation and
the gates of hell standeth open to receive such when the floods
come and the winds beat upon them. Therefore, go forth unto this
people and declare the words which I have spoken unto the ends of
the earth.[8]

THE LAW OF CHRIST

6 The greatest instruction given by God at any time, to
any generation,[9] is a rule of community found in the Sermon
on the Mount and in the Sermon at Bountiful.[10,11] The Law
of Christ is found there.[12]

ORDINANCES
BAPTISM

7 As to the commandment to be baptized, even Jesus
Christ went to be baptized by John *to fulfill all*
righteousness.[13,14] Nephi taught: *And now, if the Lamb of God,*
he being holy, should have need to be baptized by water to fulfill all
righteousness, O then, how much more need have we, being
unholy, to be baptized, yea, even by water?[15] Denver said
Baptism has always been required from the days of Adam
until the present. Baptism is always the sign of acceptance of
what God is doing in each generation. Whenever there are

people of faith on Earth, they have always been invited to perform the ordinance of baptism as a sign of their faith.[16]

8 The Lord commanded, *And he said unto them, On this wise shall ye baptize, and there shall be no disputations among you. Verily I say unto you that whoso repenteth of his sins through your words and desireth to be baptized in my name, on this wise shall ye baptize them: behold, ye shall go down and stand in the water, and in my name shall ye baptize them. And now behold, these are the words which ye shall say, calling them by name, saying,*

9 *Having authority given me of Jesus Christ, I baptize you in the name of the Father, and of the Son, and of the holy ghost. Amen.*

10 *And then shall ye immerse them in the water and come forth again out of the water. And after this manner shall ye baptize in my name, for behold, verily I say unto you that the Father and the Son and the holy ghost are one; and I am in the Father, and the Father in me, and the Father and I are one. And according as I have commanded you, thus shall ye baptize. And there shall be no disputations among you.*[17]

11 Any who want to be baptized should be. Before baptism, teach [them] the Doctrine of Christ.[18] This living ordinance should be performed in living water, if possible. Connect with God by using the things He provides.[19]

12 Little children are not accountable before God, and therefore their mistakes, offenses, and errors are covered by their innocence, and the atonement of Christ. Anyone who thinks otherwise does not understand God.[20,21] Mormon said, *It is solemn mockery before God that ye should baptize little children ... this thing shall ye teach: repentance and baptism unto those who are accountable and capable of committing sin. ... but little children are alive in Christ.*[22]

13 A record needs to be kept of the names of those baptized. Record their name[s] and submit them to the central recorder's clearinghouse.[23] A single volume with names will be deposited in a temple to be built before the Lord's return.[24]

14 Once baptized, we can receive the Father's testimony of His Son by the power of the holy ghost. It comes as a result of baptism [and is] given according to the Doctrine of Christ to any who repent and are baptized following His direction.[25]

15 *If ye will enter in by the way and receive the holy ghost, it will show unto you all things what ye should do.*[26]

SACRAMENT

16 The sacrament should be taken in the way God commanded. Partake of the sacrament in your families and in your gatherings. Use wine. If you are opposed to alcohol or have a medical condition that prevents you from using wine, use red grape juice (see T&C 9:1). Use the symbol of the blood of our Lord.[27]

17 The Book of Mormon recounts: *And it came to pass that Jesus commanded his disciples that they should bring forth some bread and wine unto him. ... And when the disciples had come with bread and wine, he took of the bread, and brake and blessed it, and he gave unto the disciples and commanded that they should eat. And when they had eat and were filled, he commanded that they should give unto the multitude ... And this shall ye do in remembrance of my body which I have shewn unto you ... And it came to pass that when he had said these words, he commanded his disciples that they should take of the wine of the cup and drink of it, and that they should also give unto the multitude that they might drink of it. And it came to pass that they did so, and did drink of it and were filled. And they gave unto the multitude, and they did drink and they were filled. And when the disciples had done this, Jesus said unto them,*

Blessed are ye for this thing which ye have done, for this is fulfilling my commandments, and this doth witness unto the Father that ye are willing to do that which I have commanded you. And this shall ye always do unto those who repent and are baptized in my name, and ye shall do it in remembrance of my blood which I have shed for you that ye may witness unto the Father that ye do always remember me. And if ye do always remember me, ye shall have my spirit to be with you. And I give unto you a commandment that ye shall do these things.[28]

18 *And they did kneel down with the church and pray to the Father in the name of Christ, saying,*

19 *O God the Eternal Father, we ask thee in the name of thy Son Jesus Christ to bless and sanctify this bread to the souls of all those who partake of it, that they may eat in remembrance of the body of thy Son, and witness unto thee, O God the Eternal Father, that they are willing to take upon them the name of thy Son and always remember him and keep his commandments which he hath given them, that they may always have his spirit to be with them. Amen.*[29]

20 *The manner of administering the wine. Behold, they took the cup and said,*

21 *O God the Eternal Father, we ask thee in the name of thy Son Jesus Christ to bless and sanctify this wine to the souls of all those who drink of it, that they may do it in remembrance of the blood of thy Son, which was shed for them, that they may witness unto thee, O God the Eternal Father, that they do always remember him, that they may have his spirit to be with them. Amen.*[30]

MARRIAGE & FAMILY

22 After the creation, marriage was the first ordinance.[31] All the elements of the gospel point back to marriage as God's final purpose for mankind.[32] If we will love our husbands or our wives, we will please God. Do so and God can preserve your marriage into eternity. Above all else,

marriage is what God wants most to preserve. Marriage is the image of God.[33]

23 The Lord said, *Marriage was, in the beginning, between one man and one woman, and was intended to remain so for the sons of Adam and the daughters of Eve, that they may multiply and replenish the earth. I commanded that there shall not any man have save it be one wife, and concubines he shall have none. I, the Lord your God, delight in the chastity of women, and in the respect of men for their wives.[34] Marriage by me, or by my word, received as a holy covenant between the woman and I, the man and woman, and the man and I, will endure beyond death and into my Father's Kingdom, worlds without end.[35]*

24 This should be the description of all our houses and families: a family of prayer, a family of fasting, a family of faith, a family of learning (therefore a family of glory), which brings a family of order, and therefore a house of God.[36] Our children will be the means to preserve Zion. Without their conversion, Zion has no chance of surviving.[37]

25 The Lord has commanded, *Teach your children to honor me.*[38]

PRIESTHOOD

26 Priesthood in its highest form is an opportunity to serve and bless others.[39] Power can only come from Christ.[40] The reason authority is given is to make men more like God; to lift and to elevate them.[41] Priesthood is confined to men because of the Fall and the conditions ordained at that time. Until things are reversed at the Millennium, it will remain for men alone to perform the public ordinances thus far given to us.[42]

27 There are three steps. The first is ordination. Any man holding priesthood can ordain another man. Man alone can do this first step.[43] Because John the Baptist laid his hand on Joseph and Oliver, we have continued the practice to lay hands to confer priesthood. We should continue to respect that tradition. No one should baptize until they have had priesthood conferred on them by someone who can trace their authority back to John the Baptist, through Joseph and Oliver.[44,45] The second, if you're functioning outside of a family, is sustaining, which requires seven women.[46] Seven women must sustain, one being the wife if the man is married.[47] And thirdly confirmation must come from Heaven. Heaven must ratify.[48]

28 Keep a record of the line of authority from the one who does the ordination. [Maintain in your] possession a written certificate signed by the seven women proving the sustaining vote, and everyone involved should record it in their personal records, particularly the day when the Lord confirms the authority to the man.[49]

29 Wait until the spirit ratifies your ordination before you act.[50] Ask God to give you the power. Get his "word" through the spirit, just as Alma did. After Alma repented, but before using authority to baptize, he asked God to give him power. God, seeing his repentance, accepted it, and poured his spirit upon Alma to give him power to baptize. The proof of God's approval was in Alma's experience and the effect of the ordinance on both Helam and Alma.[51,52]

30 If we get power to baptize, we get it from Him. Power is required. It must come from Christ. The pattern must be followed.[53]

31 Joseph Smith wrote: *No power or influence can or ought to be maintained by virtue of the Priesthood, only by persuasion,*

by longsuffering, by gentleness and meekness, and by love unfeigned, by kindness, by pure knowledge which shall greatly enlarge the soul without hypocrisy and without guile.[54]

32 The Lord said, *And again, the husband is to hold priesthood to baptize and bless the sacrament of bread and wine in the home, and the husband and wife are to bless their children together. For the husband to use authority to administer outward ordinances outside his own family, his wife must sustain him. I have told you that to remove authority to use priesthood outside a man's family requires a unanimous decision by twelve women. A council of twelve women must be convened either in the man's home fellowship among those who are acquainted with his daily walk, or in private at a general conference, also including among the twelve women from the conference those who are acquainted with his daily walk, so that no injustice results. Reinstatement of the man's authority must be considered by the same council of twelve women when the man petitions for the decision to be rescinded, and requires seven of the twelve to agree upon his reinstatement, which can occur at any time. During the period of suspension, nothing affects the man's duties and responsibility in his own family.*[55]

FELLOWSHIPS & GATHERINGS

33 The Lord said, *Whosoever repenteth and cometh unto me, the same is my church.*[56]

34 We read in the Book of Mormon: *And the church did meet together oft to fast, and to pray, and to speak one with another concerning the welfare of their souls. And they did meet together oft to partake of bread and wine in remembrance of the Lord Jesus. ... And their meetings were conducted by the church after the manner of the workings of the spirit, and by the power of the holy ghost, for as the power of the holy ghost led them, whether*

to preach, or exhort, or to pray, or to supplicate, or to sing, even so it was done.[57]

35 The Lord said, *And behold, ye shall meet together oft, and ye shall not forbid any man from coming unto you when ye shall meet together, but suffer them that they may come unto you, and forbid them not.*[58]

36 We must become precious to each other.[59]

37 True religion, when it is present on the earth, always exists in a community of believers.[60] [Fellowships are] informal, based only on the Doctrine of Christ, and require acceptance of Christ's simple statement of His doctrine, faith to believe and act, repentance from sin and baptism. Every denomination in the world can be represented in these fellowships. This is not designed to limit the possibilities of shared faith, but to greatly expand them.[61] We are all equal believers accountable to God.[62]

38 There can be conferences that can be called by anyone, but must include seven women if the business includes priesthood ordination. There is no need for any building to be purchased or built. Meetings can be anywhere.[63]

39 We cannot allow ourselves to be drawn in to inequality when the result of this labor is to make us one body equal with one another. We cannot imitate the failures of the past by establishing an hierarchy, elevating one above another, and forgetting that we must be of one heart, one mind and with no poor among us.[64]

40 The Lord said, *Although a man may err in understanding concerning many things, yet he can view his brother with charity, and come unto me and through me he can with patience overcome the world. I can bring him to understanding and knowledge. Therefore if you regard one another with charity then your brother's error in understanding will not divide you.*[65] *Study to learn how to respect your brothers and sisters and to come together*

263

by precept, reason, and persuasion rather than sharply disputing and wrongly condemning each other, causing anger. ... Even strong disagreements should not provoke anger nor to invoke my name in vain as if I had part in your every dispute. Pray together in humility and together meekly present your dispute to me, and if you are contrite before me I will tell you my part.[66]

41 *I have given you a former commandment that I, the Lord, will forgive whom I will forgive, but of you it is required to forgive all men. ... If you forgive men their trespasses, your Heavenly Father will also forgive you; but if you forgive not men their trespasses neither will your Heavenly Father forgive your trespasses ... But again I say, judge not others except by the rule you want used to weigh yourself.*[67]

TITHING

42 The primary purpose of collecting the tithes and the yield upon it is to bless and benefit the lives of those in need. Assist the poor directly, looking for God's guidance in so doing. Help provide for those who need housing, food, clothing, healthcare, education, and transportation, or children that need care. Take the money the Lord intended for the poor and administer it for the poor. [The Lord desires us to] have no poor among us.[68,69]

43 One tenth of your surplus after you have taken care of all your responsibilities, all your needs, whatever's left over - one tenth of that is your tithe. After you gather your tithe, look at your brothers and your sisters who are there in your meeting, and help those who have needs Christians should take care of the poor among them, and no one should be looking at the flock and saying, I need your money to support myself.[70]

44 The relief of "the poor among you" refers to the poor among the individual fellowship. If there are no poor among

264

you, then excess donations should go to the temple, but they can be shared as your fellowship determines by common consent.[71] God's people are always required to build a temple. Therefore, there needs to be preparation for the coming commandment.[72]

ZION & THE COVENANT

45 Zion consists of people living in harmony with God. It is defined in revelation as *the pure in heart* (see T&C 96:7). Prophecy also confirms it will be an actual location, and a place of gathering.[73]

46 God alone will establish Zion. His instructions are vital and necessary for us. Once He instructs us, the scriptures can then be used to confirm that His direction to us now is consistent with what He prophesied, covenanted, and promised would happen. But the path to Zion is to be found only by following God's immediate commands to us. That is how He will bring it. He will lead us there.[74]

47 Zion and the New Jerusalem are a place, occupied by covenant people, and not something an individual can be or become. People who gather there will all need to be individually redeemed, individually penitent, individually connected to God, but will only belong to the community if they belong to the covenant and are of one heart and one mind and have all things in common between and among them.[75]

48 The Lord said, *I covenanted with Adam at the beginning, which covenant was broken by mankind. Since the days of Adam I have always sought to reestablish people of covenant among the living, and therefore have desired that man should love one another, not begrudgingly, but as brothers and sisters indeed, that I may establish my covenant and provide them with light and truth.*[76]

49 *The Book of Mormon was given as my covenant for this day and contains my gospel, which came forth to allow people to understand my work and then obtain my salvation.*[77] *The Book of Mormon is to convince the gentiles, and a remnant of Lehi, and the Jews, of the truth of the words of my ancient prophets and apostles, with all the records agreeing that I am the Lamb of God, the Son of the Father, and I was sent into the world to do the will of the Father, and I am the Savior of the world. All must come unto me or they cannot be saved.*[78] *Hear therefore my words: Repent and bring forth fruit showing repentance, and I will establish my covenant with you and claim you as mine.*[79]

50 Those sustained by seven women (or a man inside his own family) who receive [the covenant] also have authority to administer the ordinance to others who want to be numbered among God's people. To administer to others, repeat the ordinance. Read aloud the Lord's *Answer* (see T&C 157) and the words of *The Covenant* (see T&C 158). Ask them to stand and say, Yes, and they will become one of the Lord's covenant people. Do not change the words of the covenant, for to change an ordinance is to break it.[80]

51 The Lord said, *It is not enough to receive my covenant, but you must also abide it. And all who abide it, whether on this land or any other land, will be mine and I will watch over them and protect them in the day of harvest, and gather them in as a hen gathers her chicks under her wings. I will number you among the remnant of Jacob, no longer outcasts, and you will inherit the promises of Israel. You shall be my people and I will be your God, and the sword will not devour you. And unto those who will receive will more be given, until they know the mysteries of God in full. But remember that without the fruit of repentance, and a broken heart and a contrite spirit, you cannot keep my covenant; for I, your Lord, am meek and lowly of heart. Be like me.*[81]

52 He concludes, *Cry peace. Proclaim my words. Invite those who will repent to be baptized and forgiven, and they shall obtain my Spirit to guide them. The time is short and I come quickly, therefore open your mouths and warn others to flee the wrath which is to come as men in anger destroy one another. The wicked shall destroy the wicked, and I will hold the peacemakers in the palm of my hand and none can take them from me. Be comforted, be of good cheer, rejoice, and look up, for I am with you who remember me, and all those who watch for me, always, even unto the end. Amen.*

STATEMENT OF PRINCIPLES
ENDNOTES

1 Teachings & Commandments (T&C) 157:55

2 T&C 157:50

3 T&C 157:3

4 T&C 157:10

5 T&C 157:45

6 T&C 157:19

7 T&C 158:20

8 Restoration Edition (RE) 3 Nephi 5:9; LDS Edition (LE) 3 Nephi 11:31-41

9 RE Matthew 3; LE Matthew 5-7

10 RE 3 Nephi 5; LE 3 Nephi 12-14

11 Snuffer, Denver (Sept. 3, 2017) *Opening Remarks - Covenant of Christ Conference*, p. 3

12 Snuffer, Denver (Oct. 19, 2017) *2nd Address to Christians*, p. 8

13 RE Matthew 2:4; LE Matthew 3:43

14 Snuffer, Denver (Sept. 21, 2017) *1st Address to Christians*, p. 8

15 RE 2 Nephi 13:2; LE 2 Nephi 31:5

16 Snuffer, Denver (2015) *Preserving the Restoration* (PTR), pp. 502-

503.

17 RE 3 Nephi 5:8; LE 3 Nephi 11:22-28

18 Snuffer, Denver (2015) *PTR*, pp. 516-517

19 Snuffer, Denver (2015) *PTR*, p. 515

20 Snuffer, Denver (June 6, 2012) *"Mosiah 3:16-17"*, blogpost

21 RE Moroni 8:4; LE Moroni 8:17-20

22 RE Moroni 8:2; LE Moroni 8:9-12 (see also RE Genesis 7:30; T&C 55:5; LE Doctrine & Covenants [D&C] 68:27; "when eight years old.")

23 The website is www.recordersclearinghouse.com

24 Snuffer, Denver (2015) *PTR*, p. 521

25 Snuffer, Denver (2015) *PTR*, p. 517

26 RE 2 Nephi 14:1; LE 2 Nephi 32:5

27 Snuffer, Denver (2015) *PTR*, p. 521

28 RE 3 Nephi 8:6-7; LE 3 Nephi 18:1-11

29 RE Moroni 4:1; LE Moroni 4:2-3

30 RE Moroni 5:1; LE Moroni 5:1-2

31 Snuffer, Denver (2015) *PTR*, p. 391 (see also Joseph Smith Journal, 1835-1836, entry on Tuesday, Nov. 24, 1835)

32 Snuffer, Denver (2015) *PTR*, p. 385

33 Snuffer, Denver (2015) *PTR*, p. 422

34 T&C 157:34

35 T&C 157:38

36 Snuffer, Denver (2015) *PTR*, p. 401

37 Snuffer, Denver (2015) *PTR*, p. 398

38 T&C 158:11

39 Snuffer, Denver (2015) *PTR*, p. 172

40 Snuffer, Denver (2015) *PTR*, p. 512

41 Snuffer, Denver (2015) *PTR*, p. 175

42 Snuffer, Denver (2015) *PTR*, p. 510

43 Snuffer, Denver (Mar. 19, 2017) *Things to Keep Us Awake at Night*, p. 14

44 Snuffer, Denver (2015) *PTR*, p. 508 (see also T&C 1 - Joseph Smith History [JSH], Part 14:1; D&C 13:1)

45 Snuffer, Denver (2015) *PTR*, p. 513

46 Snuffer, Denver (Mar. 19, 2017) *Things to Keep Us Awake at Night*, p. 14

47 Ibid.

48 Ibid.

49 Ibid.

50 Snuffer, Denver (Sept. 9, 2014) *40 Years in Mormonism Lecture 10: Preserving the Restoration*, p.16

51 Snuffer, Denver (2015) *PTR*, pp. 508-509

52 RE Mosiah 9:8; LE Mosiah 18:12-14

53 Snuffer, Denver (2015) *PTR*, p. 509

54 T&C 139:6; D&C 121:41-42

55 T&C 157:57

56 T&C 1 - JSH, Part 10:21; D&C 10:67 (see also Snuffer, Denver [Nov.

12, 2010] *"3 Nephi 18:16"*, blogpost)

57 RE Moroni 6:2; LE Moroni 6:5-6,9

58 RE 3 Nephi 8:8; LE 3 Nephi 18:22

59 Snuffer, Denver (Sept. 3, 2017) *Opening Remarks - Covenant of Christ Conference*, p. 6

60 Snuffer, Denver (2015) *PTR*, p. 504

61 Snuffer, Denver (2015) *PTR*, p. 519

62 Snuffer, Denver (Sept. 21, 2017) *1st Address to Christians*, p. 8

63 Snuffer, Denver (2015) *PTR*, p. 513

64 Snuffer, Denver (Sept. 3, 2017) *Opening Remarks - Covenant of Christ Conference*, pp. 6-7

65 T&C 157:53

66 T&C 157:54

67 T&C 157:58

68 Snuffer, Denver (2015) *PTR*, pp. 258-259

69 Snuffer, Denver (Sept. 21, 2017) *1st Address to Christians*, p. 6

70 Ibid.

71 Snuffer, Denver (Mar. 19, 2017) *Things to Keep Us Awake at Night*, p. 14

72 Snuffer, Denver (Dec. 29, 2016) *"Temple Fund Website"*, blogpost (see also www.TheTempleFund.net)

73 Snuffer, Denver (Nov. 6, 2016) *"All or Nothing, Part 6"*, blogpost

74 Snuffer, Denver (Sept. 3, 2017) *Opening Remarks - Covenant of Christ Conference*, p. 3

75 Snuffer, Denver (Apr. 6, 2017) *"Covenant"*, blogpost

76 T&C 157:2

77 T&C 157:20

78 T&C 157:21

79 T&C 157:23
80 Snuffer, Denver (Sept. 3, 2017) *Opening Remarks - Covenant of Christ Conference*, p. 2
81 T&C 157:48-49
82 T&C 157:65-66

Authors, Editors, and Contributors

Jana May

Juli Rees

Nichole Sair

Russell Anderson

Carleen Loveland

Tyler Kelly

Chris Hamill

Andrew Gore

Eva Gore

Craig Richards

Nancy Richards

Adrian Larsen

Nancy Genys

Sean May

Patrick May

Justin May

Evan Bennett

Nelson Whiting

Dan Pratt

John Keyworth

Claudia Keyworth

Tiegan Corbridge

Raven Corbridge

Aliyah Corbridge

Samantha Corbridge

Bret Corbridge

<u>Third Edition</u>

The *Remnant Missionary Pal* was first published in 2018 and is again offered with updated references and additional ministry sections.

As the restoration continues and prophecy is fulfilled, it is anticipated a third and final version may be published in the future.

If participants have any questions, corrections, or advice related to a future printing, your comments can be sent to: Truthworksnow@sopris.net

References

[1] Colorado Fellowship Meeting. Summer 2015.

[2] Thomas Keith Martson, *Missionary Pal: Reference guide for missionaries and teachers*, 1959. 43rd printing 1998, Publishers Press, Salt Lake City, UT.

[3] Denver Snuffer, *Answer and Covenant*. pg. 6. Denversnuffer.com

[4] Denver Snuffer, *Answer and Covenant*, pg. 7. Denversnuffer.com

[5] Denver Snuffer, *Answer and Covenant*, pg. 11. Denversnuffer.com

[6] Denver Snuffer, *Zion, Preserving the Restoration*, pg. 265

[7] Restoration Edition, 3 Nephi 5:8

[8] Denver Snuffer, *Answer and Covenant*, pg. 10. Denversnuffer.com

[9] Denver Snuffer, *Answer and Covenant,* pg. 11-12. Denversnuffer.com

Made in the USA
Coppell, TX
26 February 2024

29478273R00159